THE
ALMS
RACE

Books by Eugene Linden

APES, MEN, AND LANGUAGE

THE ALMS RACE: THE IMPACT OF AMERICAN
VOLUNTARY AID ABROAD

THE
ALMS
RACE

*The Impact of
American Voluntary
Aid Abroad*

EUGENE LINDEN

Random House 🏠 *New York*

Library of Congress Cataloging in Publication Data

Linden, Eugene.
  The alms race.

  Includes index.
  1. Care, inc. 2. International relief—Lesotho.
3. Charities—United States. I. Title.
HV590.C3L55   361.7   75-40576
ISBN 0-394-49607-8

Manufactured in the United States of America
2 .4 6 8 9 7 5 3
First Edition

For Z

Contents

Introduction

Lesotho is a tiny country in southern Africa. It is a country that people and nations like to give money to. Neighboring South Africans used to drive through barren mountain tracks throwing money and candy to the villagers they passed. With more sophistication the United Nations Development Program (UNDP); the U.S. Agency for International Development (USAID); the International Development Association (IDA); the Food and Agriculture Organization (FAO); the Swedish, West German, Danish and Canadian international development agencies; Freedom from Hunger; the Oxford Committee for Famine Relief (OXFAM); UNICEF; CARE; Save the Children; Catholic Relief Services; Miserior and a host of missionary services are throwing self-help projects and advice at villagers and government alike. Britain underwrites whatever shortfalls occur, should Lesotho have trouble balancing its budget, and contributes heavily to the capital budget. Peace Corpsmen and UN experts are sprinkled throughout the bureaucracy, sometimes helping to allocate money given by their own home governments. Yet despite the fact that Lesotho is offered more money than it can absorb, in the last few years there has been no discernible increase in the standard of living, nor has the country become any less dependent on outside assistance. Lesotho now has commitments of more aid per capita than its economy generates domestically, but for the villager this money might as well evaporate; economically, he'd be better off if the various donors drove through the countryside throwing money out of car windows in the South African fashion. Lesotho is a nation on relief, and will remain so for some time to come.

Lesotho's dependent status does not explain why this nation should be the cynosure of the charitable instincts of the Western world, nor does simple incompetence or corruption explain why this aid should have so little effect on the lives of the villagers. In fact, as one looks into the circumstances that have invested Lesotho with such charisma, and as one charts the evaporation of the money and services which flow into the country, no single, simple explanation seems sufficient to account for what is happening there. Instead, it is necessary to re-examine the functions of charity in the great consumer societies of the West, and to determine how those functions direct the activities of voluntary and aid organizations during contacts with the so-called underdeveloped (or Third) world. It is also necessary to examine how the functions of charity in a consumer society fit within the constellation of forces which supplies the momentum in ever expanding the borders of that part of the world which calls itself consumers. If the massive influx of money and advice has left little economic impression on Lesotho, it has had profound cultural effects. The Basuto are now the poorest consumers on earth.

Expatriate do-gooders and technical assistants have unknowingly reworked the cultural fabric of Lesotho, and have done this far more thoroughly than might a hostile invader coming into the country with that purpose in mind. These unintentional cultural reverberations have been far more profound than the effects of decades of British administration when, before 1966, Lesotho was the High Commission Trust Territory Basutoland. Basuto values have been completely reoriented. The average citizen is developing the expectations of a consumer long before he can afford to satisfy them. Nor are consumer attitudes exclusively economic, although many have economic explanations. The changing values in Lesotho are apparent by the presence of prostitutes, abandoned children, of old age homes, the breakdown of community spirit and sense of interdependence, in the sale of land supposedly owned in common by all Basuto, in the gradual breakdown of village organization and disappearance of Basuto architecture, in ribbon development, in a growing fashion-consciousness and alienation among the young, and in hundreds of other developments too numerous to mention here. Although these phenomena are the unintentional dividends of the activities of expatriates, many expatriates are aware of them, and some welcome these changes. When told of the rising crime rate in Maseru, one expatriate with a key role in planning joked, "Good, it means they're getting interested in money."

All this, in the name of charity.

E. L.

I

Charity as a Business

ONE

"A Hard-nosed Charity"

My interest in charity coalesced around simple questions which seemed to elude simple answers. A few years ago a man I knew remarked that he had given money to a charity with the express wish that it go toward relieving the suffering of displaced people in the Middle East. A few months later he received a thank-you letter from a man in West Germany who had used the money to build an addition to his house. This seemed like a typical bureaucratic snafu, but the donor was upset, and I began to think about charity, about who benefits the most from the charitable impulse. Had all gone well, the administrators of the charity and the recipient of the gift might have materially benefited from the donation, while this man, who had accumulated some wealth before his retirement, would have gotten a nice tax deduction, and perhaps more important, he might have looked at himself in the mirror without avoiding his own eyes. With one small stroke that in no way jeopardized his wealth he might symbolically have neutralized two potential enemies—the restless poor and his own conscience. Who would have benefited more from that exchange?

But the exchange had not proceeded smoothly, and the man was deprived of his satisfaction. Had he, a hard-nosed businessman, been cheated because he was temporarily blinded by his emotions, or was the mix-up the result of bureaucratic inefficiency? In any case, this breakdown recalled him to the world of business. Charities were run by people no better than those who run munitions factories, he told me. So! He could extract some satisfaction from the gift, after all; if he could not ease his conscience with the thought of a fed child, he could console his cynicism with the thought that the do-gooders were really no better than he was. But are they?

Charity and free enterprise might be looked at as two poles of a consumer society: the excesses of greed that occur during the exploitation of human and material resources are supposedly redeemed through the concern expressed in charity—"charity covers a multitude of sins." This man's appraisal that the do-gooder was no better than he was caused me to wonder not who was better, but whether they shared the same motivations, and if they did, how that affected charitable organizations.

By this time I was not so much interested in the idea that certain charities might be corrupt or inefficient as I was in the question of what purposes the charitable impulse served in the lives of those people involved in it. Why did this man have to hedge his bets? If he looked at people as winners and losers, why give his money to the do-gooders at all? Or if he looked at the poor in the Middle East as victims, why fall back into his cynical amoral detachment? I had the feeling that this man was afraid that his epitaph might read: "Here lies a cynical, pitiless winner, hated by all he bested." Perhaps he would have been more comfortable with something like "He loved mankind." Why the profound difference between the world in which he got and the world in which he gave? If he was going to help the poor, why not help someone right here at home, or even in his own factories? New Yorkers will send money to Appalachia but will ignore the destitute on their doorstep.

Many of us dedicate our lives to accumulating wealth, a

process which often involves the discomfiture if not the out-right exploitation of our fellow-men, and then, we give a little back, making it known that our sole aim in the first place was to benefit others. We do this as a nation, as communities, as corporations and as individuals. The charitable impulse is the excuse for the entire social calendar of Manhattan. Without it, rich Americans might never be able to find men and women wealthy enough for their own off-spring to marry. Anything as pervasive as this bears looking into, and anything so seemingly absurd as the relationship between charity and free enterprise must serve some vital function. But what? From the above it should be clear that I had suspicions as to the answers to the questions I posed. But being a good thrifty journalist, I was not about to undertake a project of this size without some background work to see whether I had cause to continue.

First off I decided that the most direct way to approach the functions of the charitable impulse in a consumer society such as ours would be to take a look at the workings of some of the best-known and most highly regarded embodiments of that impulse. When one wants to identify something like the charitable impulse, a good place to start is with a typical organization charged with serving that impulse. One problem is the word "typical." There are charitable enterprises to support everything from disabled circus performers to cancer research. But there is a classic kind of giving, derivative of almsgiving, helping the poor.

The word "charity" is related to the French word for dearness or high price, *cher*, and earlier still from the Greek *caritas*, meaning "love founded on esteem." Hence we get its Christian meaning, "Man's love of God and his neighbor commanded as the fulfilling of the Law," and from Matthew 22:39, "Thou shalt love thy neighbor as thyself." From there it is but an easy step to its meaning as benevolency to one's neighbor, especially to the poor in the form of "practical beneficences." Almost as old as this meaning of charity is the phrase "cold as charity," which the *Oxford English Dictionary* identifies as referring to the perfunctory unfeeling manner in which acts of charity often are done, and public charities administered. The charitable impulse, all warm at its inception, quickly chills during the process of its practical realization. And so we see that right from the beginning charity has had a bifurcated nature. Moreover, we see that right from the beginning people have felt more comfortable giving the poor "practical beneficences" than money. O. Henry once remarked on this sarcastically: "How properly to alleviate the troubles of the poor is one of the greatest troubles of the rich. But one thing agreed upon by all professional philanthropists is that you must never hand over any cash to your subject. The poor are notoriously temperamental, and when they get money they exhibit a strong tendency to spend it for stuffed olives and enlarged crayon portraits instead of giving it to the installment man."

When the average American thinks of this classic form of charity, the sending of practical beneficences to the downtrodden, it is not unlikely that the image of the CARE package would come to mind. CARE, originally an acronym for the Cooperative for American Remittances to Europe, wrote the book on disaster relief after World War II, and thanks to millions of dollars of free advertising and positively gooey treatment by the nation's press, the image of the CARE package is all but enshrined in the American's genes. Because it is so well known, so large, and as we shall see, so representative of the meaning of charity in the American lexicon, CARE seemed to be a natural place to start when I decided to take a look at the workings of charity in a consumer society. There is another aspect of CARE that makes it an attractive vehicle, and that is its reputation for efficiency and honesty. In terms of the press, CARE's record is immaculate; nobody in its thirty-year history has said a harsh word about it. Even during the early sixties, when revelations about oversized "administrative" expenditures of the March of Dimes and other charities brought press scrutiny to bear on the entire philanthropic community, CARE survived unscathed, and as far as I can tell, unscrutinized. Recently Harvey Katz's investigative book called *Give!*, which dealt with fund-raising practices of different charities, heaped such praise on CARE that Senator Charles Percy had the chapter dealing with the organization inserted in the *Congressional Record* as a gesture of respect.

What press CARE does receive is usually of the "CARE Keeps Costs Low As It Ships Necessities to the Poor Overseas" treatment given it a few years ago in a feature story in the *Wall Street Journal*. Stories about CARE are almost always "upbeat" stories, and perhaps one reason for this, apart from any inherent virtue in CARE, is that Americans fervently want to believe that somewhere abroad we are actually going good. Indeed, a numinous aura surrounds CARE, its importance is so deeply grounded in the American spirit that it seems to neutralize the skepticism of the most muckraking editors and enlist the press in that aura's perpetuation.

I noticed this aura, because, to my annoyance, when I first visited CARE headquarters in New York and began to ask questions, I felt like something of a killjoy, as if merely asking questions were to impugn something sacred, something that the cynical citizen is entitled to hold on to and revere. Why pick on CARE, I asked myself; isn't it possible, especially with true horrors and bureaucratic nightmares littering our overseas involvement and begging to be exposed, that no matter how objective my investigation, if my conclusions are anything but fervid praise, I will be driving the public deeper into cynicism and literally taking food from the mouths of the hungry? On the other hand, I chose CARE for its virtues, not because it was an easy mark. Furthermore, CARE's programs play an important role in the lives of millions of people around the world, and determining the nature of that role, and the nature of the spectrum of charitable activity of which it is a part, seemed far more important than preserving the illusions of donors. If that wellspring of charitable impulses which invigorates CARE translates into something inimical by the time it reaches the recipient, then we might well think twice about the charitable impulse and the purposes it serves in consumer societies. And so I set to investigating. Just as one might outfit for a safari, I equipped myself with CARE's history and all that one might divine from its home-office workings before I carried my investigation overseas.

CARE's offices are located at 660 First Avenue, just a couple of blocks south of the United Nations. The address sounds suitable for a skyscraper, but the building CARE uses for its world headquarters is crummy to the point of decrepitude. The building used to be a brewery, and in an age of tube-and-leather furniture and sleek black office fittings, CARE's offices are depressingly anachronistic and make you feel that the past was not so hot, after all. The office is terrific public relations; rarely does a visiting reporter fail to remark admiringly on the building's slovenliness and how little CARE wastes on frills in its desire to exploit each donor dollar to the maximum. The building also seems to satisfy the Peter Principle about buildings and the health of corporations. I know about this principle because on one occasion in New York when I asked a cabdriver to take me to Random House, the cabbie advised me to change publishers. Random House now occupies a shiny new glass building, and this, the cabdriver said, indicates that it is a dying organization. Once they have reached maturity and are beginning to fade, corporations erect huge streamlined buildings as tombstones, as monuments to themselves, remarked the cabdriver. The sign of a vital organization is an office bursting with activity and papers in which not a thought is given to appearance. By this criterium CARE is the liveliest organization in town.

The home-office people dress in a manner befitting the drabness of their surroundings. Narrow ties, shapeless suits, white shirts, pencil-thin mustaches abound. The constituency might have just arrived from a "Salesmen for Wallace" rally. Most nonsecretarial employees are men. CARE was recently successfully sued by its female employees for its discriminatory hiring and promotion policies.

To get an idea of what the present-day CARE man is like, I sifted through 131 biographies of CARE's overseas operatives. Forty-six of this group had studied business at college. Thirty-four of the 131 came to CARE after prior experience in the Peace Corps, while the next largest group—twenty-seven—came to CARE from the American Institute of Foreign Trade (now called the Thunderbird Graduate School for International Management) in Phoenix, Arizona. Only about fifteen had studied "development," and only a few had formally studied anthropology or the specific cultures which they might find themselves helping. Quite a number of CARE's people came to the organization from the lower white-collar and skilled blue-collar ranks of the business world, whether or not they had studied business in college. From its beginnings CARE has prided itself on being a hard-nosed, businesslike outfit in the midst of a lot of good-hearted but ineffectual dandelion gazers, so it is no surprise that its staff is heavily sprinkled with men with no-nonsense business backgrounds. Its reputation as a model of business efficiency is such that through the years, major articles flattering the business aspects of the operations have appeared in *Fortune* and the *Wall Street Journal*.

This tradition of business efficiency grew out of the tremendous logistical obstacles CARE had to overcome to get food packages from the United States to the relatives of American citizens living in the ruins of postwar Europe. However, while business efficiency might be dramatically vindicated in a relief operation where the sole aim is to get food to starving people, other aspects of the businessman's view of the world begin to obtrude when this business efficiency is employed not in the organization of a pipe line of commodities, but in the framing and execution of "self-help" projects in what is called the underdeveloped world.

TWO

From Relief to Development

CARE was formed as a cooperative. Even as the war was drawing to a close, Arthur Ringland, who was head of the President's War Relief Control Board, began to investigate the possibility of starting a food-package service similar to the one Herbert Hoover and the American Relief Administration initiated to meet relief needs after World War I. Ringland pressed the American Council of Voluntary Agencies for Foreign Service to begin something similar at the end of World War II. After Hiroshima the U.S. Army was left with huge amounts of unused ten-in-one ration packages—rations which feed one person for ten days or ten people for one day. In October 1945 the War Relief Control Board had managed to get several million of these ration packages set aside. On November 27, twenty-two of the member organizations of the American Council of Voluntary Agencies for Foreign Service adopted a constitution and bylaws, and incorporated as the Cooperative for American Remittances to Europe (CARE) for the specific purpose of distributing those packages. The member organizations, which spanned religious, labor, cooperative and civic organizations, committed $750,000 to launch CARE as an emergency relief organization.

At first both religious and nonsectarian agencies affiliated themselves with CARE, which was to be a means by which ten-in-one rations paid for by subscribers in the United States might be relayed to designees in war-devastated Europe. It was never intended that CARE become a competitor, in fact a usurper, of the functions of its member agencies. CARE was to be temporary, a conduit to serve its members until normal logistical channels might again be used. There is no question that CARE's early achievements in getting food to the needy were remarkable, but CARE's success at disaster relief bestowed an identity on the organization which some of its member agencies began to find menacing. And so, even as early as 1947, member agencies began to suggest that CARE had fulfilled its mission and that it should be dissolved. Some agencies actively lobbied that CARE fold its tents, some tried to limit the nature of CARE's work, and others, like the Jewish Joint Distribution Committee, resigned from the cooperative.

However, these attempts to contain CARE were insignificant in comparison with the forces working for CARE's expansion. CARE was staffed by businessmen and run as a business, the basic credo of free enterprise being growth: that not to grow is to shrivel and die. Second, CARE was a bureaucracy, and nothing in American life is as tenacious as a bureaucracy. Although CARE officials knew that it was intended to be a temporary conduit serving a temporary need, to these officials, flushed with CARE's spectacular success and ever expanding list of contributors, it was inconceivable that CARE be dissolved. On the contrary, even then CARE began to look beyond designated relief packages as its basic commodity, and beyond Europe as its theater of operations. By the time CARE's donors began to perceive the lessening of the problems caused by the war, and CARE's contributions began to dwindle, CARE was firmly entrenched as a permanent organization and had new sources of revenue.

The frustrations felt by CARE's member agencies are

apparent in the charges leveled during a board meeting convened to discuss CARE's future on December 17, 1947. Charles Bloomstein, who wrote an unpublished *History of CARE*, relates:

> Charges were made that it [CARE] did not indicate any understanding of the basic religious motivation of relief work; that CARE's overseas personnel were ill-equipped for such operations having been selected on the basis of their training in the movement of merchandise and in administration rather than in the selection of needy individuals; that CARE, as a child of the member agencies, should not presume to compete with its own parents in activities in which they had a long and honorable record; that a potential market existed for designated remittances which CARE had not yet fully exploited, . . . and that CARE partook in general of the nature of a business activity, paying high salaries and not drawing on those people who entered the field because of their own inner dedication.

The pressures which brought the member agencies to this crisis pitch were a natural product of CARE's success. By early 1947 CARE was well on top of the situation in Europe and was thus receptive when requests came in from elsewhere. Moreover, CARE decided in principle to extend its services to places where the need was chronic and not necessarily the result of the war. As stocks of surplus ten-in-one rations were depleted, CARE sought other substitute low-cost packages. By the end of the year CARE was shipping woolen-cloth packages, household linens, kosher food —eleven different packages to different areas. Just as depleting supplies of ten-in-one rations had forced CARE to broaden its operations, so did the success of its public relations campaign gradually force CARE into general relief and into competition with its "parent" organizations. Ad campaigns on CARE's behalf used slogans and short, highly emotional spots, and often the fact that the CARE package was supposed to be designated for a relative or friend was lost as the donor reached for his wallet. And so CARE received increasing amounts of undesignated funds. CARE also received money to be spent helping what it called "similarly situated persons"—that is, money not designated for a relative or friend of an American, but for a "needy schoolteacher in Poland" or an "unworthy person, preferably young and female," or as in one case, for a European spy through the good offices of an American spy.

There were external pressures on CARE as well which pushed the organization toward general relief. With the passage of the Marshall Plan, the Economic Cooperation Administration provided for dollar reimbursement for ocean freight of relief goods, and for counterpart funds to be used to help pay for internal delivery charges. CARE had filed for similar claims under an earlier act, and both these claims and future claims under the ECA depended on the CARE board's recognition that the organization was a legitimate relief agency and not just a temporary cooperative. At this same time the U.S. Army had come to the conclusion that unless CARE got more involved in the business of general relief, its utility was at an end and it should be replaced with another agency. Both the State Department (through Robert Lovett) and the Advisory Committee on Voluntary Foreign Aid prodded CARE to continue its shift toward general relief, with ACVFA noting that only if CARE increased its general relief volume would the committee recommend CARE for ocean-freight reimbursements.

Faced with the prospect of liquidation in 1947–48 at a time which promised terrific growth, CARE, behaving like a business, opted to adapt and grow. By 1950, designated relief contributors began to receive notification from their beneficiaries that relief was no longer needed; consequently, contributions to CARE began to fall off sharply. General relief contributions diminished as well because donors believed that government aid was adequate to meet those needs, and CARE began to suffer net losses because the package volume was not sufficient to pay for the world-wide distribution network CARE had established. While in 1948 CARE had survived on the momentum generated by its attributes as a vigorous growth industry, with flagging contributions the forces working for CARE's continued existence derived from its attributes as an established bureaucracy.

CARE's original charter expired on November 27, 1950. This was extended first until May 27, 1952, and then through May 27, 1955, a victory for those on CARE's board who wanted the agency to expand. But it did not solve the immediate problem, that of declining contributions. To deal with this, CARE took a leaf from its own book—it went on the dole. In its very early years CARE had been extremely sensitive about receiving goods or reimbursements from the government, fearing that this might compromise the voluntary aspects of its operations. However, when contributions began to decline sharply, CARE overcame this sensitivity and decided that since the government-contributed goods were of relief character, they fitted into CARE's mission. As American, enthusiasm to contribute to CARE started to wane, CARE began to fill the gaps in its budget through the somewhat less voluntary medium of tax dollars, specifically through government donations of surplus foods released by Public Law 480. Just before the passage of PL 480, a resolution was brought before the CARE board stating that the cooperative should be dissolved if CARE was ever to receive more than 45 percent of its business from the government. CARE historian Bloomstein notes in his early history that the motion was defeated, but that no great cause for alarm existed because government business then only accounted for about 1 percent of CARE's purchasing. Since the passage of PL 480, the amount of CARE's revenue that comes from government as opposed to voluntary contributions has risen to nearly 90 percent. If we discount inflation, voluntary contributions are today less than half of the diminished levels of 1951–52.

While remittances were decreasing in 1950, CARE officials were sure that there would be a certain constituency willing to continue to contribute. Writes Bloomstein: "The phenomenon can be explained only by assuming that there exists a widespread and unorganized desire to help the downtrodden, and that the satisfaction of this desire is in itself a pressing need, a need for which CARE allows outlet." Thus early in its history, CARE realized that as much as it was helping the downtrodden, it was also providing a necessary service for Americans, and that with proper reinforcements this American need might be exploited.

Despite the abatement of the severe refugee problems caused by World War II, it is safe to say that political turmoil, wars, droughts and other natural disasters over the past twenty-five years made sure that there was no dearth of peoples in need of emergency relief. Nor was there any time during this period when CARE might have satisfied all needs for emergency relief and still have had excess capacity to "upgrade" the lives of others with less immediate problems. Yet almost from its beginning, CARE strained to move from emergency relief into self-help projects and technical assistance.

By 1950, when there were still an estimated sixty million refugees scattered through various countries around the world, CARE had already begun to provide books, plows and other self-help materials to nonrefugees in so-called underdeveloped countries. CARE could have remained a pure relief agency for all these years; it could have confined its mission to feeding the indigent and the displaced, as it was set up to do. Indeed, this is what most contributors to CARE feel that it is still doing. But CARE moved relentlessly away from relief and toward self-help. To do so, CARE self-help advocates had to fight a few battles with members who wanted CARE to stick with its original mission. More specifically, someone had to make the decision to divert some resources to self-help *instead* of emergency relief. Bloomstein is quite vague about this shift. He writes: "While relief packages remained the core of the operation [in 1950], attention was being gradually shifted to more fundamental aid, to self-help in the best sense of that word." On another occasion he describes CARE as a young giant which, "by this time self-disciplined and assured of its own capabilities, began to turn its attention to more basic solutions than those provided by transient relief . . ."

Both these quotes imply that transient relief was no longer needed and that CARE might without ignoring its original purpose turn its attention elsewhere. But this was not the case. With limited resources, CARE decisions to get involved in self-help projects such as libraries or giving plows to Greece meant ignoring emergency needs elsewhere. What does come through the Bloomstein quotes is the widely shared skepticism about emergency relief. There seems to be an absurd conjunction underlying the charitable impulse: the desire to help the downtrodden is tempered by the skeptical judgment that their situation is of their own making. Once we have satisfied our pressing need to give, we are immediately suspicious of the recipient. This is borne out by surveys showing that Americans prefer to see charities give technical assistance, school equipment, advice to the poor rather than food or money— the idea being that we shouldn't give away something for nothing. Or it is evident in Andrew Carnegie's explanation of his largesse: "The rich man should give during his own lifetime for public purposes everything not needed by his own family. But he must give in such a way as to encourage self-help . . ."

To find this attitude in a philanthropist or in the general

public is not surprising, but it is something else again to find this attitude in an organization set up for the very purpose of providing emergency relief. After all, the people CARE was set up to help were those who normally would be perfectly able to take care of themselves, but who because of postwar conditions found themselves forced temporarily to ask for food. What Bloomstein and a host of CARE officials seem to do is to equate the situation of people disadvantaged by war or some natural disaster with the situation of those disadvantaged because their society is "underdeveloped"; with any examination this equation is insulting to both groups, and it is an attitude that continues today.

CARE officials I spoke with talked about the "pauperizing effects of relief," and in his book *Give!*, Harvey Katz approvingly notes the philosophy summed up by CARE's Washington staffer Suzanne Wright:

> I suppose the thing I like best about CARE is that we don't degrade people by just handing out alms . . . If people are in a crisis situation, if they're unable to produce enough food or cope with a natural disaster, then we give emergency relief with no strings attached. But they just can't sit back and live off CARE and our contributors. They have to work with us, develop their own capabilities so that we can go out of business in that country and move on to another one.

The associations in this quote are enough to boggle the mind, but they illustrate the complex feelings CARE people have for the people to be helped. First Ms. Wright says that CARE doesn't degrade people by handing out alms. Thus our first impression of the CARE recipient is that he is a person of immense dignity who would rather starve than receive food he hadn't bought himself, and that CARE isn't going to force him to that ignominy. Also in this sentence is a curious judgment on CARE's purported mission; isn't that what CARE is supposed to do, feed the starving? One can hardly imagine CARE running an advertisement that read: "Give to CARE and degrade the starving." But then in the next sentence the tone begins to change. The sense of the "if-then" conditional sentence about emergency relief is "you prove to us you're a victim and we will feed you 'no strings attached.' " And before we get to the last sentence our starving man of immense dignity has become a skid-row bum and welfare cheater of the first order: "But they just can't sit back and live off CARE and our contributors." We imagine a well-fed Bengali recumbent on a Barcalounger, lolling and burping with indolent contentment.

This unresolved impression of the relief recipient comes through CARE ads as well. One television spot currently in use shows a middle-class family watching a CARE ad on television. The spoiled and unbearably cute daughter says, "What's CARE, Daddy?" The father gives a sanctimonious little speech which ends with the line ". . . maybe if we care enough, someday these people will be able to stand on their own two feet." The ad does not give any indication whether the recipient is the victim of a natural catastrophe or just happens to be "underdeveloped" by our standards, but what comes through loud and clear is that the recipient is either unwilling or incapable of standing on his own two feet without merciful Americans willing to guide and prod him into that position. In a sense CARE is giving its donors a chance to degrade the poor, offering the opportunity to feel superior through the act of giving. The recipient is not some disadvantaged peer, but rather some sniveling, lazy, untrustworthy native who must be coaxed into the twentieth century, and the best way to do that is to give him tools and advice, not money or food which he might squander without in any way improving his situation. It was acceptable to give food to Europeans after the war, but we've got to be careful with the natives!

Inexorably and gratuitously, CARE moved from straight relief into development work. One motivation was an un-

THE ALMS RACE / 19

stated distrust of the peoples of the underdeveloped world, another derived from encouragements from the government and the availability of donated materials that might be useful in development projects, and yet another was invitations from underdeveloped countries. A natural bureaucratic evolution also encouraged this shift; it helps an official's self-image more to be able to say that he is attacking the root causes of poverty than it does to say that he is handing out food. All of these motivations work of a piece with something proselytizing in the nature of charity, the idea of "carrying the American way of life beyond where the pavement ends," as Ambassador Ellis Briggs once remarked sardonically. Indeed, CARE people are often referred to as economic missionaries. CARE was not content with merely feeding hungry Europeans, it wanted to move into the "underdeveloped" world and into development work, into something more "fundamental" than the aid brought by "transient relief." It was when CARE moved into development work that its businesslike characteristics began to obtrude, and it becomes clear that in CARE's bureaucratic evolution, the focus of CARE's attention has become ever more "introspective"—that is, the donor in the act of giving is more interested in his own well-being than in the well-being of the recipient of his gift.

THREE

Economic
Missionaries

The desire to proselytize has always been a part of charity.
One goes out into the bush and works for the welfare of a
native in order to win a convert to Christianity, or if one is
not a missionary but a philanthropist, perhaps to convert the
native to our way of life as Mackivre did in 1828 when he
founded a school in order that Mexican Indians might be
educated to "a knowledge of the useful arts and the habits
that may fit them to rule and to obey." (One suspects that
Mackivre was more interested in the "obey" part than with
the idea of eventually being ruled by his beneficiaries.)

This desire to win converts, whether they be religious or
economic, suggests that there is something "introspective"
about the charitable impulse. I quoted Bloomstein earlier
to the effect that for the donors, the act of giving is itself a
pressing need which CARE helps to accommodate. Bloomstein was content to let the matter rest there, but when we
examine the pressing need to give, it begins to become
evident that this property of the charitable impulse has a
direct bearing on whether or not charities actually accomplish their humanitarian aims, or for that matter, whether or
not the aims of a charitable mission are humanitarian at all.

When the missionary goes out into the Mato Grosso in
the Amazon jungle to win converts to Christianity, is his

motive altruistic or is his desire to save souls indicative of a
fundamental insecurity in his beliefs? If a person has nagging doubts about the validity of some enterprise or
whether he should wholly commit himself to it, one way to
put those doubts to rest is to get everybody who might
verify those doubts to join him in that undertaking. No commitment to any enterprise is more intense than a person's
religious commitment, and for the believer, there is nothing more inimical than worship of opposing faiths. The
history of religious movements has been for the usurping
religion to undermine as evil the tenets of the religion it
intends to replace. For instance, in a book entitled *The God
of the Witches,* an anthropologist named Margaret Murray
explains how Christianity took elements of some of the
animistic religions it replaced in Europe and identified
these elements with the devil. The horns of the goat, a
fertility symbol, become the horns of the devil. Similarly
demonified were the antlers of the deer, used in fertility
dances throughout Europe. It was no accident that God, in
talking with Moses on Mount Sinai, made a point of saying
that the Israelites "shalt worship no other gods before me."
The gravest threat to the righteous Christian's sang-froid is
a primitive celebration of the flesh. To convert the carnal
savage is not to save his soul, but to reaffirm the missionary's faith, to enhance the power of his beliefs by ex-
tending their sway, and to neutralize threatening chthonic
temptations.

Missionary fervor is not some intense altruistic desire,
but rather a pressing need on the part of the missionary. By
spreading disease, by undermining tradition, by opening
areas for colonization and slave trading, and by outright
exploitation, missionaries have killed more aborigines and
spread more ruination in their desire to save souls than
they might have had they willfully set out with inimical
purpose in the first place. There have always been missionaries who go native, of course, and lately there are indica-

tions that Europeans at missionary depots like the Summer
Institute of Linguistics in the Mato Grosso are beginning to
accept the fact that the tribal peoples have a right to their
own way of life and perhaps even their own beliefs. But
their re-enchantment comes at a point which author Robert
Cotlow calls the "twilight of the primitive," and the leading
edge of the combine that has so effectively milled non-
Western cultures has been the missionary.

But what about the economic missionary? The CARE
man out to bring the tribesmen into the world market
system?

At the time when CARE began to move into development
work, the United States was just entering the cold war. The
competition for souls was between the free world and god-
less Communism, and CARE, if Bloomstein's history is any
guide, was acutely aware of its role in that competition. In
his chapter entitled "Behind the Iron Curtain," Bloomstein
writes:

> In the hard realities of the international situation there is
> no such thing as unpolitical relief. It is true that aid can be
> rendered solely on the basis of need, without respect to
> race, creed or political affiliation. But it is also true that the
> very giving of help carries with it, implicitly if not explicitly,
> a message of friendship and international human solidarity.
> In these precarious times such a message is loaded with
> political implications of the most fundamental sort . . .
> CARE's relations with governments has been profoundly
> affected by the universal recognition of this phenomenon . . .
> As the international tension increased [the cold war], the
> role of the Advisory Committee [on Voluntary Foreign Aid]
> began to resemble that of its predecessor, the PWRCB
> [President's War Relief Control Board, which designated
> where relief supplies were distributed]. While not pos-
> sessed of the statutory power to regulate, it achieved the
> same control through its ability to withhold recommendation
> for subsidies under various foreign aid laws. Since official

American policy is to gain friends overseas by relieving distress, this power has been used to stimulate private agencies wherever possible. CARE, for example, has been granted significant amounts of agricultural surplus commodities and ECA reimbursements, as well as assistance at other points. The United States Government recognizes that the cooperative, while pursuing its own ends of simple humanitarianism, is also an effective instrument of American foreign policy by its work in breaking down barriers between nations and creating everywhere a feeling of friendship for America and Americans.

Even if we accept this somewhat simple-minded description of American cold-war foreign policy, and CARE's role in it, it is clear that CARE sees itself as an instrument in the competition with Russia for souls, and hence sees its humanitarian mission as contributing to the security of the United States. This of itself is slightly different from simple humanitarianism; it is charity not so much for the sake of the needy as for the security of the donor. The focus shifts even further away from the recipient when we consider development work and the motivations that brought CARE into it. Here what one is trying to do is radically change the recipient's way of life. As we shall see in Lesotho, the changes wrought by economic missionaries are in many ways more profound than those wrought by their religious predecessors.

What galls many critics of the role of missionaries in the non-Western world is the arrogant and insensitive way missionaries dismiss as invalid both the beliefs and culture of the people among whom they are working. At best a child, at worst a heathen, the native had nothing to contribute to the missionary and everything to learn from him. Early Christian thinkers such as the exceedingly ill informed Albertus Magnus did not even credit such races as the Pygmies with humanity. For instance, in one taxonomic work Albertus Magnus described the Pygmies—who are now renowned for the sophistication of their culture—as the missing link between monkey and man. This same insensitivity often applies to those working to "develop" the underdeveloped peoples.

A culture might be looked at as the way a group of people solve the environmental and metaphysical problems with which they are confronted. The ultimate face any culture puts to the world represents these solutions, and more than that, a series of trade-offs, made consciously or unconsciously by the group of people in that culture. For instance, we in America rank material comforts far above nonmaterial satisfactions, and are willing to sacrifice the environmental and cultural resources which contribute to what people are now calling the *quality of life* in order to maintain those material comforts. On the other hand, in India, traditional Hindu culture placed a higher valuation on nonmaterial solace than it did on material comfort, and the devout Hindu was unwilling to make the same trade-off as the American. From the American point of view the Hindu is "underdeveloped" because he lacks the technology, the material benefits and the health benefits enjoyed by the average American. However, the reason the Hindu is underdeveloped has to do with his choices in the trade-offs describing his relationship to his environment. Should the Hindu share the values of American material culture, his situation indeed would be underdeveloped, but the question is whether American culture describes the Hindu's aspirations or whether he is underdeveloped in terms of his own culture.

From the first, those in development work have tended to *act* as though the aspirations of different cultures throughout the underdeveloped world were identical to our own. When Bloomstein writes about the pitiable existence of the Indian or the Korean, he is writing from our point of view, and with any rhetorical skills it is possible to make almost any culture pitiable by our standards. Take Abkhazia in southern Russia, for example. There the average daily caloric intake is about 1,800 calories, and the Abkhazians spend their lives engaged in backbreaking labor in the fields. A typical brutish and impoverished peasant existence. Bloomstein describes any diet that contains less than 2,100 calories as one of slow starvation. In Abkhazia such starvation must be extremely slow, since many live for more than 120 years. Many men retain their potency through their nineties, and they rarely frequent doctors because they don't need them. Almost any of the material benefits—such as cars, a change of diet, vacations on the Lido—that we might offer Abkhazians would shorten their life span.

The point is that it would be easy to make a case for the desperate need for development in Abkhazia, but to do so, given the Abkhazians' enviable situation, would only prove that in this case the charitable impulse would not be directed toward helping the poor, but would rather reflect some constellation of internal pressures. The need to help would be selecting evidence for its own purposes. The above example is extreme but by no means unrepresentative. I have heard people argue the case for development in Tahiti, of all places. What on earth can we offer a Tahitian?

When CARE decided to go into development work in 1950, it selectively marshaled such evidence as it needed to prove the necessity of its decision, e.g., the competition deriving from the cold war. CARE, of course, was not the only relief agency founded after World War II to remain in business and move into development work. Church World Service, also founded as a temporary conduit for relief goods to ease the crisis caused by the war, remained in business. In fact, Church World Service had been a member organization of CARE, but broke off during the argument over genearl relief. It, too, followed the trend into development work; it, too, benefited from official American largesse once private donations began to dwindle.

There seems to be a general progression that has characterized vogues in programming in a preponderant number of agencies since World World II. Within the broad move from relief to development, there have been smaller fashions in development conditioning the types of projects the agencies have undertaken—cooperatives, energy-intensive agriculture (mechanization, fertilizers, etc.), green revolution, infrastructure (roads and the like), labor-intensive industry, community development, etc.—that the voluntary agencies have subscribed to from time to time and subsequently abandoned. CARE's shipment of books to Europe in 1950 set the stage for its entrance into development work, but officials like Burt Smucker, the assistant director, generally date CARE's development work from its shipment of agricultural tools to India in 1954. Earlier CARE had shipped plows to Greece, but India was the first non-Western country in which CARE's principal concern was development. Burt Smucker says that the decision to move into self-help was generated by the staff. It was Murray Lincoln, CARE director in 1954, who shouldered the responsibility for the move into development work. Lincoln was a leader of the cooperative movement in the United States. In his desire to attack the root causes of poverty and not just treat the symptoms, Lincoln felt that cooperatives might also be a suitable device to upgrade the "natives' " lives. This was the first of a series of ideas to prove unsuitable for the countries in which CARE operated.

The organization which mediated between the various voluntary agencies and the U.S. government was the Advisory Committee on Voluntary Foreign Aid. The committee was organized by Charles Taft to replace the President's War Relief Control Board and to respond to President Truman's request of May 14, 1946, that a committee be formed to make provision "for coordinating relationships with voluntary relief agencies and to tie together the Governmental and private programs in the field of foreign relief . . ." Until 1953 the committee was responsible to the Department of State. Then it was transferred to the Mutual Security Agency, which later became the Agency for International Development (AID). It was Arthur Ringland, director of the committee, who used both carrot and stick in encouraging CARE to move into general relief, a first step in CARE's move toward development. The committee became hugely important to CARE when the government began to use the voluntary agencies for the shipment of surplus goods. By its ability to withhold recommendations for the subsidies which were becoming increasingly important to the agencies as a source of revenue, the committee had de facto power to regulate the private agencies.

The question of using the voluntary agencies as a conduit to distribute surplus foods first came up in 1950. Surplus was accumulating and a group in Congress thought one good use of this surplus might be to distribute it to the hungry through voluntary agencies. In 1952 Congress passed Public Law 480, the Agricultural Assistance Act. The Department of Agriculture alerted the private agencies to the availability of surplus through a presentation to the American Council of Voluntary Agencies (a private organization not to be confused with the Advisory Committee). Because of the Korean War it was 1954 before the act, popularly called Food for Peace, was inaugurated. The act has two titles, which call for 60 percent of the foods available to be sold to countries for blocked currencies, and 40 percent to be distributed through donation.

Howard Kresge was until recently the executive director of the Advisory Committee, which endorses those organizations which might be used for distribution of surplus. Today, out of eighty-four voluntary agencies registered with the committee, only six distribute Food for Peace commodities, and two agencies—CARE and Catholic Relief Services—account for 80 percent of the food distributed by voluntary agencies. Another large portion of Food for Peace is administered by the World Food Program or donated directly.

I spoke with Howard Kresge about the way CARE goes

about securing a donation. CARE will initiate the request. After consultation with CARE New York, its man in Sarkhan, for instance, will put up a list of requirements. This list is brought to the AID mission of the American embassy in Sarkhan and copies are forwarded to CARE New York, and to Washington. There, says Kresge, the list is examined from the standpoint of availability and other considerations. An interagency committee with representatives from the State Department, the Office of Management and Budget, AID, the Defense Department, and from Agriculture, each arguing their particular interest, serves as what Kresge calls a "supreme court" and puts the final stamp on each request.

Thus there are three levels of backstopping governing each request. First there is the local AID mission, which reviews voluntary-agency requests from an in-country perspective, then CARE New York, and then finally interagency-committee approval in Washington. Actually, according to Bill Langdon, Care's assistant director of programming who for the last seventeen years has been the liaison with PL 480, the process is practically *pro forma*. All CARE requests for a given year are submitted at the same time, needs are drawn up through consultation between CARE New York and the field offices, and, says Langdon, rarely does CARE propose a program that is not acted upon positively. This is surprising, since it is hard to imagine that a strict humanitarian approach to the distribution of food would not bring a voluntary agency into conflict with some of the interests represented on the interagency committee, for example, the Defense Department. For one thing, Food for Peace has limited amounts of food to distribute. Langdon admits that there is "no question that Food for Peace goes largely to strategically important countries." It seems logical that voluntary agencies would inevitably run afoul of food-distribution priorities tied to particular foreign-policy objectives. Langdon stated several reasons why they don't:

AID writes guidelines each year which detail the types of programs they wish to stress; this year the guidelines emphasize preschool nutrition. The voluntary agencies know in advance the types of programs AID is interested in. More important, Langdon described a type of self-censorship which the voluntary agencies employ and which prevents them from pushing programs that are going to run afoul of the interagency committee. He said that there is an "understanding on the part of the voluntary agencies about countries in which program proposals might not be well received. The voluntary agencies just don't put themselves in the position of pushing programs in a 'sensitive' country." In other cases, such as India, where relations with the United States are in a flux, the political situation may have an effect on the timing of a proposal. The image this self-censorship presents is hardly one of robust independence on the part of CARE and other voluntary agencies, especially since PL 480 contracts and reimbursements, and other government projects, now dominate CARE's budget.

In fact, it appears that the worst fears of the dissident CARE board members are realized in CARE's dependence on the government and its foreign policy. When approached with this question, officials reacted with various explanations. Langdon admits that given this dependence, it is a constant problem to maintain "CARE's identity and autonomy," and that in recent years—as surplus disappeared and Food for Peace became more closely controlled—the problem has become more pronounced.

Howard Kresge of the Advisory Committee emphatically denied that this dependence made the voluntary agencies extensions of foreign aid with all its political implications. On the other hand Frank Goffio, who is the current head of CARE, felt that it was "fair to say" that CARE was an extension of foreign aid. "As a collector of resources," said Goffio, "I have no aversion to taking it from anyone. Your integrity is compromised when you start doing things *because* money's available." When Harvey Katz asked this same "government aid leads to government control" question, Goffio replied, "That's nonsense. If you're doing what you want to do without compromising your principles, you're not prostituting yourself by taking money from the government and you're not being controlled by anyone. Look us over and let me know if you think we've compromised on anything."

Perhaps one reason CARE can feel that it is not compromising its independence in its dealings with the government is that to a large degree CARE people share the biases of official policy and thus find it very easy to temper their programs to suit the priorities of the government. Remember that in the early days CARE enthusiastically accepted its role on the American front lines of the cold war. Once an agency accepts its relationship with the broad goals of foreign policy, it is easy to make the minor adjustments in program decision making necessary to conform, especially in CARE's case, given the enormous rewards for so doing. Still, as Langdon indicates, some CARE people are uneasy about this conformity. Relief and development aid as a means to preserve American security and expand American markets is different from relief directed solely towards alleviating the distress of the hungry. As our attempts at coup making, our arms sales and our efforts to wreak economic havoc in such places as Chile indicate, our foreign policy is not the simple humanitarianism that CARE historian Bloomstein contrasted with Soviet policy. There are voluntary agencies, like World Neighbors, which have refused all blandishments of government contracts and food for fear of losing their independence, and have consequently remained relatively small. Church World Service has limited the amount that it would accept from the government. Dr. Jan Van Hoogstraten, who directs the Africa department of this agency, states frankly that "to be dependent on PL 480 too greatly is corruptive." To limit this danger, Church World Service has had to limit its size. Without government contributions CARE, too, would be very small today.

FOUR

The Rush
to Sarkhan

For five years the voluntary agencies distributed PL 480 commodities on a relief basis—providing food and demanding nothing in return. But with voluntary contributions of cash which might support development projects leveling off, if not diminishing, and with increasing proportions of budgets coming from the U.S. government by means of PL 480 commodities and reimbursements, the volunteer agencies began to look to Food for Peace to finance their whetted appetite for development work.

The Ugly American, published in 1958, sent huge shockwaves through all those concerned with the American image overseas, acquainting the public with the insensitivity that characterized our dealings with non-Western societies, and the counterproductiveness of our efforts to win friends in our battle with Communism. The book acted as a further spur to those who wanted more "activist" involvement in the underdeveloped world. The book is set in a fictional country named Sarkhan which draws on characteristics of many Southeast Asian nations. Lederer and Burdick's Ugly American is, ironically, a retired engineer, a proto–Peace Corpsman who through patience and a canny understanding of machines and men manages to devise a simple pump which the natives of that area can afford to build, and which greatly reduces the labor involved in rice planting. Stories about this man, about a priest, about a savvy major who uses his understanding of astrology to attempt to influence the crown prince's attitude toward Communism, etc., are contrasted with stories of hack ambassadors offending natives and undercutting the efforts of people like the Ugly American.

All this is set against the fall of Dienbienphu in Vietnam. The message was crystal-clear: get out into the bush, Americans; learn the language and culture of the people we hope to influence; organize cheap projects at the local level rather than pushing massive aid programs; use the Communists own techniques in propaganda and war. The book was all that was needed to get thousands of Americans overseas and into development. Many believe that the book was the spur that led to the development of the Peace Corps in 1961.

Voluntary agencies which had been drifting away from relief into development took encouragement, and in 1961 they found that PL 480 offered a way to turn relief into development. Food for Work began in spite of AID, which administered the Food for Peace commodities the voluntary agencies distributed. What happened was that voluntary-agency field operatives began to feel that food distributed over time as relief would "pauperize" the communities they were trying to help. Mr. Van Hoogstraten says that Church World Service first came up with the idea to use PL 480 commodities as wages on development projects. This was in a tree-planting program in Algeria in 1961. The idea was that if the food was used as wages in return for work performed, the needy would receive food but without the shame of the dole, and that development projects would be accomplished in the same stroke. At the time—1961—this was strictly against AID regulations; however, once AID representatives began to visit these projects and report back approvingly, food for work became an accepted, even vaunted, aspect of Food for Peace.

In the move toward food-for-work, as in CARE's original move toward self-help, there are indications of distrust of the recipient. When relief goes to white Americans displaced by a tornado or drought, I doubt that the question of "pauperizing" the community ever comes up. But in the underdeveloped world we do not give food just to tide things over until the weather gets back to normal, because "normal" in the non-Western world is what is regarded as the "root causes of poverty" here in America. Given that feeling, there is no more natural conclusion to draw than that implicit in food-for-work: that a crisis period in which people are hungry enough to work for food as wages is a good time to get people to lay the groundwork which will help them to "enter the twentieth century."

On the surface, this evolution seems sensible, yet this refinement of the concept of relief might be compared with policies of the International Bank for Reconstruction and Development (IBRD, also known as the World Bank) that economist David Baldwin has termed "economic blackmail." Baldwin leveled this charge in his book *Economic Development and American Foreign Policy, 1943–1962*. He was writing about the World Bank's policy of "strategic nonlending" which the bank used to exert great influence on poor countries by *not* lending to underdeveloped countries whose economic policies were not tailored to the specifications of foreign investors—a group not known for their altruism. As Baldwin put it, "In the eyes of IBRD officials, withholding a loan from a country with 'inequitable' legislation concerning business is a way to avoid subsidizing such a practise, but in the eyes of a potential recipient, the Bank is trying to blackmail him into changing governmental policy."

Similarly, it can be argued that to offer food as a wage for a specific project of development is to take advantage of a person's poor diet to blackmail him into helping to effect a particular type of development. Frank Goffio of CARE has termed PL 480 the "most humanitarian law on the books of any government, anywhere on earth." But there is a big difference between the law's original intent to get surplus food to those suffering malnutrition, and its later use as wages in the construction of such projects as roads and dams. Goffio told me that CARE's food-for-work projects are not social blackmail because such a project has to be one the people need. However, Goffio admitted that often the need for a project is perceived at a higher than local level, and that sometimes the need is not felt at the village level. Even when people express a need for a project, this is no sure indication that it actually exists. When a villager's interest in a project, an organization or an idea derives from his desire for food, that is corruptive, Mr. Van Hoogstraten believes. I am certain that groups of people with inadequate diet might see a pressing need for a project building surfboards on the Sahara if they knew that to do so might get them food. As we shall see, the question of who determines local needs is almost a hall of mirrors.

With hindsight, Mr. Van Hoogstraten, who initiated the idea, has decided that the concept of food-for-work is fraught with serious problems. He agrees that there is the danger of such projects amounting to "social blackmail," he worries about wages corrupting the basis of self-help, and he notes that once we give the food as wages for work, we then tell the villager that he cannot sell it, which is in effect telling him what he is allowed to do with his wages. Once at a reception in Washington in the early days of food-for-work, labor leader George Meany accosted an official connected with the tree-planting project in Algeria and said, "Are you the guy that's using slave labor in Algeria?" The official laughed, but he remembered the incident.

As CARE moved further from refugee relief in Europe and into development work in the non-Western world, so did the humanitarian focus of the work become ever more dimmed, so did the ultimate effects of its projects become ever more open to question, and so did CARE, with its strong business bias, move further away from its area of expertise. The years between 1947 and today have been patterned by decreasing voluntary revenue, increasing dependence on the American government, increasing involvement in development work, and within development, involvement in ever more elaborate types of projects and contractual agreements with governments.

The move away from straight relief into more elaborate development strategies brought CARE into an area where there is danger of producing cultural effects quite different from those intended within a project design. Indeed, it was possible that a voluntary agency might be inadvertently creating the very emergency conditions that it was set up to help relieve.

It was with this question in mind that I set out for Lesotho. The truth of my hypothesis about the function of charity in a consumer society would only be determined by the effects of CARE's form of charity on the people to be helped.

The urge to help Lesotho is quite powerful. Actually it was through CARE that I first heard of the country, in 1972. Five years earlier, CARE had been invited to Lesotho to help relieve the effects of a drought which was afflicting the country at the time of independence. In response to this request from Lesotho's Ambassador to the UN, CARE sent a team over to investigate. This team, headed by Ralph Montee, discovered that Catholic Relief Services, the World Food Program (the relief arm of the UN Food and Agricultural Organization) and the British organization OXFAM were on top of the relief situation, so Montee set about to determine whether there was some other area in which CARE might offer assistance. There was, in development, and that day when I first visited their headquarters in New York, CARE officials suggested that if I was interested in pursuing what they were up to overseas, I might consider visiting Lesotho, because CARE's involvement there represented the vanguard of what CARE hoped to be doing in the future. This was a far cry from what CARE was doing twenty-seven years before when it was founded.

CARE officials put me in touch with the Lesotho country director when he came back on home leave. Following CARE's suggestion, I did some background preparation on Lesotho. I discovered that Lesotho was an ideal place to continue my investigation from my point of view as well as CARE's. The country is small (about the size of Maryland), most of the population speaks English, and development was so recent that as one anthropologist put it, a man's memory would be a suitable index of change.

By the time I got around to going to Lesotho, in 1974, the Five-Year Plan with which CARE was dovetailing its activities was in its last year; it seemed a good time to determine how well CARE had fulfilled its ambitions. Oddly enough, though, CARE's attitude toward the country seemed to have changed between the time I formed my plans and the time I came back from Lesotho. On my return several people asked me why I had chosen Lesotho to investigate CARE's performance. One high official muttered that CARE's suggestion that I go to Lesotho was an incredibly stupid thing to do. Some seemed surprised when I told them that it was CARE that had suggested I go there in the first place. Having been there, I could understand both their earlier enthusiasm and their later chagrin.

II

Working at the Frontiers of the Consumer Society

FIVE

Lesotho as Job

To establish a historical perspective from which to view change in Lesotho wrought by development requires a lessening, if not an outright suspension, of one's disbelief. Lesotho is a freak nation. It owes its independence to pity in the British Foreign Office, and in a sense it is the continuing pity of the West that sustains it today. From its founding as a defensive alliance of tribes which was formed in the early nineteenth century under the legendary African leader Moshweshwe (or Moshesh, as he was commonly called), through its tenure under British administration from 1868 through 1967, and even today, Lesotho has had a most precarious existence. Its security has been its poverty. For the Zulus, the half-breed Koranna and Griquas, the Boers, and now South Africa, the costs of taking this mountainous kingdom have far outweighed whatever benefits the conqueror might reap from its barren, eroded soil. Indeed, half a century ago, when some natives found coal near Mohale's Hoek, the chief ordered the mine closed up, reasoning that if it ever became known that Lesotho held resources, the country would lose such independence as it then had. One of Moshesh's descendants, the late Paramount Chief Griffiths, acted similarly on the report of the discovery of diamonds in the mountains.

If poverty is security, Lesotho has the brightest future of all newly independent nations. The country consists of 11,000 square miles bounded on all sides by the Republic of South Africa. Thus it shares borders with the Orange Free State, the Cape Province, Natal, and the Bantu homeland called the Transkei. The territory is mostly mountainous; no one has yet found mineral resources in commercially exploitable quantities. In a few generations the country may not even have topsoil if its increasingly severe erosion is not halted (some people jokingly remark that Lesotho's biggest export is topsoil, which flows down its rivers and into the Republic of South Africa).

Paradoxically, although severely overpopulated, Lesotho is greatly lacking in human resources as well. At any given time some 40 percent of the male population (which means some 70 percent of the labor force) is out of the country working in South African mines—people rank only just behind topsoil as Lesotho's biggest export. Population pressure on the land is one impetus for men to work in the mines, but once gone, the villagers lack the manpower to effectively crop their lands. This spurs an interest in having more children. As a result, Lesotho is both overpopulated and underpopulated at the same time, and each problem feeds on the other. (This labor migration illustrates how Lesotho's poverty is her strength. South Africa draws on Basuto labor because it can pay migrants less than it can residents. For this among other reasons South Africa is complacent to allow Lesotho to persist as an independent nation.) The country's social institutions and land could not survive were all the Basuto to return from the mines, but the present lack of manpower limits agricultural yields. A country without men, without resources and with diminishing soil on which to support an exploding population is indeed an unlikely candidate for invasion.

And yet, at one point the country did have a shot at real independence. Eighty years ago Lesotho was a wheat bowl, feeding not only itself but boom towns in South Africa. Since then, game and trees have disappeared, topsoil is rapidly depleting and the yield per acre of uneroded land has decreased radically as well. Lesotho is an ecological nightmare, a vision of what might happen throughout Africa, Asia and South America. And the Basuto themselves are only partly responsible for their dimming prospects.

The Basuto are one of the youngest tribal groupings in Africa. Their ancestors were pastoral Bantu peoples who migrated southward, crossing the Zambesi River some seven or eight hundred years ago. The Bantus gradually displaced the aboriginal Bushmen and Hottentots who inhabited the plains. At first the Bantus and Bushmen coexisted amicably because the Bushmen cared nothing for grazing rights. Basuto lore recalls a Peter Minuit type exchange in which a Bushman, having been introduced to the joys of smoking *dagga* (the local cannabis), approached Kali, a Mosuto chief and said, "Give me some dagga, my dear Mosuto, and I will give you my country [the Caledon Valley]."

The Bushmen, like all people who live by hunting and gathering, were diminutive, and when relations with the Basuto deteriorated over competition for game, they were driven west into the Kalahari Desert, by the larger, more numerous Sothos. Similarly, the steatopygic Hottentots were driven south toward the Cape of Good Hope. The Basuto, like the Zulus and whites who came later, were invaders.

The Basuto as a tribe date back only to 1823, when Moshesh united under him an agglomeration of Sotho-speaking clans living west of the Drakensberg Mountains in South Africa. (Basuto are the Sotho-speaking peoples; Lesotho is the place where they live; Mosuto or Mosotho is an individual Basuto, and Sesotho is the language they speak.) Moshesh came from the Bamokoteli clanlet, which inhabited the Caledon Valley in the vicinity of the Lesothan village called Leribe. The clan was an offshoot of the Bakwena (Crocodile people—each clan had its totem; e.g., Wild Cat people, Dew people) tribe of Botswana and was held in subjugation by their neighbors, the Basekake. Moshesh's original name was Lepoqo. He earned his adult name in celebration of a successful cattle raid in which he "trimmed the beard" of a neighboring and much feared chief named Moeletsi. The name, given by a clan storyteller, onomatopoetically captures the sound of shearing Moeletsi's beard.

The Basuto were a notably easygoing collection of clans, and clan life was relatively democratic. Unlike the Zulus, for whom sneezing in the presence of the Paramount Chief meant death, Basuto could interrupt, even argue with their chiefs. Each clan paid or exacted tribute from the others according to their fluctuating fortunes in the skirmishes and raids that went on between the groups. Decisions were made in *pitsos,* congregations somewhat like a New England town meeting, where the chief and his counselors would argue the pros and cons of a decision. Disputes were settled in *kgotlas*—courts—where everybody would join in the interrogation and discussion of the merits of the case. In the admiring words of Rivers Thompson, the leading expert on Basuto law, "the system quite often got to the truth of whatever matter was at hand."

Moshesh's rise to power began during the "Difaqane," the Great Tragedy, which began in 1822 and continued through 1828. The Difaqane was a series of convulsions sent through the Sotho-speaking world by the activities of the great Zulu leader Shaka. Fleeing the southwestward push of his armies, hordes of Wild Cat people and Zulu renegades stormed through the Caledon Valley and beyond, massacring the clans they came upon and plundering their crops and livestock. During this period more than a score of clans disappeared altogether. Refugees created by the Difaqane plundered in turn, and it is estimated that six thousand valley people turned to cannibalism rather than face certain starvation. During the Difaqane, Moshesh moved a small collection of clans from a relatively vulnerable hill near present-day Buthe Buthe to a large flat-topped hill farther south. On the way to this mesa, Moshesh's grandfather and some infants were captured and eaten by cannibals. They arrived late at night at their destination, and upon scaling its slopes named the mesa Thaba Bosiu, "The Hill That Grows Larger at Night"; at night the hill loomed impressive over the plains. Thaba Bosiu, three to four hundred feet high, half a mile wide and a mile long, was accessible by six passes, each easily defensible. It was covered by sweet prairie grasses which could support great numbers of cattle in an emergency. From this fastness the Basuto, in relative security, watched the nightmare of the Difaqane.

Refugees, hearing of Moshesh's impregnable fortress, gradually began to arrive, petitioning Moshesh that they be allowed to remain. Moshesh welcomed them, demanding only that they fit themselves into clan life. Moshesh even offered sanctuary to bands of former cannibals who prostrated themselves. In response to arguments offered by edgy elders who claimed that cannibals were beyond taming and would pose a threat from within, Moshesh, reports historian Peter Becker, replied that "he had been advised by the spirit of Mohlomi, the seer [who when alive had predicted the Difaqane], to have compassion on cannibals, for they carried within their bowels the remains of departed souls. Cannibals were living sepulchres, and had to be protected in much the same way ancestral graves were protected from desecration."

In this way Moshesh became known as a compassionate leader and pieced together a nation from the rabble left in the wake of the Difaqane. The consensual and democratic aspects of this union are two important themes which run through Basuto history and form the backbone of Basuto culture. By 1827 three thousand people lived atop the hill, with thousands more occupying kraals strung along its base. By 1829 this admixture of clans began referring to itself as the Basuto, and to Thaba Bosiu and environs as Lesotho.

Not content to rely solely on physical defenses, especially with the tyrants Mantiwane and Shaka ever present on the horizon, Moshesh actively sought to play his enemies off one against the other. He offered himself as a tribute-paying vassal to Shaka in order to secure the conquerer's protection against the renegade Zulu leader Mantiwane. Often when he had won a battle, Moshesh would disarm the anger of the attacker by sending tribute and by begging that the Basuto be left in peace. Indeed, later in the century, in dealing with Europeans, Moshesh relied more on diplomacy than on military might to preserve his kingdom's independence, and played the British against the Boers in much the same way he had played Shaka against Mantiwane.

Although Europeans had entered southern Africa in 1652, it was not until 1831 that Moshesh first saw a white man. Before then, however, Moshesh had heard of whites and had even captured a horse which another tribe had stolen from a white farmer. In many respects, including the relations between natives and whites, Lesotho resembles the American Southwest. It is tableland and mountain, and it is territory ideally suited for horse-mounted people. The Basuto immediately took to the horse, and became the most adept at riding of all the tribes of Africa. The Basuto resemble the Indians of the Southwest in other respects. A mounted Mosuto, with a rifle cradled in his arms, wrapped in a blanket decorated with elemental geometric designs in bold blues and reds, with his faintly Asiatic cast to his eyes, might be mistaken for an extremely weathered Hopi from New Mexico.

From 1833 until independence, two great forces acted to change the cultural fabric of the Basuto. First, there was Christianity, inculcated by the missionaries, and then, later, the administrative changes imposed by the British. Moshesh seems to have had a sophisticated view of missionaries. On the one hand he sent hundreds of heads of cattle to an intermediary in his efforts to secure a missionary, and when he eventually did, Moshesh called the arrival of Eugene Casalis the most important day in the history of Lesotho. But on the other hand, he viewed much of what Casalis preached with humorous detachment, and gently chided the missionary for his arrogance. On one occasion, Peter Becker notes

> Casalis recited the Ten Commandments, emphasizing their significance as a basis for moral behavior. The chief was amused. There was nothing unique in these laws, he smiled teasingly, for the Basuto although unfamiliar with the white man's Christ knew "it was very wicked to be ungrateful and disobedient to parents, to rob, to kill, to commit adultery, to covet the property of another, and to bear false witness." Referring to the sixth commandment—"Thou shalt not kill"— he asked Casalis if the great white nations ever waged war. Told that they did he feigned surprise. Surely then, he said, Christians must be hypocrites of the first order . . .

While Moshesh encouraged his people to attend church services, until his last days he resisted conversion to Christianity. He felt that the spirits of his ancestors had served him during his life and wondered why he should forsake them. However, on his deathbed, senile and after incessant pleading and browbeating by Casalis' daughter and other missionaries, Moshesh finally consented to be baptized.

Moshesh, before his dotage, said that tribal custom was inaccessible to white minds and beyond the reach of Christianity. One senses that Moshesh's active solicitation of missionaries was another shrewd diplomatic move and a means by which he thought he might bring to his people some of the benefits and expertise enjoyed by the Europeans. In fact, Eugene Casalis served as an able intermediary and scribe for Moshesh and quickly displaced the influence of the elders as counsel to the chief. Partly because of their waning influence and partly because they saw the alien ideas of Casalis as threatening to tribal authority and their beliefs, many of the elders and prominent Basuto sought to have Casalis expelled or killed. But Moshesh, who probably never realized the potency of the toxin he had invited into his kingdom, protected Casalis and invested him with ever more power. He used Casalis as both an instrument of protection from white domination and a means to "civilization." Casalis was indeed instrumental in protecting Lesotho from being overrun by the Boers; however, the civilization brought by the missionaries consisted of different clothing, the end of polygamy, firearms, literacy, and a new set of superstitions that suggested that most of what the Basuto had previously enjoyed was evil.

The missionaries who met Moshesh fell in awe of his perception and kindliness, as well of the pacific nature of all Basuto. Political scientist Richard Stevens writes: "To the missionaries, the Basuto owe in no small measure their written language, their literature, the preservation of their oral traditions, and their recorded history." Few would dispute this, but like most pre-literate people, before the arrival of the missionaries the Basuto possessed exact memories, and tribal life had praise-singers who served as vessels of clan history—they did not need a recorded history. Moshesh himself would regularly spend hours recounting to dismayed visitors the history of his people, not ignoring even the most minute detail. The great enemy of such a mnemonic facility is overwhelming change. It was such change that the missionaries brought, and it was against such change that the elders intuitively rebelled. Today the Basuto I spoke with complained that because their history has been recorded exclusively by Europeans, it seems alien to them—they feel no sense of cultural identity. How can they when they have to rely on accounts which subtly suggest that Lesotho's pre-Christian history is in some sense shameful. Ironically, today the European might be better equipped to understand Basuto history than the Basuto himself, and unfortunately, he might also be more motivated to defend Basuto culture. Many educated Basuto, as is the case with deculturized Africans throughout the continent, are embarrassed by their tribal heritage.

Moshesh's protracted negotiations with the British led to a treaty in 1843 when Sir George Napier, the governor of Cape Colony, signed an agreement making Lesotho a "Friend and Ally." At that time Moshesh had fifty thousand people in his domain. This agreement signed, the Basuto, the British and the Boers squabbled and fought for the next forty years. One often cited indication of Moshesh's diplomacy occurred in 1852 after one such squabble. After successfully fighting off a British force, he wrote High Commissioner General Sir George Cathcart: "You have chastised, let it be enough, I pray you; and let me be no longer considered an enemy of the Queen." Moshesh would never crow over a victory.

Most of the ensuing fighting with the British and the Boers devolved ultimately to the issue of borders. Stripped of their vast pastures, the Basuto lands became increasingly congested with cattle and horses. Such pressures intensifying over the next hundred years led to grotesque transformations of the face of the country. Moreover, Moshesh's unruly sons constantly raided Boer farms for additional cattle in efforts to increase their own prestige. Much of the problem with the British and the Boers was that they simply did not believe that Moshesh could not control his sons.

Although possessing one language, one army and a unified system of chieftainship and laws, Basuto unity essentially coalesced in response to external threats, while for the most part the principal chiefs ran their respective domains with some autonomy. After forging Lesotho out of an agglomeration of clans, Moshesh, as he grew older, was constantly tested and defied by his sons. The British or the

Boers sometimes suspected duplicity on Moshesh's part because warriors would raid neighboring farms despite Moshesh's assurances that raiding would cease. More often than not, Moshesh would hear of the raid only when it was a *fait accompli.* The British had difficulty understanding the freewheeling autonomy of the Lesotho chief system.

It was under the British that the semianarchic character of Basuto government took on a more formal and rigid cast. The British ostensibly were trying to preserve the traditional structures of Basuto life. They wanted to run Basutoland indirectly through the chief system, in part because it would be less expensive to do things that way and in part because British philanthropic organizations were becoming sensitive to the vulnerability of African cultures to outside forces. The British had agreed to take Lesotho under imperial protection because they wanted to dampen the incessant turmoil in that part of Africa. They never expected to make money out of this protectorate, and a succession of British administrators assiduously honored Moshesh's wish that no Basuto land be alienated. This was in contrast to Swaziland, protected by no such guarantees, where at independence nearly half of the land was owned by foreigners. Consequently, the British did not invest any money in the country and were content to rule indirectly.

Lesotho became the High Commission Trust Territory Basutoland in 1884. As such it was governed not by the Colonial Office but by the Commonwealth Relations Office. This left the country in political limbo with regard to its future, but Britain eventually looked to turning the country over to South Africa and only hoped that it would not become a pecuniary liability in the meantime. However, despite Britain's disinterest in the nation's economic development, and their desire to protect Basuto land and institutions, indirect British administration left its marks on Basuto society.

Richard Stevens, in his study of Lesotho, Botswana (formerly Bechuanaland) and Swaziland, suggests that indirect rule failed both to protect tribal custom and to equip the Basuto to deal with the West. "The preservation of tribal law and custom," writes Stevens, "without reference to the complexity of modern society, could only leave the country to the mercy of external economic and political forces which nullified the substance of British protection." Then, later, Stevens notes the erosion of tradition under the British system:

> The initial advantages of British administration, adapted as it was to the existing social and economic organization of Basuto society, were lost, however, with the emergence of a new range of social, political, and economic problems. Although the normal routine of Basuto life seemed to survive intact, forces at work were subtly altering its content within the traditional framework. The great increase in population became a serious factor in this undifferentiated agricultural society. The availability of land decreased and soil erosion reached staggering proportions. Traditional Basuto society was unequal to the new burden of monetary taxation and was forced to sacrifice the cream of its manpower to meet the need.

There were many other subtle alterations as well. If Moshesh (who died in 1870) ensured a line of succession, it was the British who ensured the paramountcy of his successors. Lerotholi, who succeeded Letsie, who had succeeded Moshesh, ultimately quelled rebellious chiefs in 1891. Stevens points out that unlike other Territories such as Swaziland, in Lesotho the king (Paramount Chief) was a totally political entity, "there being no mystical quality involved which would link the personality of the Paramount Chief in magico-religious rites with either soil or subjects." The British gave the Paramount Chief many of his powers. While Moshesh may have labored to merely contain the opposition, with time so many key positions were controlled by his successors that they could "govern more autocratically, and with less danger of opposition than Moshesh."

Similarly, the British rigidified the lesser chieftainships. In his article "Defining National Purpose in Lesotho," Richard Weisfelder notes that before British rule, the chieftainship functioned as a forum through which communities could adapt to external challenges, but that "colonial [sic] rule transformed them into citadels of selfish interest." A 1958 Report on Constitutional Reform and Chieftainship Affairs notes a tendency of the chiefs to look "upwards to the government for authority and support rather than as before, to the people." The local *pitsos,* in which the people would hash out their affairs, withered as another British import, the Basutoland Council, intruded ever more into domestic affairs.

In summary, the chief system which had been a two-way street through which local chiefs represented their people to the principal chiefs, and the principal chiefs to the people, became a one-way street through which the British and the chiefs administered the affairs of the country. Today in independent Lesotho, there are two principal political parties, and according to Weisfelder, one reflects the chief system of Moshesh's day, and the other the chief system that developed during British tenure. The Basutoland Congress party "emphasizes the egalitarian, consensual, cooperative, and innovative aspects of the national political heritage," while the Basuto National party (which is in power by virtue of a 1970 coup) reflects more the realities of the chieftainship during the days of British administration.

British presence produced noncultural changes as well, although these changes ultimately were to produce cultural dislocations. Peace and European medicine drastically reduced the death rate, and the population skyrocketed. From 1891 to 1904 the population increased from 218,900 to 349,500. Migration to work in South African mines, which began with the opening of the Kimberly mine in 1878, went up as well. In 1904, 86,155 passes were issued to migrants from Basutoland. The Basuto farmers who had been exporting bumper crops of wheat began to notice soil deterioration in the first decade of the twentieth century. Population pressure inexorably reduced that amount of land allowed to lie fallow and reconstitute, and crop yields began to fall. However, the incredible erosion which gives the country the scarred, barren look it has today had not yet appeared, nor had the land been denuded of trees. Then, in 1932, with the depression, the enormity of Lesotho's problems began to surface. Prices dropped, wiping out export of mohair and wool, a drought wiped out crops and livestock, and the rains which broke the drought carved huge gullies through the overcropped ground cover. Pressure for land drove farmers into the foothills, and the resultant runoff increased erosion. With declining acreage and yields, more and more Basuto left to work in South Africa's mines.

If the British wrought changes in the chief system and traditional way of life, and if population increase eventually transformed the face of the land, one institution survived until independence relatively unscathed. This was land tenure, which, perhaps, even more than the *pitso* system, was the basis for the egalitarian and communal aspects of Basuto life. In Richard Stevens' words, the "cornerstone" of British policy in Basutoland was to honor Moshesh's "express wish" that the territory be exclusively reserved for the Basuto. The British looked at the Paramount Chief as the trustee of the lands on behalf of the nation. Land was apportioned (generally three noncontiguous fields per family) through the principal chiefs and subchiefs to a person for life. Livestock grazed communally. The chiefs kept records of who had been given what land in their memory.

Even today the most striking thing about Lesotho is the orderly distribution of people throughout the country. There are some 7,100 villages in all. Sometimes one has to look for a moment at the base of a hill or mountain before realizing that there is a village nestled at its base, so well do Basuto architecture and design harmonize with the environment. Until just recently there were no large concentrations of people, nor were there any large concentrations of money. The principal chief lived in a kraal no more lavish than his neighbor. Moreover, the villages were relatively autonomous, self-sufficient entities. People pitched in together in the building of huts, and in the harvesting of fields (Moshesh once had to chastise missionaries not to pay for services the Basuto performed, fearing that the villagers might come to expect to be paid for all work).

From the circular organization of the village around the *pitso* tree and communal animal enclosure, or *lesaka,* through cooperative efforts such as harvesting or a sitting of the *kogtla,* every level of village life emphasized the interdependency of the villagers. No orphan was abandoned, nor elder turned out; the village was the unit, not the individual, and such wealth as there existed was spread evenly among members. Given the closeness of community life, negative forces such as envy reinforced this equality as well. One European told me that a few years back their gardener had refused a gift of some seed because he feared for his wife's welfare if his family should seem to prosper disproportionately to the rest of the village.

Rondevaals, the traditional Basuto huts, were built of branches covered with thatch and then evenly smeared with clay. As trees disappeared and the influence of Europeans seeped through Lesotho, the Basuto adapted native stone to their circular design. Often now there are half-stone, half-clay structures in the mountains and foothills. The Basuto have earned the reputation as excellent stonemasons. This gradual assimilation of stone into native design indicates that change might come to Lesotho without overwhelming local traditions. That the pace of change has quickened is evident as Basuto increasingly abandon native design totally in favor of rectangular, concrete-block and zinc-roofed structures.

Village organization and hut design both are part of a subsistence adaptation to a harsh environment. Yet harsh though that subsistence may have been, accounts suggest that village life used to be extremely tolerant of transgressions. Adultery brought nothing more than a beating of the errant wife by the offended husband, and a fine to the offending male. Missionary François Laydevant reports that if a child was born from adultery, the aggrieved husband sometimes exclaimed, "Certainly, she is guilty; but I readily pardon her because she has enriched our family with another child [although I doubt the aggrieved husband used precisely these words]." Laydevant goes on to note that natural children were never disinherited and that orphans were always taken into someone's care. The Basuto were also legendary in Africa for both hospitality and sharing. Says Laydevant: "[The policy of mutual aid] went hand in hand with solidarity which united all the inhabitants of a village against the common enemy. This sentiment was so strong that native courts would severely punish an entire village for hiding the faults of one of the community. Native courts always considered common good before any particular interest."

And, of course, basic to this pervasive collectivity was what the British called land tenure. It gave the Mosuto the security of knowing that none of his neighbors might envy the others' holdings. Land tenure has been tested and twisted under pressure from population growth, pressures for development, and changing Basuto values.

We tend to think of subsistence adaptations as conserving, and without disruption many such systems are, if only because without some natural balance between a people's numbers and the resources available they would starve and disappear. However, when this balance is thrown out of kilter—say, by a decrease in the infant-mortality rate or by confinement—flaws might surface that otherwise would be glossed by nature's reconstitutive powers. In the case of the Basuto, both the careless use of land and communal grazing tended to hasten erosion. Moreover, although traditionally pastoral, the Basuto increasingly turned to cultivation as they slaughtered the game which used to supplement their food supply. Lesotho used to teem with antelope, buffalo, zebra, hippo, monkey, hyena, leopard and lion. Since the Zulu wars drove the Basuto into the country, Lesotho has been virtually cleared of wildlife. But while there is no doubt that ill-conceived practices in Basuto agriculture, greatly intensified by population pressures, have been responsible for the denuding and scarring of the landscape, it is not clear that these wasteful practices would have overtaxed the reconstitutive powers of the environment had not improved medicine caused the Basuto population explosion, and had not the Zulus and Boers confined this population on the marginal land that is Lesotho today.

At independence in 1966 Lesotho was already an environmentalist's nightmare; however, its social institutions, though somewhat altered, were still intact. The country was beset with staggering erosion problems, lack of manpower due to labor migration, a greatly changed chief system, and a huge burden of population. But the country was still decentralized; the social institutions held together these thousands of communities. At independence Maseru, the capital, was still a small village, and the country had four miles of paved roads. It is the great changes that have occurred since independence that I was concerned with—the people who have introduced change, why they introduced it and who has benefited from it. However, any consideration of change in Lesotho must take into account the direct and indirect influences of its giant, racist neighbor, South Africa.

As far back as 1909 the Union of South Africa began to lobby for the eventual transfer of the High Commission Trust Territories (Basutoland, Bechuanaland, and Swaziland) to its control. There is no indication that before the Nationalist party victory in 1948, the British saw any future for the Trust Territories other than transfer to the Union. With that victory, however, and the development in South Africa of the policy of apartheid, the transfer of the Territories became a prospect that the British could not stomach. It is easy to guess South Africa's reasons for wanting the Territories. Independent, they might become hostile states harboring dissidents and exporting revolution; British unwillingness to turn them over was a nettlesome rebuke to South Africa's racial policies; the relative political autonomy of blacks within these Territories offered uncomfortable comparisons for South African blacks to ponder; and finally, Swaziland at least had manifest resources. However, Richard Stevens feels that in recent history other considerations came into play—namely, the late Prime Minister Hendrik F. Verwoerd's desire to give credibility to apartheid and the development of native reserves. The Tomlinson Commission Report, published in 1956, disclosed that all three Territories were intended to be part of the Bantustan system. Without the Territories, white South Africa would be offering the black majority only 13 percent of the country. With the Territories (with Bechuanaland's healthy chunk of the Kalahari Desert), South Africa would seem to be offering its blacks some 47 percent of its area— never mind that the Trust Territories were already densely populated.

When it became apparent that incorporation was out of the question, South Africa quickly summoned a smile and sought to make it clear that when independent, these countries would have everything to gain from close cooperation with South Africa, and everything to lose from hostility. South Africa was not unduly disturbed by its failure to gain control of the Territories because at the time of their independence it had all three economically hamstrung and could apply tremendous pressure should any of them export African nationalism to the Republic along with their manpower and resources. Since independence, great mineral resources have been found in Botswana as well as in Swaziland, which has timber and agricultural potential to boot. These discoveries make the prospects for their eventual economic independence ever more realistic. On the other hand, population increase and the dawning realization that Lesotho is impoverished both agriculturally and in terms of exploitable resources have made that country ever more dependent on its wealthy neighbor.

South Africa sees its security in the economic interdependence of all of southern Africa. In the words of Anton Rupert, the head of Rothman's International and a South African noted for his philanthropic efforts: "If they do not eat, we cannot sleep." In more pragmatic terms, this means that economic decisions are political decisions in South Africa. According to the political scientist Barbara Johnson, in the implementation of this policy Lesotho gets thrown about like the tip of a bullwhip as South Africa juggles agreements to economically enmesh neighbors more powerful than Lesotho. By manipulating import quotas and subsidies, and through control of rail traffic, South Africa can exert considerable influence over what industries will be developed in Lesotho, Botswana and Swaziland. South Africa does not want these three countries competing with or underpricing its own indigenous industries, even if the developer is South African. In 1962 Verwoerd warned that "any industry which goes into [Lesotho, Swaziland or Botswana] in the hopes of using cheaper labor will find itself in deep trouble." John Vorster changed this in 1967, but South African manipulations have in recent years prevented the development of a fertilizer factory in Swaziland, dissuaded the Japanese from starting a Honda venture in Lesotho, and more recently forced the tabling of the construction of the Oxbow Dam, which would have been the largest undertaking in Lesotho's history.

Part of South Africa's forced smile toward the newly independent Territories was the offer of legions of experts to

help guide their postindependence economic development. Lesotho was a particular beneficiary of this kindness.
In Lesotho there were many South Africans on secondment
(temporary assignment) placed in sensitive positions of the
newly independent government. Wynand Van Graan was
loaned by Anton Rupert to head LNDC (the Lesotho National Development Corporation); Fred Roach came in to
head the Police Mobile Unit, which serves in Lesotho as
both army and political police; the radio station was run by
a South African. In 1969 there were also South Africans
serving as Resident Magistrate, Chief Justice, Attorney
General, Prosecutor, and Master of the High Court. In some
cases South Africans worked outright to hamper the work of
the offices to which they were attached. For instance, on
one trip to Vienna, a South African attached to the LNDC
was reported to buttonhole the people with whom Prime
Minister Leabua Jonathan talked and to follow up Jonathan's pitch by telling potential investors that investment in
Lesotho was ill-advised. In another instance of this type of interference, the South African on secondment to the Lesothan
radio station censored UNESCO reports that were offensive
to the Republic, but did not bother to tell the Lesothan government that he had done so. Finally, while not completely
verified, it is widely believed that South Africa backed the
coup (there is no question that South Africa supported Jonathan before the coup) that put Jonathan in power. Jonathan
had lost the 1970 election in which he ran for a second term
as Prime Minister, but before the results were in, he seized
power. The winner of the election, Ntsu Mokhehle of the
Basutoland Congress party was at that time strongly na-
tionalistic and thought by South Africa to be a dangerous
man. I might note that there was a touch of the surreal in
this coup. Chief Peete Peete had been a constable before
returning to Lesotho from the Republic. To be a constable
in South Africa is far more lucrative than being a principal
chief in Lesotho. Another principal chief who benefited

from the coup, Maseribane, had been a chef in South Africa. (Chief Peete Peete and Chief Maseribane were reputed to have talked Jonathan into going through with the coup rather than conceding the election.)

It must be pointed out in balance that many South Africans came to Lesotho to help, with no interest other than genuine concern.

Actually, South Africa has little need to use heavy-handed tactics to influence the internal policies of Lesotho, so deeply is the country dependent on South Africa for its economic survival. In 1970–71 the Lesothan gross domestic product was about 42.5 million rand (R = $1.50) of which some 29 million rand was monetized! The rest consisted of the value of subsistence agriculture. That same year Basuto workers in the Republic sent back some 20 million rand from their mine earnings. Contract workers sent back an amount equivalent to two thirds of the money generated domestically by the Lesothan economy. They earned a hell of a lot more than the economy generates domestically. Moreover, that money in the form (common to many countries) of Post Office deposits and savings is the capital base for the projects of LNDC and Lesotho National Bank. Those remittances that don't go into savings filter through the economy in the form of consumer spending (although most of the money ends up in the hands of non-Basuto traders). If a significant number of miners were to return to Lesotho, the banks and LNDC would suffer a net outflow of deposits rather than enjoy the present net inflow, and the nation would be faced with a desperate liquidity crisis. Lesotho belongs to the South African Rand Customs Union, which means that in the event of such a crisis, the government could not issue currency to meet its obligations.

Belonging to the Rand has its benefits, to be sure, because South African currency is one of the strongest in the world, and more important, Lesotho's share of the Customs Union pool—some 14.6 million rand estimated for 1973–74—

accounts for nearly 70 percent of government revenue. But this points out Lesotho's dependence on South Africa even more sharply. The price of mine-labor remittances is the loss of Lesotho's manpower and the loss of flexibility in policy toward South Africa. The price of Customs Union revenue and enjoying the strength of the Rand is the loss of a vitally important policy instrument—control over currency. Yet Lesotho hesitates to issue its own currency because it realizes that with nothing to support its value, no one would want to take it, and that the government would quickly succumb under the burdens of attempting to control an inevitable black market that would arise.

The only thing worse than losing its manpower to South African mines would be to have the miners come home. In the spring of 1975 Lesotho inadvertently suffered a sobering reminder of what might happen should South Africa decide to employ any of the legal weapons it possesses against its tiny neighbor. After a spate of mine riots in which Basuto clashed with Xhosas (members of a Bantu tribe in Transkei with whom they have never enjoyed good relations), some ten thousand miners returned to Lesotho. Even this small number brought near-chaos to Maseru. Crime soared as the returnees overwhelmed the capital's already saturated capacity to employ and house its inhabitants. The crisis abated only when the miners were allowed to return to the mines.

Finally, if South Africa's complete economic domination of Lesotho were not enough, all Lesotho's commerce must pass through the Republic. South Africa can control what enters and leaves Lesotho, as well as what goes on within the country through seemingly harmless manipulations of rail traffic and tariffs. Lesotho must make almost all of her import purchases either in South Africa or through South African intermediaries. Some observers believe that upon independence the Transkei will provide Lesotho with an all-African corridor to the sea (as well as with land for

Lesotho's population); however, others have pointed out that the Transkei has no natural harbor suitable for development, and that relations between Xhosas and Basuto might turn out to be considerably worse than relations between Basuto and South Africans.

However, for Lesotho there is, believe it or not, a bright side to all this. If Lesotho were surrounded by an African-ruled country, it would probably not receive a tenth the aid it receives today. But because of South Africa's racial policies, Lesotho is a very popular place to help: without much investment, a nation or organization can strike a blow against apartheid. The thrust of all aid efforts is to make Lesotho less dependent on South Africa, and regardless of the prospects of achieving this goal, to make the attempt makes good copy at home and in the rest of black Africa. In the words of Cyril Rodgers, the vice-chancellor of the University of Botswana, Lesotho and Swaziland, "Lesotho is dependent on world understanding of circumstances of history and geography. We must tap the conscience of the world if we are to exist." This pity, however hypocritical, is indeed essential to Lesotho's survival.

Besides the political attractiveness of striking out against apartheid, there are other reasons why nations and organizations find Lesotho such a charismatic place. It is one of the twenty-five poorest nations on earth, and one of six singled out by the UN for special attention. There is little of the corruption that is endemic throughout the underdeveloped world. Consequently donors can give with reasonable confidence that their money is not going to end up in the wrong hands (in fact, much money ends up in the hands of people of the same nationality as the country that originally did the giving). Moreover, the government lets high-power donors like UN, AID and the World Bank do what they want to do. There is still a great deal of deference toward Europeans in Lesotho, and experts find it easy to push through

their ideas. There are also great numbers of whites sprinkled throughout the government, and this presence, in spite
of protestations to the contrary, further reassures donors
that their funds will be efficiently allocated. Finally, there
is a type of competition which has developed between different agencies simply because Lesotho is such a basket
case among nations. Each agency coming in wants to be the
one that cracked Lesotho. As Hy Helman, head of planning
and evaluation for the giant Thaba Bosiu project, put it,
"Nobody knows about one successful project in Lesotho.
We want to be the one that succeeds."

When we consider the number of experts and programs
that are part of this unofficial competition, we begin to see
how fierce the contest is, and to wonder why, so far, it has
not produced any results. The UN Report on Development
Assistance for 1973 counts some 270 expatriate* experts in
the country at the end of that year, plus some 75 volunteers.
This figure is exclusive of private-organization personnel
such as officials for CARE, Catholic Relief Services, Save
the Children and OXFAM, as well as of missionaries. Besides 104 experts funded by the United Kingdom (which as
donor of last resort fills any gaps left by the government or
other donors), the UN has 74 people in-country, filling sensitive posts:

> Emphasis continued to be placed in the agricultural sector
> with 8 technicians assigned to programming, coordinating,
> and policy supporting functions in the Ministry of Agricul-
> ture, and 21 working in a variety of administrative and tech-
> nical roles in the three area-base programs—Leribe, Thaba
> Bosiu, and Senqu—which at present constitute the main
> thrust of Lesotho's rural development efforts. UN experts
> were also placed in high level roles close to policy in sev-
> eral other fields, e.g., Commissioner of Mines, Managing

* For convenience, non-natives who have gone abroad to assist a country refer to themselves as "expatriates" or "expats."

Director of the LNDC, Vice-Chancellor of UBLS [University of Botswana, Lesotho and Swaziland], Director of Posts and Telecommunications and two advisors to the Central Planning and Development Office . . .

There were 92 other experts filling different posts and coming from South Africa, Taiwan, the United States, the Netherlands, Canada, Sweden, Belgium, Israel, France, Korea, Germany and Denmark.

Altogether the report estimates donor commitments for 1973 and beyond which amount to some $70 million, and this figure is exclusive of large donations expected from Iran and Libya. That figure is significantly larger than the dollars the home economy generates in a year.

This figure would be even higher were it not for the limiting factor of what the experts call the "absorptive capacity" of the economy. In economic jargon, it is lack of "paper" that limits the largesse of the donors. "Paper" consists of plans for what to do with the money, and a bureaucracy to serve as conduit and administrator for funds once committed.

Given this panoply of aid, one might well wonder whether it is safe to make general characterizations or safe to examine an organization like CARE as typical, especially since the different expatriate agencies are constantly disparaging each other's programs and personnel. However, there is an incredible cross-fertilization of money and personnel as well as a host of shared assumptions and vogues in development that elide these disagreements and give a general character to the spectrum of development assistance in Lesotho. When the different agencies spot what they consider a winner of a project, like Thaba Bosiu or Thaba Khupa (projects we shall encounter), a host of them jump in, offering money and assistance. Agencies like CARE, the Catholic Relief Services and OXFAM which might be critical of each other in private will find themselves supporting the same project. Field personnel often move from agency to agency while remaining in Lesotho, or might be funded by a succession of different agencies while working on one project. Similarly, a major donor like AID might use several different agencies as conduits for its money. AID is keeping a low profile these days and is sluicing a lot of money ("laundering," in the words of one expatriate) through private agencies like CARE.

These interconnections form a web between the different agencies. From the Basuto point of view, the expatriates are a common puissant front.

SIX

First Impressions,
First Questions

In August of 1974 a small Hawker-Siddeley prop engine
plane took me into Leabua Jonathan Airport, which is an
airstrip and series of low informal buildings cut into the
plain just north of Maseru, Lesotho's capital. Going through
customs, I was asked to fill out a detailed form listing
every item purchased during my stay in South Africa. I
was wary because elsewhere in Africa such forms are a device for extracting heavy duties, or more common, bribes.
However, in Lesotho these forms serve not to exploit the
traveler, but to help Lesotho determine her share of the
Rand Customs Union revenue pool. A new agreement with
South Africa, retroactive to 1969, redistributes customs, excise and sales duties according to the former Trust Territory's actual share of imports, and production and consump-
tion of excisable and dutiable products. Lesotho's share is
then multiplied by 1.42 (as are the other former Trust Territories' shares), a factor of compensation for the loss of fiscal
discretion which accompanies Lesotho's use of the Rand.
The result of this new arrangement has been to multiply
Lesotho's revenue from the customs and revenue pool by
nearly a factor of ten. Every item reported on the form
handed to the visitor at the airport contributes a minuscule
amount to Lesotho's share of the pool. The dimensions of

these earnings are such that in 1973–74, Lesotho received five times as much from this arrangement with South Africa as she raised through direct taxes. Customs and excise now account for some 70 percent of the government's revenue and have enabled Lesotho to show a surplus for the first time in many years. These earnings have also freed Lesotho from a dependence on British grants-in-aid, but, of course, at the price of increasing her dependence on her hated neighbor. In short, I didn't mind filling out the form.

The drive into Maseru from the airport took us past warrens of squatter huts and dusty stands, and then into the main street of Maseru itself. Before I left for Lesotho, I had extensive briefings from a number of people who had been there over the past few years, and all had described Maseru as a small frontier-type town. Although the main street still had the flavor of a small town in the American Southwest, I was surprised by the number of people and the amount of building going on. The Lesotho National Bank building, an expensive-looking concrete structure, is faced with native red and blue designs. The government buildings and many other buildings on Moshoeshoe II reflect the Basuto skill in working with native stone.

It was the original King Moshesh who built the first stone house. That was atop Thaba Bosiu and it was in emulation of the design constructed by missionary Eugene Casalis at the base of the hill. Until recently, Basuto stoneworking talents have been ignored. This has led to some sad ironies. While I was in Lesotho the first edition of a new newspaper entitled the *Comet* appeared. On the front page was an article heralding the commencement of a low-cost housing scheme. Above the article were two pictures. One showed a simple but not unattractive dwelling in native stone, and the other an elaborate modern structure. The caption read: "The LNDC scheme would tear down eyesores like this [the stone house] . . . and replace them with something like this [the new house]." The modern house pictured, far from low-cost, was one of the more expensive homes in Maseru. On the other hand, the Lesotho National Development Corporation is currently building a hotel which will be faced with stonework.

The first night in Maseru I stayed at the Holiday Inn. In the summer of 1974 there were three hotels in town; four years earlier there had been one; by next summer there should be five. The Holiday Inn is the subject of some controversy. Several of the expatriates and volunteers I talked with refused to eat or stay at the hotel. When necessary, they would lodge at the Basuto-owned hotel located near the airport. Some expatriates and Basuto regard the Holiday Inn as the wrong type of development: critics claim that the amount of benefit to the Basuto does not outweigh such negatives as the fact that the profits go to a foreign-controlled company, that the hotel is white-managed, with Basuto filling only low- and intermediate-level jobs, and that its casino is as much a lure for poor Basuto as it is for rich South Africans. Others see the hotel as a significant contributor to the Lesothan economy. When I spoke with Cyril Rodgers at the University of Botswana, Lesotho and Swaziland, he remarked that Lesotho was probably the "only country in the world that can balance its budget on the basis of one hotel. Take away the Holiday Inn, and you are back to British grants-in-aid." Lesotho does realize a substantial sum from the hotel through direct and indirect taxes. The figure for 1973–74 was unofficially pegged at 800,000 rand, which would make the hotel the government's second biggest domestic source of tax revenue. Still other critics see the hotel's effects on the country's values as far more significant than any possible revenue gain.

The hotel is a sprawling structure which occupies a several-acre wire-enclosed compound. The compound extends from the Caledon River, which is Lesotho's western border with South Africa, up a hillside where it abuts on the relatively posh section of Maseru called Europa. Europa and Maseru West used to be exclusively European reserves for British administrators. The hotel offers swimming, gambling, horseback riding, torrid strip acts and "racy" shows such as *Hair*. Books and magazines banned in South Africa are readily available in the lobby across from the main desk. In certain ways the former Trust Territories that are now Lesotho and Swaziland provide services for South Africa that such border towns as Tijuana and Nuevo Laredo used to provide for Americans. South Africans now come to Lesotho and Swaziland as much for sin as they do for backpacking. Swaziland took advantage of this potential market earlier than Lesotho, but with the Holiday Inn, Lesotho has been making rapid strides. Nearby is Lancer's Inn, where curious South African whites can meet black prostitutes without fear of the law. (Although Lesothan prostitutes export a particularly persistent strain of gonorrhea.)

One of the people I spoke with before I left on my trip was William Edgett Smith, who spent a number of years in Africa and is the author of a book about Tanzania's Julius Nyere entitled *We Must Run While They Walk*. When we met and talked about what I might expect in Africa and what I should avoid, the conversation eventually turned to the question of development and charity. We argued a bit about such things as urban migration, and then Smith said that in his mind, the lowliest bellhop in a hotel in downtown Nairobi was better off than a chief in a village, because that bellhop had joined the Western economy and might "benefit" from it, while the chief had not. In effect, Smith is saying that pandering to the appetites of foreigners outweighs the satisfactions of a non-Western way of life because it offers the promise of money and Westernization.

Tourism is a major route to development throughout Africa and the non-Western world. Still, that first day it made me uneasy to see Basuto in bellhop uniforms, and it made me uneasy to wander through the Basuto Hat, where the road to the Holiday Inn meets the Kingsway. The

Basuto Hat is where Basuto handicrafts are marketed for tourists. It contains rugs with classic bold Basuto designs, fine jewelry, moccasins and the like. The display is airy and artful, there is nothing gaudy about the room or the goods, but still, it is with mixed feelings that one confronts a culture marketing its arts.

I remember my first impressions of Bali when I arrived there a few years ago. Bali is one of those places commonly associated with paradise. It has a rich cultural life in which Hinduism and native arts blend in a series of performances and ceremonies which every day give the Balinese something to do and further marry him to his religion and culture. By appearances, Bali is what the brochures call enchanted, but upon inspection, it turns out to be cursed. Sukharno and the Intercontinental Hotel chain have succeeded brilliantly in teaching every person on the island the English word "Hello." At first this seems like hospitality, but I came to believe that it represented the spreading of a cancer. Young Hindus now attempt to sell Americans Balinese women, something that was unheard of in pre-tourism days. When I went into the mountains on a motorcycle to a village noted as the home of religious artists, I encountered hawkers and signs in English reading "Primitive artist within." Later I paid a stiff fee to see a barong dance and watched along with fat tourists as a myth of good and evil was played out before our uncomprehending eyes. Depressed by the weight of my shattered dreams of Bali, I, perhaps unfairly, came to look at the island as a cultural whorehouse, and left as soon as I could.

I say that my indictment of Bali was perhaps unfair because at that time I was projecting the destruction of a culture that was still largely intact. But my projections were not so unreasonable. Bali now has a jetport which has brought the island on line in the world-tourism nexus. Later I had a minor argument in Hong Kong with a man named Toddy Wynn who was planning to add to Bali's tourist capacity by building another luxury hotel. He could not understand the sadness with which I greeted this news. After all, he was providing employment, helping to bring big-spending tourists into Bali, which by any measure has a low standard of living. Much as I felt sad for the impending destruction of another non-Western way of life, I also felt claustrophobic in the face of what was happening in Bali. Greed, or the money instinct, seemed to be universal. Was there a culture that could not be bought?

A person will not sell something he cherishes or believes in. The war veteran will not sell the lighter that carried him through World War II, perhaps because he associates that lighter in some way with his survival. The Kom tribe suffered the theft and sale of their Afo-A-Kom totem; it was the soul of the tribe. When an individual or a culture sells its heritage, it indicates a changed relationship with that heritage. When people who produce artifacts for religious reasons begin to produce those artifacts for money, it is a safe bet that their religion has lost its authority. I do not know how a people can sell or mass-produce their religious patrimony for sweating tourists and still claim that they are developing without sacrificing their heritage.

The counterargument to my sense of claustrophobia is that a society can Westernize without sacrificing its cultural heritage. When I was in Lesotho I thought about that question in somewhat more immediate terms. The Basuto's decorative spirit is now geared toward the tourist market, as are the native dances that interrupt one's ruminations in Maseru on Saturday afternoon; ancestor worship has all but succumbed to seventy-five years of Christian threats and promises. As in most "developing" nations, handicrafts in Lesotho are viewed as an important adjunct of tourism, and a voluntary project related to handicrafts was one of the first things I encountered when I made contact with CARE on my second day.

The CARE offices are part of a compound set behind a new hotel. The compound consists of three low buildings set in a rough arc. One outer building houses Catholic Relief Services, the center building houses CARE, and the other outbuilding houses the World Food Program. The CARE offices consist of four rooms: assistant director Bob McCullam's office; a small office where, alternately a Mosuto on secondment as assistant field representative from the government of Lesotho named Daniel Marite and a Peace Corpsman on secondment named Kent Black worked; a central office where three or four Basuto employees performed various clerical tasks; and director Ray Rignall's office. The official staff consists of the two Americans and three Basuto. Bob McCullam greeted me (he had been advised by CARE New York that I was coming) and explained that the director was on home leave. McCullam was an excellent host throughout my stay, and responded to all my questions and requests in an open and forthright manner.

McCullam is in his mid-forties, a former engineer with a background in the merchant marine, the Navy and engineering-consultant work. In 1962 he and his wife joined the Peace Corps and worked in Chile on urban community development projects. His Peace Corps contacts brought him to the attention of CARE, which he joined in 1967. Previous to his assignment to Lesotho as assistant director, he served in Guatemala, Indonesia and Nigeria.

McCullam is a tall, folksy, unaffected man. Whether he agrees with you or not, he begins every other sentence with a long thoughtful "Nooo." He has a number of self-deprecating gestures, and his accent and manner provide a source of entertainment for some of the British expatriates who amuse themselves by mimicking their non-British colleagues. Most of them are fond of McCullam. On his days off he often goes duck hunting or golfing with some of the people he works with.

The first thing McCullam did was brief me on the basic CARE program in Lesotho. His direct contact is with the

Department of Community and Rural Development, or
Comrudev, as it is known to acronymic wags. Comrudev
was called the Food Aid office during the drought in
1966–67. Desmond Taylor, a British expatriate with two
decades' experience in Lesotho, is the director; John Hurst,
another British expat is the project officer and CARE's direct liaison on actual projects; and yet another Englishman,
Bob Phillips, who like Taylor had been in Lesotho for a
long time, is CARE's liaison on road projects. While it is not
easy to fault the qualifications or knowledge of Lesotho of
men like Phillips or Taylor, it is interesting that CARE's
basic contacts in Lesotho are with non-Basuto.

McCullam divided CARE's program into four categories,
all of which fit within that new CARE umbrella, the Multi-
Year Plan. The Multi-Year Plan is supposed to replace the
ad hoc nature of previous CARE programming in the Third
World by putting project decisions on a longer-term basis
and allowing station directors to develop an in-country
focus. In New York the MYP means budgetary differences,
and differences in accounting procedures. Overseas it
means different paper work, and as we shall see, little else.

McCullam said that the biggest project category was a
school-desk factory that CARE was sponsoring in conjunction with the Ministry of Education. This was the project
that Kent Black, the Peace Corpsman, was on secondment
to assist. At that moment the project had been in the works
for six months. Food-for-work labor was leveling the site.

The second category was continued food-for-work road
building under Desmond Taylor for which CARE was sup-
plying material for culverting (food-for-work wages coming
from Catholic Relief Services and the World Food Program), and warehouses for materials, and CARE was also
"upgrading and putting in drainage on existing track."

The third category was small industries, which McCullam said CARE was easing into under the encouragements
of John Hurst. CARE was to become involved in a mohair

processing plan in which the British voluntary agency OXFAM was also involved. The project involved building simple spinning wheels from local materials so that Lesotho, a major exporter of raw mohair, might free herself of the ironic necessity of importing expensive processed mohair for the Royal Lesotho Carpet Weavers.

The fourth category McCullam termed "community improvement," a catch-all category including the ad hoc programming which CARE was hoping to phase out. The category now includes all unfinished business such as health clinics, water systems, classroom construction, and assistance to the Thaba Khupa Farm Institute.

As is the case with most grand ideas contrived in the United States for application thousands of miles away—whether they be counterinsurgency programs, or in CARE's case, MYPs and "dovetailing into the five-year plan of a developing nation"—translate into something less grand when one considers specifics. A few weeks after I first met McCullam, I was able to secure an itemized list of the CARE program for 1972–74 through a UN official who keeps tabs on voluntary assistance in Lesotho. The budgeted amount was $142,108.72 for school construction, road construction, radio equipment, agricultural equipment, hand tools and industrial arts. I present the list here to illustrate the nuts and bolts behind CARE's various categories and descriptions:

1) Itekeng Primary School
    Roofing Materials 3,729.15
2) Road Construction (Food
    Aid) Bulldozer . . . .   29,925.—
3) Radio Equipment (F.D.S.) Generators
    and Batteries 4,404.40
4) Food Storage Buildings (Food Aid) 9,511.50
5) Secondary School. Const. (Min. of Ed) . . .   18,900.—
6) Secondary School Const. (Min. of Ed)
    Steel Const. /cement/windows-
    door frames . . . .   49,350.—

7) Thaba Khupa Farm Inst.—Oxen and oxen equip.	1,977—
8) Hand Tools (picks, shovels, wheelbarrows, Food Aid)	14,464.36
9) Stone Crusher (Food Aid)	4,500.—
10) St. Paul 2nd School Roofing Material ...	1,664.67
11) 3 Rural Primary Schools—Kyanyene-Toloone-Maliele Roofing materials	2,912.12
12) Industrial Arts Hand Tools, St. Monica..	770.42
	$142,108.72

The preponderant amount of money is devoted to school construction, with road construction running a close second —pretty much what CARE is doing throughout Africa. Whether or not CARE's budget increases, as it claims it will with the new MYP, remains to be seen.

Shortly after McCullam and I discussed the CARE projects, he asked me where I was staying. I told him the Holiday Inn, and added that I was thinking about moving. Kent Black then mentioned that he knew of a British expat who was about to depart on home leave and would like to have someone look after his place. To find this man's house we had to contact Mike Bevins, an IVS (International Volunteer Service) carpenter who was working on the spinning-wheel-factory end of the mohair processing project in which CARE was to become involved. And so we set out for the Maseru crafts center to give me an idea of the project, and hopefully to help me find new digs for my stay in Lesotho.

The Maseru crafts center is a series of government-owned workshops built around a small square. Craftsmen may come in and use tools and buildings for low rent; the spinning-wheel factory occupies one of these workshops.

The idea of the spinning-wheel factory was to produce a machine that was sufficiently inexpensive that Basuto could afford it, and at the same time sufficiently reliable to produce mohair yarn comparable to that which could be produced on imported spinning wheels. This, according to

Comrudev, would create an export market, free local industries from reliance on imported processed mohair, shift
"agricultural emphasis" from crops to sheep and goats and
perhaps help check soil erosion, and provide a cash income
for Lesotho's women and perhaps offset the income loss
that occurs through the repatriation of Basuto miners. Given
such breath-taking benefits, the spinning-wheel factory
seemed like a masterly stroke. Its simplicity and practicality
recalls Lederer and Burdick's parable of the Ugly American, who with his native colleague Jeepo devises a water
pump powered by bicycles. In fact, the spinning wheel,
which was designed by OXFAM, is also constructed from
bicycle parts. However, reality is not quite as smooth as
parable.

Mike Bevins, the IVS carpenter, was at work in the shed
when we arrived. Bevins is a sincere, no-nonsense Englishman who is very good at his job. McCullam reported that he
had improved on the OXFAM design by introducing a re-
movable bobbin. Bevins had two Basuto working with him.
Together they could turn out one spinning wheel in a day
and a half.

The spinning-wheel project was my first introduction to
the incredible cross-fertilization of agencies and people, a
cross-fertilization which made it difficult to speak about
"good" or "bad" voluntary agencies, because several agencies might be involved in the same project; or, on the other
hand, an expatriate might work for several different agencies during his tenure in Lesotho. This intertwining also
makes it easier to picture the "nature" of voluntary-agency
involvement abroad.

The original money for the spinning-wheel factory came
from OXFAM, according to McCullam. Then the Lesothan
government took over and attempted to administer the project. Reportedly, bureaucratic considerations made it difficult to market the machines through the government, so responsibility for the project shifted to the U.S. Save the Chil-

dren. Now CARE was to get involved. CARE agreed to buy spinning wheels from Save the Children and mohair from local traders. CARE would then donate these articles to the Lesotho Cooperative Handicrafts, which in turn would sell them to women's groups; in turn, these groups would pay for the machines and mohair with money borrowed from the Credit Union League. The money paid to the Lesotho Cooperative Handicrafts could then be used to expand mohair-related activities, and the women's groups purportedly could pay back the Credit Union through profits realized by the sale of processed mohair. This complicated arrangement is called a revolving fund.

Bevins interrupted his description of the spinning-wheel operation to complain to McCullam about Pauline Woodall, who was involved with the mohair processing scheme at the Roma Valley Cooperative, and the way she had thrown Bevins' operation into a bad light. According to Bevins, the trouble had begun three weeks previously when Ms. Woodall "demanded" whatever machines were ready. Bevins responded that the machines were not completely tested and ready to be sent out. Purportedly, Pauline Woodall said to send the machines anyway, and that if there was any trouble they would take care of it in Roma. Bevins sent the machines, and for a while there was no word from Pauline. Then an OXFAM inspection team visited Roma, and according to Bevins, Pauline "complained about the quality of the spinning wheels." OXFAM then gave Bevins "bloody hell." I asked Bevins what the motive of such behavior might be, but he would only speculate.

Before we departed, Bevins told me how to find the British expat's house and contact his boss if my prospective host had already left for vacation.

Back in town McCullam introduced me to John Hurst, CARE's liaison in Comrudev on small industries, who had been encouraging CARE to become involved with the spinning-wheel factory. Hurst noted Bevins' complaint and remarked that he had to go out to Roma, anyway, and he invited me to accompany him that afternoon.

I had heard a lot about John Hurst before I arrived in Lesotho. He was one of the expats the American volunteers I spoke with remembered, and he was remembered with considerable resentment. One volunteer described him as a lackey of Prime Minister Leabua Jonathan, another said that he had ingratiated himself with the Prime Minister. Everyone I spoke with remarked that for an eighteen-year-old British IVS volunteer with 0-level education (the equivalent of high school), Hurst had achieved a lot of power with awful rapidity. While he was still in his teens Hurst was put in charge of well drilling in Lesotho; a few years later he was put in charge of water-supply systems. One former Peace Corpsman remarked that Hurst was glib and managed to convince people that he knew a lot more than he did. Another described him as a "real neocolonial" who looked rather rugged riding around in his land-rover, and that the Prime Minister liked the image Hurst projected.

Hurst was known as a "big idea" man, a dreamer who was careless about designing projects and who did not really care whether or not the beneficiary villages were interested in the projects he was administering. Dan Hogan, a former Peace Corpsman, remarked that there was no reason why Hurst could not have trained a Basuto to replace him within six months, and Hogan claimed that a volunteer named Larry Roth was kicked out of the country for suggesting this.

Altogether, my preconceptions about Hurst were about as unflattering a portrait as one might compose: I expected Hurst to be the paradigm of the self-seeking soldier of fortune who goes to a poor country to play out his fantasies of power and maneuver himself into a position far more exalted than he might ever achieve at home. Upon meeting Hurst I made a strange discovery. I could readily understand how he could inspire such resentment, and from watching him in operation I could well imagine him making the mistakes ascribed to him by former volunteers, and yet Hurst is a remarkably likable character, and delightful company.

The Americans I talked with before coming to Lesotho were speaking about the John Hurst they had met five to seven years before. I considered the possibility that he had changed radically in the intervening years, but then I had to discard that thesis. The composite image of Hurst presented by his present colleagues was not dissimilar, except that tales of his foibles were tinged with genuine affection. McCullam, who dealt with Hurst almost daily, remarked that Hurst was a "big picture" man as opposed to a man like himself who was more concerned with logistics and practical problems. Everyone seemed to know Hurst liked to exaggerate, yet these same people obviously valued his company and enjoyed his humor. Hurst himself would freely admit that he exaggerated, and he would also freely admit that he could and perhaps should be replaced by a Mosuto. Often when called up on one of his more outrageous statements, Hurst would grin shamefacedly and accept this defeat with good humor.

What these impressions of Hurst showed me was that I was susceptible to the same false impressions of good and evil that surround the volunteer with his protective noumenon and which make charity so difficult to investigate. Because I liked Hurst, I at first tended to dismiss the negative conception his former colleagues had given me. When we think of someone as causing harm in volunteer work overseas, we expect to find that person fired by blinding ambition, or blinded by messianic fervor perhaps, but we would not expect to peel back to the last veil concealing this Dr. Moriarty of development and find a good-hearted, outrageous but likable jokester. "What!" we say to ourselves, "you can't be our villain!" and we go off looking for a more traditional fall guy: the corrupt expert, the self-serving bureaucrat.

There is a powerful logic to this reaction because journalists, as well as everyone else, need to be able to peg good and evil, and in contrast to the standard pegs for evil—corporate and political spies, assassins, military dictators—the volunteer and the AID expert look quite good. Regardless of what we intellectually come to know about the effects of development or aid programs, we still contrast them positively with the sordidness that characterizes economic and political power play in foreign affairs. That is why the journalist who one week writes an article showing how development programs indirectly led to starvation in the Sahelian drought might the next week write an article arguing that our foreign policy should downplay military assistance and concentrate on development aid. In the sub-Saharan area called the Sahel he might be horrified by the short-sightedness of a particular development program, but when he looks at development in contrast with the other things we do overseas, our journalist decides that development assistance might be characterized by inefficiency and mistakes, but taken as a whole its motivation is good. Or to take another example, the *New York Times* might on the same day have articles about the nightmarish consequences of development, and editorials pressing for more industrial development in the Third World. This happened on September 2, 1975, for instance. On page ten an article headlined "Expert Warns of Acceleration in Extinction of Animal Species Despite Conservation Bids" was devoted largely to the antidevelopment warnings of an ecologist named Ian McTaggart Cowan. Dr. Cowan noted:

> It may well be that the nonindustrial societies are fortunate in that they can seek to follow paths of development less destructive and more sustainable than those followed by the so-called developed nations . . . Industrialism is the peculiar product of the temperate lands. Although some tropical environments are responsive to its methods and technologies, many are not and suffer irreparable damage from

their application. The spread over the world of the industrial objectives of northern peoples can be seen as a most destructive event. Almost inevitably diversity is sacrificed to a spurious efficiency.

That same day an article about a Kissinger proposal of new institutions and funds for development was displayed prominently on page one. These proposals called for, among other things, "The establishment of an international industrialization institute to aid developing countries with research on industrial development." In its lead editorial that day, entitled "Welcome Initiative," the *Times* warmly endorsed the Kissinger proposals and totally ignored the dissent on development it had relegated to page ten. After all, the cautionary words of scientists do not much matter when considered in contrast to Kissinger's "welcome" interest in the poorer lands. Moreover, if our urge to assist in economic development is not good, then what is?

And so I had to fight a powerful urge to make the same mistake—to look for a few villains sullying an otherwise noble enterprise—and I had to steel myself to the idea that people I found likable and well-motivated might be bringing misery to the lives of the very people they were trying to help. My thesis was that it was not the personalities involved, but basic properties of voluntary assistance that accounted for its many failures. If economic development projects in Lesotho had the negative repercussions one might imagine, then the flinty appraisal given Hurst by his former colleagues was entirely justified, regardless of his personal virtues.

By the way, Hurst was not the rugged neocolonial that I had been led to expect. He is cherubic, blond and entirely harmless-looking. When we drove out to Roma, I noticed that once his tendency to bloviate was discounted, Hurst did have a perceptive view of Lesotho's situation, and his situation in Lesotho.

The drive from Maseru to Roma takes you from the plains bordering the Caledon River to the base of the forbidding Maluti Mountains. At first we saw shacks, concrete-and-zinc stores and homes strung out along the road, then as we moved farther away from town, the roadside settlements thinned, and we passed through ravaged farm and pastureland. It was August, winter in Lesotho, and a bright sun brought the temperature into the fifties and warmed the Basuto treading beside the road in their heavy karosses.

The countryside looked like a demonstration model for the effects of a Malthusian ecocatastrophe. The lowlands were denuded of trees and scarred with gigantic gullies, or dongas, as they are called. The mountains had only spare cover. Everywhere I traveled there were stumps where trees might have matured. Without wood for fuel, the Basuto burn dung which deprives them of fertilizer for their crops; with diminishing yields per acre, the Basuto farm marginal areas which increases soil erosion: it seems that in Lesotho you can't turn around without encountering a situation that might be summed up in one of those damn vicious circles.

The size of the dongas was staggering. Some cut sixty-foot-wide swaths through fields, and there might be two or three such ravines cutting through one small holding. Passing these huge gullies brought my mind back to the mohair project and caused me to wonder about Comrudev's statement that "the direct benefit from correct grazing control and less ploughing will be the *checking of soil erosion*." Before coming to Lesotho I had read a World Bank report which analyzed the country's economy. Paragraph 89 of that document reads:

> Under present husbandry practices the number of live-stock exceeds the carrying capacity of the land. Lack of grazing control has led to a serious deterioration of mountain pastures. Together with uncontrolled breeding, this has affected

the quality and productivity of the animals. Not only has output stagnated, but there is now a severe shortage of sufficiently strong animals at ploughing time. The worsening ecological situation in the mountains has led to a movement of people and animals to the lowlands and foothills, adding to the pressure on the land there.

Earlier the report referred to the Basuto's use of livestock:

> Studies in connection with the Leribe Pilot Agricultural Scheme revealed that cattle are held principally for traction at ploughing time, to meet social obligations, and as a store of wealth and prestige. Sheep and goats are principally held for domestic slaughter, and only in the second place for their wool and mohair. Small stock are also very important as everyday currency and are often used in sale or exchange for school fees, clothes, government taxes, etc.

These considerations cast a shadow over the innocent, optimistic speculations offered by Comrudev concerning the mohair project. The two key phrases are "providing correct management is undertaken" in the Comrudev handout and in the World Bank report, "under present husbandry practices." There is no question that the same qualifying phrase "providing correct management is undertaken" might be applied to crops, and one might again claim that this would lead to the checking of soil erosion. However, as Hurst himself is one of the first to point out, twenty-five years of effort expended to introduce correct management of crops have had insignificant effects. One wonders why Comrudev should think that it would be any easier to introduce proper management procedures to herding, especially since Basuto methods of and problems with livestock management are no less tied to traditional constraints of village organization, land tenure and Lesotho's archvillain, overpopulation.

It was overpopulation that originally pushed both Basuto

farmers and herdsman into the mountains. Now the ecological misadventures that have resulted from overcropping and overgrazing marginal mountain areas are pushing these same Basuto back into the lowlands, further increasing pressures on Lesotho's already overburdened fertile plain. To commit lowland farmland for grazing purposes would be to trade off an inevitable increase in costs for importing additional food for a potential increase in cash gains for mohair and wool exports.

There is also the question of what alterations in village structure and traditions "correct management procedures" entail. Lesotho law contains provisions for resting overgrazed land. That such provisions are not effective is the fault of overpopulation, not poor management. Would "Western management" demand the abandonment of land tenure and communal grazing; would it demand the formation of large livestock operations with high capital inputs and the end of small independent herds? Without going into the details of the Basuto's relationship to his land—we will deal with that later in terms of other projects—it is clear that even a superficial consideration reveals cracks in the façade of Comrudev's forthright proposal.

I asked Hurst about the dangers of overgrazing. He replied by mentioning the South African wool board experiments referred to in his Comrudev proposal. He said that the problems with livestock herding in Lesotho involved livestock grazing too long in the same pasture, burning grasses, and not planning for winter feed. Put this way, these problems seemed suited to remedial programs, but still they remained unremedied.

Throughout Lesotho I was to come across expatriate experts who spoke with confidence and command about Lesotho's problems, and about how they must be solved. And yet for all this talk—and I assumed that it had been preceded by decades of similar talk—the problems under attack have remained if not worsened.

The image was that there were two different worlds in Lesotho: the insular world of the expatriate expert and his memoranda and proposals, and the world of the Basuto. My first impression was that there was some breakdown, or lack of transfer, between the two worlds. Hurst was quick to agree with this impression. "There have been thousands of pilot projects," he said hyperbolically, "involving vast sums, but they all fail or disappear because they have no people involvement. What happens in a pilot project when the experts and the money pull out?" Hurst said that the classic pilot project had begun in Liphiring in the south to attack the problem of soil erosion. It was started by the British, said Hurst, then picked up by a succession of donors, all of whom failed because the project did not attempt to involve the Basuto. Incidentally, Hurst's pet mohair scheme was a pilot project itself. Its success depended on whether a host of different women's groups could produce a processed mohair sufficiently standardized to be marketed, and if they did, whether they would produce enough income to cover costs, repay their loans and generate enough profit to keep people interested.

Hurst pictured Lesotho as a place in which projects are devised to give experts a job, in which the majority of the money committed ends up back in the pockets of donor-nation corporations and expats through salaries and perquisites, in which massive amounts are committed because it is easier to commit millions than thousands, in which professional memoranda writers pick projects and make them donor-attractive.

Despite Hurst's predilection for hyperbole, I found that a good number of people agreed with his assessment. Lesotho was a laboratory for some people, an assignment for others; it was a place where you might experiment, where you might find material for a dissertation, where you might live well and with a sense of purpose, a place where the Basuto did not get in the way of expatriates' fulfilling their own purposes. So far the Basuto I had met were rather diffident and retiring. Rivers Thompson, was has lived in Lesotho since 1929, told me that it took him and his wife seven years to gain the confidence of the Basuto and that even then there were major portions of Basuto life which were inaccessible to him and his wife. He said that the Basuto hide their feelings around non-Basuto, and will tell them "pretty much what they think Europeans want to hear." This makes it difficult for the man who comes to Lesotho for two years on contract to plumb the real feelings of the Basuto toward the undertaking he is involved with. On the implementational level, it was hard to imagine them arguing with the aggressive, self-confident Caucasians there to help them.

After a relatively brief trip, Hurst and I arrived in Roma, the site of the University of Botswana, Lesotho and Swaziland and a bastion of Catholic Lesotho. The Roma Valley Cooperative sits just off the main road on a dusty hill. After a tour of the handicrafts center and a stilted conversation with two painfully shy Basuto women there at work, we walked further up the hill to Ms. Woodall's apartment. Pauline Woodall is a large, outgoing woman. She and her daughter occupy a spacious apartment, which is decorated in muted hippie fashion. Her husband works elsewhere in Africa. John Hurst introduced me and told Pauline that we had been talking about some of the absurd things that happen in Lesotho in the name of charity. Pauline rolled her eyes and said that in Roma itself a German organization named SOS had come up with the idea of a children's village, "and here in a country with a functioning extended family and a perfect social welfare system that takes care of all orphaned children."

Hurst said he feared that children growing up in a children's village would be utterly alienated from Basuto society because they would be growing up away from village organization and family ties. So far the village has had trouble finding children to fill the SOS village. Hurst said that now the only way an orphanage can get children is to have the child declare in court that he steals because he is homeless. Just as children are taken care of, so are the elderly revered. Leabua Jonathan's wife inaugurated an old-age home as one of her pet projects, and the home now stands empty, similarly because it is not needed—yet.

One has to wonder about the mentality that sees the need for children's homes in a country where all children are absorbed by the extended family. The need for such facilities could not have derived from a study of Basuto society. Indeed, Basuto law explicitly states that "the community through the chief is responsible for orphans." Rather, we can imagine such projects borne upon a blind tide of sentimentality and guilt—like Operation Babylift in Vietnam—a rough translation of the poignant phrase "But what about the children?" They reflect more problems of the donor society than those of the recipient.

There is, I was to discover, a complicating factor concerning such projects. Under the influence of Western values, there is evidence that Basuto society is beginning to break down. As Basuto adopt consumer values, some mothers are just now beginning to see children and aged parents as economic liabilities which compete with clothes and consumer articles for what little money they have. It may turn out that in a few years, children's villages and old-age homes will be as important in Lesotho as they are in the societies that introduced them here.

Hurst then brought up the delicate question of Mike Bevins' rage over what he considered to be self-serving actions on Pauline's part, and added that the OXFAM overseer had cooled off markedly on the project. Pauline acted very surprised about Mike's reaction, and said sweetly that she had never complained about his machines. She added as a footnote that she had just signed a new contract a year later for the next two years. Such is the fluidity of aid projects that when I returned to New York, I learned from Ray Rignall that the Roma Valley cooperative is no longer connected with the mohair project and that Pauline Woodall had left for Swaziland.

Upon my return to Maseru, McCullam and CARE's borrowed Peace Corpsman, Kent Black, helped me move into the modest house temporarily vacated by a British agronomist. The house had four rooms and was part of a new development in a prosperous section of Maseru. The Basuto woman who had cooked breakfast for the agronomist and taken care of the house agreed to stay on, so I literally found myself in the privileged situation of an expat expert.

That night, having made no preparation for dinner, I walked back up to the Holiday Inn. Clustered at the bar was a group of expatriates who had just come from a reception for Dr. Boerma, the head of the World Food Program, who was in Lesotho for the day. They were swapping stories about different projects and different places in Africa. Some of them were in Lesotho on inspection trips, people the local Peace Corps director calls the "five-day reporters." A handful of other officials were trying their luck at roulette and blackjack. Also at the tables were a number of Basuto making small and infrequent bets. I introduced myself around the group at the bar. "Ah, so you're here to report on the alms race," said John Murphy, the local World Food Program chief. "Well, you've come to the right place." At first I was wondering whether he meant the bar of the Holiday Inn or the country itself.

Perhaps the most surprising impression I gained of Lesotho was of the expats themselves, and their attitude toward their work. By the end of the day I was sure that my job was not going to be so much digging as restraining: Hurst and the alacrity with which he would dissect boondoggles and snafus; Murphy and the glint of malicious pleasure that came into his eye when I told him what my trip was about; the enthusiasm of everyone else I spoke with as well. What was confusing was the breakdown between the expats' perceptions of effects of outside assistance on Lesotho and their perception of their own role in causing those effects. The expats seemed to be functioning at two levels, or perhaps, in two different worlds. My question was whether or not information in one world transferred to the other.

SEVEN

Fantasies for Development: The Five-Year Plan

It was while I was flying into Maseru from Johannesburg that a metaphor for development began to take shape in my mind. I had just been to Liberia and Zaïre, I had heard expatriates discuss what "held the underdeveloped world back" and what were the necessary preconditions for development. Looking out of my window at the rolling South African countryside I saw hosts of little towns connected by roads with larger metropolises evenly distributed. I remembered then that while this would be a perfectly normal aerial view in the United States or in Europe, this was not something I had seen from the air in my hop to southern Liberia, or something I would see from the air in Lesotho.

This logistical organization of roads, rails and telephones foisted on the face of the earth recalled pictures I had seen of cancer cells and the way they expand their domain. Drawing off the resources of the body, cancer communities grow by sending off pathways of their own, which interconnect individual cells and act as supply routes. They depend on a logistical network foisted on the body much like the labyrinth of roads below lay on the earth and facilitated the usurpation of the earth's resources.

It was such a system of communications on which management and the consumer society depended—management can only manage if it has access to its domain. With that thought came a new way of contrasting places like Lesotho or Liberia with the United States, and perhaps a new way of judging how far along the road to development a country is.

The average businessman can reach any part of America almost instantaneously by telephone or Telex; by plane he can reach almost any domestic destination within a few hours. Thus if the United States were mapped according to accessibility of different regions to each other, it would be quite small. In contrast, a person sending a message in Lesotho, which is about the size of Maryland, might need several days to get it through to the mountain regions. The phone book in Lesotho is not much larger than a wine list in a good restaurant, roads are still few, and some towns are a packhorse ride from the nearest airstrip. Mapped according to communications, Lesotho would appear to be much larger than the United States. Viewed this way, it is easy to see how a country with such lack of communications retains a relative insularity though surrounded by the vastly developed South Africa, and it is easy to see the forces that have until now moderated the pace of change.

The idea of a Lesotho larger than the United States should be kept in mind when considering the fate of Lesotho's first Five-Year Plan.

The skeleton supposedly organizing the projects of the voluntary agencies like CARE as well as the big projects of the World Bank and the United Nations Development Program (UNDP) is Lesotho's "First Five-Year Development Plan." This was the document with which CARE was dovetailing its own program. CARE officials considered this intermeshing with the government an important policy decision, one that they would be following in the future in other Third World countries, and an example for other voluntary agencies as to what was the most advanced thinking in "giving." Produced by the Lesothan government's Central Planning and Development Office this document runs to some 262 pages, and it sets forth in ambitious detail a plan to "lay the foundations for economic development and economic independence." The Five-Year Plan set ten major development targets, the principal ones being: (1) to attain an average annual rate of growth of gross domestic product of not less than five percent; (2) to achieve a marked increase in productivity in the agricultural sector; (3) to promote as far as possible non-agricultural productive activities, putting special emphasis on small-scale indigenous industries, and to secure the economic, legal and institutional preconditions for a self-sustained development of these activities; (4) to prepare for the full exploitation of the country's water and mineral[!] resources, and in particular to carry out the first construction phase of the Malibamatso River Project; (5) to accomplish a radical and government controlled development in education and postschool training, related to the needs for economic and social advancement of the country; (6) to create 10,000–15,000 new employment opportunities, mainly in non-agricultural activities; (7) to end the dependence of the government's recurrent budget on external aid, such as British grants-in-aid.

It is unnecessary to go into this Five-Year Plan in too great detail, principally because Lesotho never got too deeply into it herself. During the first three years of the plan, both total agricultural output and yields per acre continued their inexorable decline, the promotion of nonagricultural activities and the creation of jobs crawled along at a snail's pace; if anything, the growth rate of the economy was stable or negative; and the giant dam project that was to be Lesotho's salvation was shelved because of complicated political and economic disputes. Estimates are that the government spent only about half the money targeted in the plan. In short, Five-Year Plan notwithstanding, things went on pretty much as before—they got worse.

From a look at yields, trade statistics, etc., a naïve visitor would be hard pressed to find evidence that a Five-Year

Plan existed. The one category in which the government not only met but exceeded its projections was in spending for police and prisons, a circumstance which is all the more remarkable because planning for police and prisons is perhaps the shortest section of the Five-Year Plan. What happened? Why did this plan, with which CARE and other voluntary agencies were dovetailing their programming, fail? Certainly there was change in Lesotho during the period of the plan, in some respects, great change, but the changes that occurred were not changes hoped for by the makers of the Five-Year Plan. Some of the changes that occurred were not envisioned in the plan; others were feared; and others still were changes the plan was in part intended to prevent.

Upon my arrival in Lesotho I set about to check on the progress of the first Five-Year Plan. What I found was that people did not much want to talk about it; most would rather discuss the potentialities of the second Five-Year Plan which was about to begin. However, in time I was able to coax people into discussing the plan and put together an impression of the information and misinformation which contributed to its conception and failure.

There are two basic levels upon which the Five-Year Plan should be approached: first, the practical success or failure of the plan to realize its goals, and the reasons for that outcome, and second, the wisdom of the Five-Year Plan's ambitions for Lesotho regardless of the success or failure of their realization. There are, of course, interconnections between these two levels: blindness to constraints in Lesotho's particular situation could very easily lead to the practical failure of a program just as a program which is a practical success might have negative repercussions which would ultimately reveal the inappropriateness of that program to Lesotho's situation. In Lesotho's case, starting with a practical consideration of the Five-Year Plan, we find that the answer to the question of why the program failed and what changes it brought about leads to the basic theme of what is the nature of development and what development requires.

To begin with, it is difficult to assess the worth of many projects in Lesotho. For one thing, there is a very patchy statistical base in Lesotho. Quite a few categories in the World Bank's summary of country data on Lesotho are blank because the statistics are not available, and I was told not to trust many of the available statistics by some of the people who had worked on getting the data together. The World Bank says: "Economic indicators for Lesotho are scarce and unreliable. The Government's own budget statistics are the only reliable information available. Production statistics are virtually nonexistent." Perhaps we shouldn't trust statistics, anyway—they inevitably reflect biases in collection, and because of decimal points, seem more true than they are. Even though their lack makes a global assessment of the Lesothan situation more difficult, perhaps this same lack forces us to look more honestly at the impact of individual projects.

I spoke with a UN/FAO official named Jonathan Jenness who works on secondment to the Central Planning and Development Office. When I asked Jenness whether the Planning Office had evaluated the first Five-Year Plan, especially since they were about to launch their second Five-Year Plan, Jenness replied that the Planning Office had prepared an analysis of the plan but had not released it. This was because they had no meaningful "target indicators"—they could not evaluate statistics, but only note what money was spent. When I asked the obvious question about how the Planning Office could produce a second Five-Year Plan without a thorough understanding of what had gone wrong—or right—in the first plan, Jenness replied that it was true that the Planning Office people "have not looked at past projects as much as we should have," and that lacuna was perhaps the weakest part of the new plan.

Jenness felt that the Planning Office in general in Lesotho was characterized by too little evaluation and too much interest in getting money. He explained the lack of evaluation as a function of the country's newness to development. Since there was no history of development in Lesotho on which to draw in formulating plans, each planner tended to start afresh, he said. I was to discover that this tendency often meant expatriate experts were constantly reproposing projects and techniques that had been suggested and forgotten earlier.

This limitation in assessing projects is related to a bureaucratic limitation which inhibited implementing the first Five-Year Plan. This has to do with what is called the absorptive capacity of the economy. Just as there are scant statistics which would enable the economist to use his tools in assessing the impact of the first Five-Year Plan, there is scant administrative apparatus which would permit Lesotho to effect its plans in the first place.

In its confidential critique of the Five-Year Plan, the World Bank agreed with the plan's emphasis but felt that its goals were unrealistic, given Lesotho's lack of the government framework which would permit them to implement projects even when the funds were available. This is in part due to a desire originating with independence in 1966 to rein in recurrent government expenditures in order to wean Lesotho from British grants-in-aid. In fact, goal number seven of the first Five-Year Plan specifically stated this. However, underlying the plan was the intention to build up the absorptive capacity of the economy. This in effect pitted one part of the Five-Year Plan against another. On top of all this, Lesotho could not build up its administrative apparatus because of lack of administrators and administrative apparatus to do so—a Catch-22 situation.

This lack of absorptive capacity is a product of several things: the absence of Western-style managerial expertise, of organizational methods, etc., but it is also a product of the political climate in Lesotho. The fact that Leabua Jonathan is in power by virtue of a coup d'état he led after he lost a popular election in 1970 is delicately left unmentioned by expatriates, but it permeates Lesothan life and has had a profound effect on the civil service.

Virtually every expatriate I spoke with mentioned the low morale in the civil service. John Hurst noted that his office in the Department of Community and Rural Development had 50,000 rand from villages on deposit, which languished unspent because no one wanted to take the initiative in formulating plans to use that money. Theoretically, the civil service is nonpolitical, but after the coup there was a housecleaning, and many Basuto in government felt stripped of all protection. This, plus the presence of aggressive and self-assured expatriates willing to make decisions for the Basuto has fostered a "pass the buck" mentality among civil servants, according to several of the expatriates I spoke with. However, I did not need to speak with expatriates to get a good look at the style of government administration in Lesotho.

One day I chanced to meet a Mosuto who is a high official in Organization and Methods in the government, and we discussed communication between the ministries and its effect on development. This was a point which many experts have stressed. The World Bank had noted that there was nobody in the government that would ensure cooperation and coordination between the various arms of government, and that the Planning Office at present was dependent on the eloquence of its spokesmen and its position of relative favor with the different ministries. Mr. A (as I shall call my acquaintance) agreed with this criticism; in fact, he noted that often one ministry only knows what the others are doing through informal contacts.

Mr. A is an exceedingly pleasant and articulate man. He carries himself with self-possession and discussed Lesotho's problems with reflection and some humor. He seems to enjoy his job very much, and I detected hints of a bour-

geois outlook. He dislikes cars, typewriters, and organizations that are faulty or wasteful, and conversely, likes order
and efficiency. He might serve as a paradigm for emerging
Basuto bureaucrats. After a chance introduction through an
expatriate, we agreed to meet in his offices, which lie in the
rear of the executive office complex.

On the day of our meeting, the guard let me through with
a minimum of security checking, obviously discounting the
possibility that a white American would be a potential
assassin. Mr. A greeted me with characteristic cheerfulness,
and we set about to talk. The impression Mr. A gave of the
different ministries is that they are run like little duchies
relating to each other through personal contacts and whims
of the Prime Minister. One problem many experts have
noted is the scarcity of trained people who might implement projects. Mr. A said that because of the lack of communication between the ministries, not only was it difficult
to have coherent planning, it was also difficult to know
where the good men were. Both information and people
who Mr. A felt were vital to development remained un-
tapped because no one knew where to find them or even
how one might go about finding them.

Many expatriates told me that there is a wealth of evaluative reports representing the investment of hundreds of
thousands of rand which might as well have never been
written, because once completed, they disappear into Lesotho's bureaucracy, a bureaucracy which is like a filing system without an index. Mr. A claimed that the reason this
problem remained unremedied was that few people in the
government knew "anything about looking at a bureaucratic
structure with an organizational eye—it's a severe problem." To top this off, he said, "most people have not gotten
used to the habit of reading," so that often reports went unnoticed even by the people responsible for receiving them.
Mr. A was called away by a telephone call, and I mused
over what he had said.

The image Mr. A painted gave me some notion of one

particular reason why Lesotho might receive such intense development aid and yet fail to develop: simply that the information was never "assimilated" by the appropriate people. Information was there, but little of it transferred to the Basuto, either because of Lesotho's black-hole-like filing system or because of the Basuto themselves. There was no development gestalt in the minds of the Basuto which might make sense of the proposals being thrown at the Basuto so that they would say "Aha!" and know how to carry things through where the expatriates left off.

The idea of development as a gestalt made particular sense in view of the picture of disorganization which Mr. A painted. He had clicked onto such a gestalt. It was evident in his style, the clear-sighted way he saw the organizational problems inhibiting development; Mr. A had reorganized his life for development. If the government were composed of men like him there would be no lack of absorptive capacity in Lesotho. However, the others were not less intelligent, or even less enlightened than Mr. A if, in fact, development is a gestalt, a construction of mind. Rather, they were simply sorting their experience according to a different pattern, and that different pattern was not constructed to "understand" the significance of development projects. Perhaps they were fortunate, but still it meant that information necessary to development remained unappreciated.

My ruminations along these lines were interrupted by the arrival of two men from the Ministry of Education—Mr. B, an Indian in charge of the curriculum department, and his Basuto associate, whom I'll call Mr. C. Mr. B was preparing a textbook for Lesotho's schools. He and Mr. C had come to discuss the organization of the government so that Lesotho's schoolchildren might know how their government works. I got up to leave, but all insisted that I feel free to remain. I'm glad I did. What followed seemed like a drama constructed to help me better understand how the political

situation in a developing country warps both formal governmental structures, and the ambitions of a five-year plan.

Mr. A began by drawing a chart of the government. It
looked something like this:

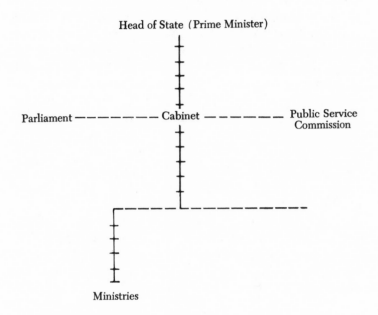

Mr. B began asking questions, and there the trouble began.

MR. B: What about the auditing office; isn't it independent
of Parliament?

MR. A: Well, no.

MR. B: Then, how can it audit?

MR. A: Well . . . it can't.

MR. B: The Planning Office is under who?

MR. A: Well, it's strange. It *was* under the Ministry of
Finance, but the Prime Minister was told that it was getting too independent, so it was brought into his office

under the Deputy Permanent Secretary. Then he discovered that Planning was not getting too independent,
so now it is under Commerce and Industry. It's a question of personalities, really. (*Mr. A said this in his casual
way with an amused smile.*)

MR. B: But personalities shouldn't really matter in a strong
official structure. Take Permanent Secretaries, for instance. Presumably they are modeled on the British system. They are in civil service and can't belong to a political party.

MR. A: Not here—in fact, the civil service is politicized
down to the level of district administrators—which can't
be good for the village.

At this point Mr. B started amending the government
organization chart so that it conformed to what Mr. A had
told him. First he drew a little series of dashes to show how
the head of state might directly intervene in the ministries
without going through the cabinet. It looked like this:

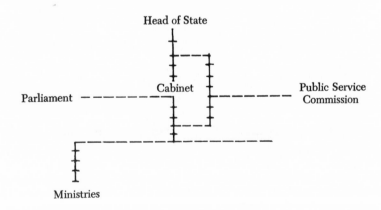

Mr. B was a miracle of tact. As Mr. A was explaining
things, Mr. B kept looking for euphemistic ways to explain
Lesotho's peculiar adaptations of British government to
students.

MR. B: Well then, we can say that we have a British system partly influenced by the American system.

MR. A: Well, no, not influenced. It's a coincidence, things just happened to work out that way. For instance, Organization and Methods [Mr. A's office] was once intended to govern all ministries, but when the head [of O & M] moved up, he maintained control over our organization—wresting Organization and Methods from its proper role [in other words, placing O & M in an isolated section of the bureaucracy from which it is unable to ride herd on the bureaucratic practices of the other ministries.]

Here Mr. B paused for a moment and then picked up his line of questioning.

MR. B: Let's say the Public Service Commission viewed a cabinet appointee as unfit, could their recommendation prevent his appointment?

MR. A: No, actually they have made recommendations which have been ignored.

MR. B: Well . . . let's take the decision that was made to increase taxes and make education free. How was that decision made?

MR. A: Well, actually it came from the top.

MR. B: Well, let's say that it didn't come from the top, would it have been as the result of consultation?

MR. A: Only if he [the P.M.] knew someone, there's no formal procedure.

MR. B: What about Parliament?

MR. B: Actually, Parliament is just a token formality. Someone may make a speech, just to get his opposition on the record.

MR. B: Then there are no checks and balances.

MR. A: That's right.

MR. B (*reflectively*): The question is, How are we going to present this [to the students]?

MR. C (*with a chuckle*): That's the question.

MR. B (*after a minute's thought*): Let's say it's a mix of the British and American systems.

Mr. A looked with some admiration at Mr. B for his ability to propose that. Then Mr. C stepped in.

MR. C: Yes, but it [the organization] changes so fast, can we be sure the chart will be right?

MR. A: Also, how do you present the fact that the Constitution was suspended in 1970? And that nothing has replaced it.

MR. B: What about the Lesotho Orders [Jonathan's edicts] of 1970 and 1973? We can also say that this is a developing country, and its needs are somewhat different than Britain and the United States, and that there are countries with law that are lawless—like the United States—and countries without constitutions that are law-abiding—Lesotho—and that with time Zambia, Tanzania, Lesotho, etc., will eventually evolve a peculiarly African constitution, but that first we must reorganize ourselves for development.

It was easy to see how someone like Mr. B survived in a fluid government like Lesotho's. But now patient, easygoing Mr. A had finally heard enough.

MR. A: Didn't Watergate [Nixon had resigned just a few days earlier] show that the United States is not a lawless country, and, in fact, didn't Watergate show the strengths of a constitutional system?

From the above dialogue and from the Five-Year-Plan recommendations, it would be easy to imagine that the two referred to two different countries. One country had Sectoral Programming Units and Constructional Capacity Committees all working harmoniously for development, and the other has henchmen covetously guarding their domains. It is also easy to understand why the framers of the Five-Year Plan did not formulate it taking into account the realities of administration in Lesotho. They, like Mr. B (and I was told that the majority of the work on the first Five-Year Plan was done by expatriates), have to pretend that the reality is something other than it is. They write a program that presupposes a nonexistent bureaucratic structure, and ultimately their program founders on their false suppositions.

Even more than Mr. B writing his euphemistic curriculum, the planners of development have to ignore unfortunate political maneuvers such as coups and the suspension of constitutions. Planners and the aid organizations and voluntary agencies that help to implement the planners' ideas have to believe that development is nonpolitical, and that in working with dictators they are not abetting dictators. When questioned about political considerations, expatriates tend to get very nervous. It's almost as though do-gooders don't want to hear about any of the complicating factors that might interfere with the notion that they are doing good.

When I confronted expatriates with these disturbing questions, they generally replied with variations of the defense offered by Jonathan Jenness. When I asked him to what extent he considered the political and moral repercussions of the work he was doing in Lesotho, he responded, "With regard to the moral argument on my responsibilities: I have expertise. It's up to the people who make decisions to decide whether it contains the seeds of destruction." Another expatriate, Dr. Robert McKee, a softspoken English soil physicist at the Agricultural Research Station said, when I asked about his moral defense, "Jenness' defense is our only defense: Let them make the decisions. Before I came here, everybody told me 'Don't shoulder too much responsibility'; the last director is in a mental hospital, and the first director shot himself. I sit in the chair in which he shot himself."

It is curious to find highly moral men adopting the moral

blinders offered by the phrase "we are only following orders." Many of them gravitated toward voluntary or assistance work because they considered the moral responsibilities of alternative actions such as joining the military, yet when confronted with questions which they might throw at people in the military, they adopt the moral posture of the soldier.

Some voluntary agencies are beginning to confront these questions themselves. A *Wall Street Journal* article about Church World Service brings out this very point. Entitled "A Helping Hand? Relief Agency Ponders Ultimate Good of Aid in Despotic Nations," the article deals with doubts in Church World Service about whether there is any such thing as apolitical relief, much less apolitical development.

When I spoke with Dr. Van Hoogstraten, head of the Africa department at Church World Service, he noted that it was a consideration of the repercussions of their involvement that has kept Church World Service out of Lesotho. Besides Lesotho's political situation, there is considerable bickering between Protestants and Catholics, and Dr. Van Hoogstraten remarked that another church-related project might only exacerbate these religious tensions.

Not all at Church World Service have these doubts. The *Wall Street Journal* reports that Nancy Nicolo, who for a term served as interim director, pooh-poohed the question of such subtle repercussions: "We give in terms of those in need. Period. Regardless." This is also CARE's defense, but it is easy to see that things are not that simple either at CARE or at Church World Service. There are more people in need in the world than there are resources to help them, and so, by logic, there has to be some process of selectivity in determining whom to help. What seems to happen is that once the decision to help a country is made, neither the home office nor the in-country staffer wants to believe that they have made a mistake—and the stakes for the staffer are much higher than for the home office, because with the staffer, doubt might work its way to the very ethical basis of his career.

Lesotho is a country particularly ripe for the germination of such doubts. If the uncertain political climate and insecurity in the Lesothan civil service acts as a constraint on development, and if the personalization of the ministries also limits the country's absorptive capabilities, there are other political considerations surrounding the Five-Year Plan which becloud its goals should it have been realized. In Lesotho in 1970 only about 2 percent of the population could be said to be living in anything like an urban area. The great bulk of the population lived in villages, most of which were not even accessible by road. Because of their inaccessibility, the villages were relatively autonomous, and except for Lesotho's ever worsening population situation, they might continue to be autonomous for some time to come. Predevelopment Lesotho was as close a system of functioning anarchy as one might imagine for a semiliterate people. The Five-Year Plan hoped to change all that.

The great preserver of Lesotho's decentralization has been the chief-system and land tenure. The chiefs covet their lands and the right to distribute them through the land-tenure system. When I spoke with the Lesothan ambassador to Washington in 1972 about Lesothan planning Mr. Moshelugu said, "I don't think much can be done vis-à-vis decentralization as long as the chief system exists." What he was referring to was a government proposal to draw increasing numbers of Basuto into a series of metropolises which can serve as nexuses for development. By centralizing a good part of the population in a series of urban and semi-urban centers linked by roads, Prime Minister Jonathan intends to bring the Basuto within the administrative and economic ambit of the government. In the plan, of course, this goal is stated in terms of getting health, educational, sanitary and electrical facilities to the people, pooling labor, etc., but it is interesting to note that police and prison facilities have often been the first amenities of modern life that the government has contributed to these favored, designated growth centers.

Jonathan's hold over Lesotho is not complete, and during the last few years there have been incidents of revolt. On a ride to Nakong I passed some Basuto huts which had been burned out by the paramilitary Police Mobile Unit the year before. In terms of the ruling party, the country would be far easier to *govern* as well as develop if the population were more centralized.

Over the past few years, the chiefs have felt these threats to their hegemony and have become increasingly alarmed over their diminishing influence. The government has set up a network of district administrators responsible to the ministries, which supposedly function parallel with the chiefs. But in practice, this parallel government has served to further isolate the chiefs from administrative functions. Mr. A told me that the chiefs once complained to the ministries about this loss of power, asking rhetorically from whom the ministries derived their hereditary authority. According to Mr. A, the ministers replied by asking where the chiefs' popular mandate was, and the chiefs were taken aback.

Viewed in terms of achieving the goals of the Five-Year Plan, the most obtrusive success was toward achieving the consolidation of Leabua Jonathan's power, a goal which because it was political and therefore outside the consideration of those concerned with development, the expatriate experts have preferred not to consider or evaluate.

Apart from Lesotho's political situation, there are a number of other things that neither the Five-Year Plan nor the expatriates there to implement the plan took into account, and these omissions had a direct bearing on the plan's fortunes.

One of these neglected items is the importance of land

tenure in maintaining the communal and egalitarian traditions in Lesotho. One would think that a nation's Five-Year Plan might deal sensitively with the nation's single most enduring tradition, but such is not the case. Here is how land tenure is discussed in the Five-Year Plan:

> The land tenure system appears to be responsible for a number of major obstacles to the modernization of the agricultural production. In particular:
> a) it impedes the consolidation of scattered land holdings into larger and more efficient units;
> b) it makes individual farmers reluctant to improve the land, as there is no security of tenure; and
> c) it makes the extension of agricultural credit difficult because of the lack of individual ownership.

The plan did not call for the abandonment of land tenure, which then or now would not be tolerated by the chiefs, but it did call for a study "to test the compatibility of the land tenure system with a rapid expansion of agricultural productivity."

Land tenure has not only preserved the communal character of Lesotho, it has prevented the development of such Third World bugaboos as the alienation of land (foreign acquisition) and extremes of wealth and poverty. Until recently, land tenure evenly distributed people through the countryside and limited urban migration and the development of slums.

Given these positive functions of land tenure, one would think that the framers of the Five-Year Plan had at least done a cost/benefit analysis of the trade-offs involved in sacrificing land tenure for agricultural productivity—if in fact agricultural productivity even demands the sacrifice of land tenure. But no, I asked every person connected with planning in Lesotho whether such an analysis had been done, and I always received the same answer. One man with long experience in the Planning Office said, "No one in government that I know has faced the potential social repercussions of uneven distribution of wealth in a monetized economy in a society that presently has an even distribution of wealth . . . nor have they faced the loss of political independence that might be the trade-off in bringing more of the economy into the world market."

This man phrased his answer in terms of uneven distribution of wealth, because given political realities, such income discrepancies would almost inevitably follow the consolidation of farm holdings, the introduction of capital-intensive agricultural techniques, and the development of industry. Sadly, an uneven distribution of wealth is even now beginning, simply as a result of the contrast between village subsistence and Basuto on government salaries or hooked into the massive aid flow. One Mosuto told me that non-Maseru Basuto look with mounting resentment at the luxuries and life styles of the Basuto who work for the government.

Such discrepancies, and the emergence of a minuscule middle class, are things radically new to Lesotho. Outside Maseru even the chiefs share the lot of the villagers under them. Chieftainess Makhuabane (today women occasionally assume power when men with claim to chieftainship are disabled or absent) of Thaba Bosiu lives in a traditional Basuto hut distinguished from neighboring huts only by its prominence on a hillside overlooking her village and by the presence of a record player which she makes available to her village.

The lack of thought given to the social repercussion of development problems might seem to be a function of the presence of expatriates in the framing and implementation of development plans, but it turns out that this is only part of the problem. Once the non-Westerner flashes into the development gestalt, they seem to have less regard for the value of their traditions than even the most ignorant expatriate. In Kenya, natives I spoke with would refer dis-

paragingly to proud, tradition-bound tribes such as the
Masai as "thirty years behind us [the Kikuyu] in civilization." It seems that once the African is infected with the
spirit of development, he becomes ashamed of his previous
life. Sean Sullivan, who was director of training for the
Peace Corps for Lesotho, Botswana and Swaziland, remarked that he distrusted the ability of African leaders to
protect their heritage because "it's always the Westernized
leaders who push for development, people who are frankly
embarrassed by their traditions and the least willing to
defend them."

David Morton of the World Food Program remarked that
much of the push for blind development in Africa is political: "You can't stay in power here if you are only a 'moder-
ate developer.'" Fueled by the beneficiary government's
impatience and the expatriate experts' need to spend
money, there is a pell-mell rush to develop. This leads to
striking confusion over the critical issue of felt needs.

The expatriates' defense as expounded by Jonathan
Jenness is that they are merely helping to implement the
wishes of the people of the countries in which they work.
This sounds simple enough until you start to examine who
feels what need. For instance, CARE asserted that its programs responded to needs felt at the village level. Then it
pridefully claimed that it was dovetailing its program with
the Five-Year Plan of Lesotho. Is that to say that the Five-
Year Plan was a reflection of needs felt at the village level?

If the first Five-Year Plan was not the result of outright
authorship of expatriate planners, it was at least heavily
influenced by their consultation. Moreover, as Sean
Sullivan pointed out, the people pushing for development
in Lesotho, and the Basuto working on the development of
five-year plans, are people who have clicked into the development gestalt—and, conversely, out of the Basuto
gestalt. Finally, if the Five-Year Plan and its particular

projects are to be "donor-attractive," they have to be presented in a way that is soothing to the businesslike minds that will be donating the money. This further reinforces the conformity of five-year plans and acts to minimize whatever tempering action Basuto traditions or circumstances might have on the planner's imagination. The result is a document which donors might claim reflects the felt needs of a developing country, but which in reality reflects the Western world's perceptions of the needs of Lesotho.

The distance between Washington and Maseru is often considerably less than that separating Maseru from a mountain village twenty miles distant. The Basuto who had dedicated their lives to development and the Basuto who remained in the mountain villages lived in two different worlds, and each world selected its information, in a different way. The Five-Year Plan did not sympathetically consider the value or rationale for traditional Basuto society because it could not do so, not because of willful insensitivity on the part of the planners.

For instance, while Lesotho's own Five-Year Plan treats land tenure as nothing but an impediment, it is ironic that some expatriates are beginning to believe that land tenure need not necessarily preclude improved agricultural practices. With regard to targets such as switching agricultural production more toward cash crops, for increasing the use of capital-intensive techniques such as mechanization, fertilizers and irrigation, there have been more recent counterproposals disputing such moves or offering cheaper, less socially disruptive and more effective ways to improve crop yields.

It is hard to resist the temptation (the temptation that ensnares all planners who come to Lesotho) to try to look for the practical snag that might have caused the failure of the Five-Year Plan. The temptation is to say, "If only they had tried 'trickle irrigation,' or 'catchments' . . ." etc. But as we shall see, even the better-thought-out counterproposals often run afoul of unforeseen shoals, until the ostensible goal of helping the villager comes to appear an eldorado surrounded by an infinite succession of reefs.

Looked at another way, we can see that practical breakdowns in the perceptions and projects of the Five-Year Planners are not causes of the plan's failure, but rather symptoms of the plan's real function, which was to play out the needs of the consumer societies that entered Lesotho to help implement it. Rather than providing a design for improving life at the village level, the plan was a blueprint to help reorganize Lesotho along consumer lines, and it worked as a dynamic part in the consumer societies that sponsored it.

It might seem senseless, that in a world where the income spread between rich and poor is looked upon as a major problem, a nation without such a problem might take steps to fire private initiative in such a way as to produce that problem. Or similarly, that a country would plan for capital-intensive development with no exploitable resources to pay for it, or that a country unafflicted with slums would encourage urban migration. But what seems strange from a practical point of view begins to make sense if one looks at the goal of development as an increase in the number of buyers for the products of the consumer nations—not just potential buyers at some point in the future when development occurs, but present-day buyers of expatriate expertise and the equipment of development. No matter that for the present the U.S. or West German or Swedish government is footing the bill, the money ends up back in the pockets of the donor nations. The great preponderance (one official told me 90 percent) of the money donated ends up re-entering the U.S. economy. With regard to one upcoming project into which the United States was to put some $3 million, I was reliably informed that only $150,000 of that money would be spent locally. In fact, this type of recycling is a major selling point used by AID in its confrontations with Congress.

I do not think that the forces in a five-year plan that work to expand the perimeter of the world's consumer societies are there as the result of some Machiavellian conspiracy, but rather that they are there as the result of everyday processes working in the consumer societies which subtly warp the focus of development planning and vitiate its stated goals.

Take one example:

One aim of the first Five-Year Plan was to build up Lesotho's absorptive capacity, to beef up the bureaucracy so that the country might implement the projects for which the donors were ready to commit money. Of course, once the momentum of development became self-sustaining, Lesotho would need an expanded bureaucracy to keep things running. What happened was quite the opposite.

It quickly became apparent to both donor societies and planners that building up the implementational capacity of the bureaucracy was going to be more difficult than the Five-Year Plan envisioned. Rather than coax the Ministry of Agriculture extension services into effectiveness, most large projects in effect had chosen to by-pass the ministry altogether by setting up project authorities. The effects of this approach were debilitating. As one confidential report put it: "Most of the large projects under way are executed through separate project authorities, staffed by expatriates. This may have been the only way to achieve quick results, but there is a built-in tendency for the project to be managed independently of existing government departments and institutions and in isolation of overall sector programs."

Soil expert Dr. McKee described these project authorities as "little ministries ten times as expensive as the Ministry of Agriculture could afford." They are doubly debilitating. With their massive overhead, they give an unrealistic impression of the types of things Lesotho could do on its own. McKee says that no ministry could afford the level of staffing at the Thaba Bosiu project, a circumstance which will obviate whatever success Thaba Bosiu has if the expatriates and donors pull out.

As Jenness of the Central Planning and Development Office rightly pointed out, the presence of so many expatriates constitutes a capital-intensive approach, whereas a labor-intensive approach is needed. Moreover, the projects with their inflated salaries and need for Basuto counterparts siphon whatever good men there are in the ministries into the projects, further decreasing the ministries' effectiveness and increasing reliance on the project arrangement.

McKee noted that he spent three years to train his government irrigation man, and that now he was leaving for a more lucrative job with the huge Thaba Bosiu project. McKee sent another Basuto to Belgium for training and brought him back, only to have him grabbed by this same massive project. Desmond Taylor of Comrudev also complained about losing people to Thaba Bosiu. Once Basuto leave the ministries for projects, they find it hard to return—some then go to work for the UN or other international aid organizations. Tim Tahani, one of the Basuto who worked on the Five-Year Plan, now works for the World Bank in Washington. As Taylor said, "You cannot patch the country together through projects." But this approach is the most expedient one for the donor societies, and so it is the one— damn the consequences—that is being used.

Because of its manifest debilitating effects on the Lesothan bureaucracy, the project approach calls into question the basic goals of the donor societies supporting this approach. The project approach allows the donor societies to get their money into Lesotho, something that would have been delayed had they insisted on using the ministries, and it also allows the donor societies an enviable degree of authority over the way their money will be spent. It would seem that the donor societies' primary interest is to see the money spent.

This suspicion is supported by the lack of follow-up that characterized these projects once the money was spent. No one I spoke with could point to a project in Lesotho which continued once the donor pulled out. A high American official one night told me of some of the "horror stories" that accompanied the rush to spend money. For instance, there was one expert salaried at $30,000 plus perquisites who labored to help produce fourteen acres of alfalfa, and then, said this official, there was another case in which $800,000 was spent to explore the growing of asparagus as a cash crop —the money was to pay for expertise needed to grow asparagus on a 400-acre plot. For the most part the findings of these projects end up in the elephant's-graveyard filing system of Lesotho. In the case of the asparagus project, Dr. McKee has been fighting to prevent the generalization of its findings because of peculiarities of the soils where the project was undertaken.

Another circumstance which might be interpreted to support the idea that development projects reflect consumer-society exigencies and not the needs of the beneficiary is the pilot-project syndrome. This same high American official said that Lesotho was dotted with "hundreds of pilot projects. Most pilot projects," he said, "have three-year funding. It takes two years to do the planning, so they never get into the thing. Then they get funding for an additional two years, but by then they have new personnel on rotation, and so they have to start all over. It's like moving Sterling Library at Yale with nothing but committees planning the move." Another aspect of the pilot project is that for the money spent, their findings are minimally important to Lesotho. Dr. McKee noted that he was fighting to have his office downgraded from research to development. The British agency which financed him wanted Dr. McKee to turn out papers, but McKee felt that the only spinoff of such soil research would be for neighboring South Africa and that he would rather turn his attention to practical solutions for Lesotho's problems. All one has to do is look across the Caledon River at the beautiful, uneroded fields of the Orange Free State to see how unnecessary such papers would be.

In essence, the pilot project in Lesotho gives the expatriate expert a job, provides a means by which donor agencies might maintain their budgets and by which American manufacturers might get indirect government subsidies. In Lesotho, pilot projects have done little else. The Five-Year Plan called for a host of them.

Voluntary agencies were always eager to join hands in implementing "five-year plans" in Third World countries because they too need to get their money into projects. I spoke with David Mitchnik of OXFAM before I arrived in Lesotho. He remarked that "the voluntary agencies have to unload a certain amount of money each year. The result of having too much money for too few projects is that the voluntary agencies assume more responsibility than they should in their anxiety to spend." The effect, says Mitchnik, is to turn villagers into beggars and create a welfare mentality. In Lesotho that mentality is not just in the villages, but in the Planning Office as well.

This attitude is doubly a shame because it fosters the big project approach. This is because Michnik felt that there was a direct correlation between planning and projects which were the least disruptive of local traditions and those that obtained the maximum results.

If the Five-Year Plan was inappropriate to the needs of Lesotho, and if it might spawn a host of damaging and unintentional social repercussions, it was not inappropriate to the needs of donor nations and voluntary agencies.

EIGHT

Population:
More Is Less

There is one factor which we have not yet discussed and which the Five-Year Plan did not take into account. That factor, population expansion, made nonsense out of the Five-Year Plan's stated goals. Population is an explosive issue throughout the Third World, and its importance with regard to its effect on charities' involvement with development cannot be underestimated.

The Five-Year Plan does note the negative influences of population pressures, but seems to rate population below land tenure as a factor inhibiting crop and livestock production. For instance, the plan notes: "Poor agricultural techniques and injudicious land use in general are aggravating factors, which are also indirectly related to population pressures." But such is small notice for a problem with the immense proportions it has reached in Lesotho. The plan stops there, and makes no recommendations whatsoever vis-à-vis family planning.

A glance at a chart of crop yields over the last twenty-five years is enough to show that something other than such facts as "sandy soil with low fertility; lack of irrigation; shortage of labour . . .; primitive farming practices and lack of sufficient agricultural tools and implements; inadequate credit facilities and limited development funds" are to blame for Lesotho's declining production:

PRODUCTION AND YIELDS OF MAJOR CROPS

Production ('000 metric tons)	1950	1960	1970
Maize	214	121	67
Sorghum	49	54	57
Wheat	50	58	58
Peas	8	12	5
Beans	1	1	4
Crop Yields (200 lb. bag per acre)			
Maize	5.3	3.7	2.3
Sorghum	4.0	3.8	3.1
Wheat	4.5	3.8	2.4
Peas	4.5	3.3	1.8
Beans	1.5	1.6	1.0

What is apparent is that both gross production and yields have fallen drastically in the last twenty-five years: maize (corn) yields are down over 50 percent, sorghum 25 percent, wheat almost 50 percent, peas over 60 percent, beans 33 percent. Surely one could not argue that twenty-five years ago, farming practices were less primitive, or that there were more tools or credit facilities, or that the soil was less sandy. What is apparent from the figures is that increasingly less soil is left fallow, and that, conversely, the soil is being overworked. In 1950, some 200,000 out of 600,000 acres were left fallow, but by 1970 only 95,000 acres were being rested.

Population pressures have driven people to farm marginal land; this has increased soil erosion and in turn decreased yields. Because the landscape has been denuded of trees, the Basuto burn dung for fodder; this deprives the soil of another potential source of enrichment. Population pressures are evident in the striking increase in the number of landless households and continual shrinkage in the size of average holdings. While in 1950 a little more than a third of Basuto households had land of less than four acres, by 1970 half of the Basuto held less than four acres. By now almost 15 percent of Basuto households have no land whatsoever. In general, landless households sharecrop or graze live-stock on the already overloaded communal pastures.

Not only do population pressures place great stress on the land, they are stretching Lesotho's social institutions to the breaking point as well. With a fixed amount of arable land— 900,000 acres, of which 600,000 are under cultivation—the land-tenure system is reaching the saturation point, if it has not already passed that point, as some people believe. A communal society cannot survive encumbered with grow-ing numbers of landless and alienated people.

Lesotho already has customary law dealing with rotating pasturage to prevent overgrazing, the protection of trees, or the prohibition of burning of grasses. That they are not ef-fective is the result of population pressures; problems such as overgrazing are not the result of the nation's communal traditions, as the Five-Year Plan implies. Fields are not properly rested, not because of primitive farming tech-niques, but because landholdings have shrunk so that sub-sistence farmers feel they have no land to rest. A family of five or six simply cannot support themselves on three acres of exhausted soil, much less leave a section fallow. Using the rough formula of one acre of land needed to sup-port one person, it is easy to see how a family of five or more will fail to support themselves on less than four acres (in 1970 it was 1.37 people/acre), or a nation of 1.2 million might starve on 900,000 arable acres of which only 600,-000 are cultivable. A British Colonial Office report issued in the nineteen-sixties reckoned that Lesotho was eco-nomically viable with a population of 300,000 to 400,000 people—roughly Lesotho's population in 1911. It was around this level of population that labor migration to South

African mines began. In 1870 Lesotho's population was around 70,000; today Lesotho adds 70,000 to its population every two years.

In Lesotho the crude population-growth rate is about 2.6 percent annually, but in certain districts, such as the Leribe district, the growth rate is an incredibly high 3.6 percent, according to Dr. George Walter, field director for the Maternal and Child Health Project for Lesotho, Dahomey and Zambia. A few years ago John Williams of Regional Affairs of the Africa Division of the U.S. Department of Commerce published a booklet entitled *Lesotho, Three Manpower Problems* which attempts to show how growth rates interreact with attempts to encourage economic and agricultural growth in Lesotho.

Williams notes that a heavy endowment of raw materials can change the picture of whether or not a nation has reached the point where population becomes an overpoweringly depressive influence, but neither in 1971, when Williams published his report, nor today have there been any resource discoveries that might hold this wild card for Lesotho. Thus Lesotho's population must be analyzed in terms of its almost total dependence on agriculture. According to Williams, this reaches a point of diminishing returns at an early stage in a population cycle, a cycle which (1) has high birth and death rates, (2) high birth but lowering death rates, (3) both falling birth and death rates, and finally, near-equilibrium (4) with low birth and death rates. The United States and much of Western Europe could be described to be near stage 4 (even so, the U.S. population will still grow by 60 million before the growth rate begins to level off). The situation in stage 1 might be represented by aboriginal tribes in New Guinea or the Amazon basin, and unfortunately, a great portion of the world's population is in that period of terrific growth which occurs during stage 2.

Williams breaks up stage 2 into three parts, all of which bring down the death rate while the birth rate remains high.

First the "growth in trade and communications which drastically reduce famine," then, "the application of preventive medicine to epidemic diseases such as smallpox, typhus and yellow fever," and finally, "the extension of medical facilities such as doctors, hospitals and clinics to private persons." As luck would have it, Williams and other experts place Lesotho somewhere toward the middle of stage 2, which means that Lesotho, already severely overpopulated, will probably experience great population growth for some time to come. To demonstrate what this means, Williams points out that in Nigeria, certain areas experienced diminishing returns in agriculture at approximately half the density of people/acre that Lesotho has. Lesotho has been experiencing such diminishing returns for some time, but what is most horrifying is that the great expansion of her population is still to come. Because permanent emigration is denied, Williams feels that Lesotho has the elements of a "classic Malthusian situation."

Williams examines the effects of this population nightmare on Lesotho's economic growth through a device called the Total Dependency Ratio. "The TDR may be defined as the ratio of the number of persons under 15 and over 60 years of age (numerator) to the number of persons within the age group of 15 to 59." The ratio gives an idea of the number of people each productive worker has to support, which in turn gives an idea of how much is free for saving and the increase of capital necessary for economic growth.

In 1966, for instance, the proportion of children under fifteen in the United Kingdom and the United States, respectively, was 23 and 30 percent, while, says Williams, in Lesotho this proportion was as high as 50 percent, including absentees in 1966. This means that "each person of productive age and resident within Lesotho must support an average of 1.1 persons besides himself or 57% more than a worker in the United Kingdom."

Later Williams examines in cold economic terms the implications of this high ratio (which would be even higher if computed today because of the continuing increase in the number of surviving young children):

> Irrespective of whether expenditure on raising children is viewed as a consumption outlay or as an eventual investment in human capital, such expenditure is totally wasted if the child dies before reaching a productive age. Lesotho's high rates of infant and child mortality suggest a relatively high degree of zero return to investment in children. Although no data are available for Lesotho, it is interesting to note that as much as 20% of India's national income is expended, in one form or another, on children who die before the age of 15. Even if the child survives there will be a significant proportion of past expenditure which is normally classified as consumption expenditure.

Lesotho loses whether the children live or die. If this weren't enough, Williams notes that not only does a high TDR inhibit capital accumulation, but the high population-growth rate which goes into the TDR also demands *higher* capital accumulation merely to stay even. Williams computes that Lesotho, with an estimated 2.6 percent population-growth rate, would have to save and invest 8.1 percent of national income "simply to maintain the existing level of per capita income . . ." Of course, Lesotho's high TDR prohibits that type of capital accumulation. Population growth thus prohibits self-sustained growth.

And there are more problems on the horizon. Evidence is that the infant-mortality rate is falling in Lesotho, and this forebodes an increase in the TDR which, says Williams, "requires an additional improvement in worker productivity (to keep the additional dependents alive), which in turn demands an increase in the capital–labor ratio—additional savings and investment—just to maintain the standard of living."

Finally, the increased number of children siphons off resources from so-called productive uses in transport and credit, and into health care and primary education and other child-oriented services.

Even this cursory survey of the effects of population growth makes it easy to see why per capita income in Lesotho has suffered a sharp decline in real terms over the past few years, and how this increase would warp the projections of a Five-Year Plan that did not take it into account.

The first Five-Year Plan called for the development of 10,000 to 15,000 new jobs, mainly in nonagricultural areas. Francis Creed, managing director of the Lesotho National Development Corporation, noted that in South Africa's similar experience it cost about 6,500 rand ($10,000) for each job created in the Bantu homelands over the last thirteen years. It probably costs more now. However, even using those figures, the creation of the number of jobs specified would require the accumulation and investment of between $100 million and $150 million, an impossible goal in a country where consumption would exceed GNP were it not for outside help. Of course, this is due to the uncontrolled population growth. As it was, only some 2,000 jobs were created between 1967 and 1973.

Creed said that Lesotho would be doing well if it could create 2,000 to 2,500 new jobs a year. Every year Lesotho's population increases more than ten times that amount, while the labor force increases by about 7,500 men annually. Thus, even with the most optimum scenario, Lesotho will be rapidly losing ground in terms of the percentage of male labor engaged in wage employment, and this does not even take into account the increasing numbers of Basuto leaving the land, or the possibility of men returning from the mines. Francis Creed states flatly that "it is inconceivable that industry could ever absorb returning miners or population increase."

One reason the Five-Year Plan downplayed population as

a factor in Lesotho's economy is that Prime Minister Leabua Jonathan is a Roman Catholic, and Dr. George Walter
noted that fears of political repercussion from his government encouraged a policy of benevolent neglect toward this
problem. Oddly enough, Walter also said that because Jonathan's government is a minority government in power by
virtue of a coup, the government itself feared pushing an
idea which might be unpopular. When Dr. Walter came into
Lesotho in March of 1972 as field director for the health-
care project, he could not even use the words "family planning" but had to refer to this euphemism through another
euphemism, "child spacing."

Lately, however, the situation had become more confused, as intelligent Catholics began to appreciate the grav-
ity of Lesotho's population situation and took steps, often
sub rosa, to try and slow the population's geometrical expansion. Thus today we have people like Cyril Rodgers, the
vice-chancellor of the University of Botswana, Lesotho and
Swaziland in the Roman Catholic stronghold of Roma,
downplaying the population problem, while a mile away
Sister Rose, head of St. George's School of Nursing, spoke
to me about the importance of integrating family planning
into the nurses' regimen. Sister Rose did say that "because
of the Church's stand there are many aspects of family planning we cannot encourage," but I was told later that, unofficially, some Church representatives will encourage the use
of contraceptives. While CARE, with no religious constraints to prevent it from becoming involved in family
planning, does nothing in that regard in Lesotho, Catholic
Relief Services next door goes to great lengths and risks the
wrath of its headquarters in New York to do what it can to
encourage family planning. Said Jim Kelley, CRS chief in
Lesotho, "We are acutely aware of how population increase
wipes out economic gains."

However, this thinking does not seem to have seeped into
the Planning Office. When I spoke with Jonathan Jenness,

he said that he did not think that population was that much of a problem in Lesotho, nor that it was a problem that should enter into planning. When I pressed him on this question, he said that "we can't deal with population [meaning that there were no easy solutions to population growth], so we won't take it into account." Because of this, he said, "The Planning Office is not making population a priority, but instead placing more emphasis on more money, and more jobs."

Jenness did not allow that population might place constraints on Lesotho's ability to create more money or more jobs. Finally, when I still pressed Jenness on this question, he said, "I can't emotionally bring myself to believe in this death-and-starvation bit. It may happen in the Sahel or in India, but it won't happen under my nose. I think more about what development does to society in terms of the general disarticulation of a culture. But it's their show, not mine!" Jenness paused for a moment, and then, just before I left, he added, "Also I'm not convinced that as a whole the earth is not qualitatively and quantitatively better off than it was at the turn of the century."

Jenness' concerns for the disintegration of Basuto culture are quite sincere, although the Planning Office does not consider cultural repercussions, either. But it is astonishing that the Planning Office in Lesotho can function as though population problems did not exist. In doing so, Planning dooms itself to continually seeing its ambitions queered by that pesky variable. Such circumstances are reminiscent of some megalomaniacal general who seals himself in a bunker and plans strategic assaults while his army flees in disarray outside: the general ignores the retreat because he cannot deal with it. Bluntly put, in Lesotho, to not consider population in Planning is to be out of touch with reality, which is presumably the place where planning is done. If you do not consider the population, the political situation or social repercussions, what *do* you take into account?

Some of the ministries are beginning to become aware of the population problem, although, so far at least, the result seems mostly to be an excuse for the ministers to fly to Bucharest, Mauritius, Kenya, Ghana, Geneva and elsewhere on junkets to study the problem. In fact, it is worth a slight digression here to note that nobody, ministers or miners, seems to like to spend much time in Lesotho. My biggest difficulty in seeing people in the Lesothan government was that many of them were not there, but in Washington, London, Brussels—anywhere but home. I flew in to Lesotho with C. D. Molapo, who was then Minister of Education and was returning from some junket. Dr. Walter told me that recently Mr. Molapo had visited Mauritius, Kenya and Ghana to collect information toward formulating family-planning policy. Ghana has a statement on family planning, which I suspect Mr. Molapo could have read in Lesotho. Before I got a chance to discuss family planning with Mr. Molapo, he had left the country again. In any case, Mr. Molapo's earlier junket on population policy was undertaken at the behest of the Prime Minister, which indicates that Mr. Jonathan is beginning to wonder about the problem.

Dr. Walter said that while the official line on family planning was still cautious, the problem of population is being discussed more and more. The district administrators have pushed family planning as a priority in some sections of Lesotho. However, Walter still "cannot see the day in Lesotho that family planning will have an effect." He noted that the government seemed to "lack a cohesive sense of what they are doing," and that this and a lack of planning was at the core of the problem. No one has been able to involve family planning in the decision-making process at the cabinet level.

So far, whenever family planning entered into a project decision, it was as the result of a chance meeting between two officials. When I returned to the United States I heard of one example of this during a conversation with James McGilvray of the Christian Medical Commission, an international voluntary agency based in Geneva which has contacts with 5,000 health-care facilities in 98 countries. McGilvray holds the belief that "you will never reduce the birth rate until parents have the confidence that their children will live." According to McGilvray, this takes twelve to fifteen years, and in that time, if you bring down the infant mortality rate by 50 percent, population will reach a plateau and then decline as a new generation changes its expectations about the survival chances of its offspring. However, he admitted that in a pressure-cooker situation like Lesotho, which is already suffering from population poisoning, the great spurt given to the population during those twelve years would probably be disastrous. McGilvray had recently spoken with Chief Minister of Health Patrick Mota (in Geneva, naturally) about the possibility of the Christian Medical Commission becoming involved in Lesotho in setting up some of what McGilvray termed "Under Fives" clinics (for children under five and their mothers), which the commission thought were effective in reducing the infant-mortality rate. Because of Lesotho's critical population problem, McGilvray felt constrained to discuss with Minister Mota the potentially nightmarish consequences of reducing the infant-mortality rate. McGilvray said that Lesotho's Minister of Health was aware of the dangers they were discussing, but that he still felt that they should go ahead with the clinics. And although McGilvray had introduced the subject of those dangers, he decided to involve the Christian Medical Commission in that project.

I asked McGilvray why he went ahead if he knew that such a project might indirectly lead to consequences far more serious than the problem they were trying to control. I received the answer I received so many times when discussing projects in Lesotho: McGilvray said that he was tied to church-related projects, and that while he would prefer to get involved in countries like Zaïre, there the prospects for starting a manageable program with government cooperation were dim. On the other hand, in Lesotho it was easy to start manageable programs.

McGilvray went into his infant-mother program in Lesotho headfirst, aware that further lowering the infant-mortality rate in Lesotho without lowering the birth rate might have disastrous consequences. However, if Lesotho's Malthusian nightmare comes to pass, his hesitancy will not be taken into account when it comes time to assess the impact of his project.

To set a comparison we might consider the Sahel, where it appears that well-intentioned development efforts significantly worsened the effects of cyclical drought. Cattle vaccination, agricultural projects and other interferences with the Sahelian people's cultural ecology greatly increased the numbers of cattle and people living in this marginal region and commensurately disrupted their traditional nomadic ways of dealing with recurrent lean years. When the lean years inevitably arrived, the snowballing effect of enormous human and animal pressures on decreasing water and ground cover led to the "desertification" of the large areas in that fragile ecology, and intense human and animal suffering. With hindsight, the development and self-help projects tributary to this crisis seem ill-advised, and, like McGilvray, perhaps some of the do-gooders working on those projects could envision the unhappy results that would follow their good intentions. Perhaps they, too, were carried along by the inexorable momentum to administer manageable self-help and development projects, but one must admit it puts the clear-sighted self-helper in a peculiarly schizophrenic position. He tells himself he is acting like a saint, but he sees the potential for villainous results.

Population problems in Lesotho do not seem to interest CARE very much at all. Merton Cregger, CARE's assistant executive director in New York with responsibilities in programming and the CARE man most versed on population questions, said, "Frankly, I feel that population is not the determinant of Lesotho's problems." CARE documents echo this feeling. The Post Reports, Pre-Plan Papers, Multi-Year Plans and Project Fact Sheets I looked at on Lesotho rarely mentioned overpopulation or its effects on agriculture and economic development. During conversations about family planning in general, CARE officials in New York consistently downplayed its importance. During my first conversations, in 1972, the theme was that family planning was "overfinanced and understudied." Although in 1975 officials spoke a little more seriously about the importance of population problems in general, they still saw no reason to get involved in that area of programming.

Merton Cregger attended the population conference in Bucharest in 1974 which, he said, "reaffirmed my long held view that to deal with population the approach has to be broader than contraceptives alone," and that one should not gauge the success of family planning by the number of contraceptives delivered—which approach, said Cregger, had been the bias of aid organizations. Cregger also felt that the conference emphasized the highly politicized nature of population questions and how personal the problem is. Given that CARE planning papers speak about transforming a villager's way of life, this shyness at approaching questions of family planning because it involves personal matters seemed a little strange to me. Is it any less personal to change a mother's nutritional hygienic habits so that many more children survive than she usually expects than it is to also offer family-planning counsel in concert with health care so that the mother is not saddled with more surviving children than she usually expects?

Mr. Cregger subscribed to the thesis that a "family is more likely to be a family-planning acceptor if assured of the survival of the children they have . . . two to three children seem adequate for most families, but we don't know yet." Cregger also felt that an intensive program to cut infant mortality should have a concomitant focus to decrease fertility rate, but, says Cregger, "I said family planning should accompany health care, but I did not say that CARE should be doing it." The question is, Why not?

Cregger answered that CARE had not found a "good vehicle to make funds useful in family planning," and that CARE felt more secure in working with health, agriculture, nutrition, vocational education and the like—the types of activities that traditionally have led to great increases in population. When asked whether CARE thought that population increase would weaken CARE programs, Cregger replied that there were quite a number of countries who are facing hopeless situations unless population problems were solved. He also said that CARE was aware the population increase would weaken their programs. But, said Cregger, "You can't just throw up your hands."

This was the answer I received from many CARE officials whenever I asked a question about the wisdom of a particular program or the effects of some project, and though I found infuriating the logic that suggested that the alternative to one particular course of action was throwing up one's hands, the frequency of this answer offered some insight into the minds of CARE men and self-helpers. CARE tries to present itself as an organization that thinks through the effects of its projects, that does not "pauperize" the people it works with. Cregger is saying, like Jenness, that it is too difficult to take population into account in programming, so we won't take population into account—CARE's activist nature is overruling its critical faculties.

In 1972 when I spoke with CARE's former country chief for Lesotho, Tom Bentley, he remarked that CARE was "trying to increase child health [through clinic construction] which is going to mean an increase in the population-growth rate, but we hope for a commensurate increase in production." What has happened, of course, is just the opposite; the direct and indirect effects of population increase have obviated programs for economic gains, and the fact that CARE throws up its hands rather than taking population increase into account has had a role in this effect.

There is evidence that many CARE field people are considerably ahead of CARE New York in their perceptions of the importance of population. However, if, as I suspect, one reason CARE downplays family planning is for fear of alienating potential Catholic donors, then it will be some time before a sense of urgency reaches the planning levels at CARE. I should add also that CARE has become involved in family planning in Colombia, Haiti and the Dominican Republic, but in each case CARE was approached by another agency with the idea of using CARE's logistical network.

That population growth permeates all aspects of Lesotho's economic and social structure might well cause the expatriate activist to throw up his hands, but some agencies are taking a shot at the problem. One of these efforts was being undertaken by the Maternal and Child Health Project of the University of California Extension at Santa Cruz, California. This was the organization for which Dr. George Walter is field director. It was funded out of Title X money through USAID. In fact, just as many voluntary agencies get their money from PL 480 and USAID, so do many family planning agencies get significant amounts of money from the government. The International Planned Parenthood Fund gets about 60 percent of its budget through AID, and Pathfinder Fund in Boston gets about 40 percent. This is another example of AID's new low profile, perhaps springing from the fear of being accused of imperialistic or genocidal intentions. However, before Walter's approach to family planning, it might do well to discuss some further causes and factors which aggravate Lesotho's growth rate.

The first great spurt in population was caused by the cessation of warfare and improved medical care that followed British protection in the late nineteenth century. Lesotho with its mountain climate and running water was relatively free of parasites. Between 1920 and 1950 the population increased relatively slowly, but since then both the population and the rate of increase have been accelerating. There are factors in Lesotho that militate for population increase besides improved medical care; one has to do with Basuto customary law, and the other, ironically, is the indirect result of previous population pressures.

According to customary law, only a married Mosuto can be allotted land, and he gets as much as he needs for the subsistence of his family, so that, like welfare in New York City, the system rewards those with large families. The bride's family receives a dowry of cattle from the groom or his father—generally after it has been proved that the wife is fertile—and this further encourages childbearing. Then there is simply the fact that the Basuto love children. They have a proverb, "God gives me children, God will take care of them," but the thought behind it is not so much that God will take care of the children (the extended family does that), but that the children will later take care of them. A large family is security; a man without a family is indeed lost in Lesotho.

Population pressures add to population growth in several invidious ways in Lesotho. First, population pressures decrease the ability of the Basuto to make a living in Lesotho, and commensurately increase the flow of men to the mines in South Africa. This in turn leaves Lesotho without a male labor force and increases the desirability of having male children to serve as herdboys and partially to fill in for their absent fathers. These herdboys, of course, later grow into men who, faced with further diminished opportunities in Lesotho, migrate to the mines and create the need for more herdboys to replace them. Adding to this vicious circle is the fact that the Mosuto does not trust his wife while he is away in the mines, and generally resists the use of contraceptive devices because he feels that they will allow his wife to cheat with impunity while he is away. Many wives cheat with or without contraceptives, and these children are often adopted by childless relatives.

Walter's project is aimed at halting this locomotive before nature steps in with her harsh controls. Revolving around mother- and child-care clinics, it integrates nurse and midwife training in family-planning counseling and techniques. Besides having to overcome religious resistance on the part of Roman Catholics, Walter had to overcome the resentments that followed previous heavy-handed attempts at family planning. Lesotho's first attempt to contend with population growth, the Family Planning Association had a bad start, because, said Walter, the head "tried to force the issue rather than quietly go about her business." The issue became charged and the organization had to call themselves Family Welfare associations, and when Walter came in, in 1972, he essentially had to start from scratch to overcome distrust built up from previous contacts.

Walter noted that at public meetings, middle-level people of both principal political parties brought up the argument that family planning is an imperialist trick to control the black population. It is truly amazing the way this argument (and its off-the-wall companion argument that birth control is part of a disguised genocidal conspiracy to depopulate the nonwhite world) circulates throughout the world. Everywhere I have been—from New York, where a doctoral student in sociology from Chile told me that family planning was a conspiracy of the Rockefellers and the Mellons, to Indonesia, and to Lesotho—someone will look at you with a knowing, pitying smile and unspool the *real* story behind birth control, as if they had discovered the horrifying truth themselves.

For all our corporate and political meddling in the non-Western world, we deserve the suspicions that greet our every action, and like most mesmerizing conspiracy theories, if you omit certain facts, it is even plausible when taken in the specific, for there is almost always an element of truth. However, often that element of truth serves as a smoke screen masking more obvious dangers. For instance, it is apparent that the CIA has from time to time used voluntary agencies and aid organizations as covers for its agents. However, as in the practice of using news organizations as covers for agents, the cover serves to hide the agent rather than pervert the mission of the organization. It is widely suspected, for example, that a CRS operative in Vietnam in actuality worked for the CIA. However, this does not justify the assumption that the CIA pulls the strings that govern the actions of CRS and other voluntary agencies. And it is misleading to look for the nefarious influence of the CIA as an explanation of what goes wrong with charity in the Third World when one might find more obvious explanations right before his eyes.

With regard to Lesotho's population-conspiracy fantasy, an exploding and desperate Basuto population could pose an increasing threat to political stability in southern Africa, and relieving that strain might be tributary to postponing the day of reckoning for the white regime in South Africa. Keeping neighboring blacks complacent, fed and economically entangled with Praetoria is already South Africa's overt policy—"If they do not eat, we cannot sleep." In this sense, rather than being a nefarious conspiracy, birth control should be considered no different from any of the other economic-aid projects South Africa offers and Lesotho accepts.

But rather than go on and detail how South Africa might enlist the United States and Western Europe in this imaginary conspiracy, take one counterargument: it would be to Lesotho's ultimate good for it to reach the point of desperation, where through unlawful emigration or war her population might burst into neighboring South African provinces or homelands. We might predict various outcomes, some of which could lead to the Africanization of South Africa (which would not necessarily be a boon for Lesotho), but all of which would depend on the massive human, animal and environmental catastrophe that would be necessary to reach that point of desperation—an interesting argument to offer in the interests of the Basuto.

Other conspiracy theories are based on the assumption that Lesotho does not have a population problem and will grow stronger with each additional Mosuto; this argument might be dispensed with in the light of previous descriptions of Lesotho's situation.

Still other people do not believe that family planning is an imperialist plot, but feel that future resource discoveries will change the picture of Lesotho's future, or that Lesotho might some day export business expertise like Lebanon, or that South African manufacturers might someday need a black "label" for their goods, and consequently use Lesotho's population as labor in this type of export platform. In all, Walter has not had an easy time talking to people about population.

Dr. Walter suggested that I go to the Mafetang region of Lesotho, which he said had originally resisted family planning on a "we can not be bought" basis. Mafetang is a stronghold of the ousted Basuto Congress party. CARE loaned me a car and a driver, assistant field representative Daniel Marite, who was delighted to make the trip because it would give him a chance to see his family. Matron Maile of Mafetang Hospital told us where we might find Ivy Monoang, a midwife attached to the Tsakhola Clinic, and on the way over to her house, Daniel sidetracked to show me the site where he plans to build his new house. It was one of dozens of neat little rectangular tracts laid out, suburban fashion, on the outskirts of Mafetang. Land tenure and the nation's communal traditions might survive pressures for agricultural development, but it was hard to imagine how it might survive the development of a middle class. Already some chiefs have found the potential for profit irresistable and have sold choice lands on a bid basis. The suburbanization of Lesotho's towns could only enhance those pressures.

Ivy Monoang was a delightful young woman. She lived in a small house protected by two large, illusorily ferocious dogs. The clinic where she worked as a midwife had only been open two months, but Ivy believed that so far the results had been encouraging. She said that a lot of women had long wanted to limit the number of children they had and had previously tried to "space" their children by such ineffectual devices as withdrawal, which demands consistent self-control, and by prolonging breast-feeding for up to three years. Some women who want big families still will not have intercourse during breast-feeding because they feel that to do so would produce a spoiled child.

For Ivy, males are clearly the villains in Lesotho's or any country's population tragedy. She described us as selfish, because we don't trust our wives when we are away, because we like big families which we leave for the women to produce and take care of, because we don't like the idea of women having the increased freedom that might accompany smaller families, because we will force the women to keep having children until we have a son. Daniel and I both felt very guilty at the end of her recitation. In Mafetang, said Ivy, the extended-family system was still quite healthy, so big families were not yet perceived as a burden—except by weary mothers. She noted that she was taking care of her brother's three children, and Daniel interjected proudly that he was educating two of his brother's children. Also, in the Mafetang area most children were still born at home which meant that many families were still beyond the reach of Ivy's counseling.

Ivy customarily tried to work on promoting family planning while the women were pregnant. She said they were more receptive then. Some of these women came back for postnatal care and then had an IUD inserted. Some women came in for IUD insertion while their husbands were away at the mines (unfortunately, there was the possibility that some of these women would have the IUD taken out before their husband's return). Most of the women who came had already had two children or so, and this might be interpreted in support of the "precious child" theory of family planning offered by McGilvray, CARE and Dr. Walter. For the most part, said Ivy, women had been coming alone, but more and more husbands were beginning to accompany their wives.

Consequently, Ivy had hopes for family planning. She felt that the next generation would definitely accept family planning, and if that generation comprised women as strong-minded as she, there might be some substance to her hopes. However, there was another, less positive interpretation that might be used to interpret future acceptance of family planning. This has to do with changing values which, while they may have some small effect on the birth rate, will produce a host of other repercussions that could well leave Lesotho in a less favorable position than it finds itself now.

Dr. Walter, a firm believer in development, saw family planning as but one component of what should be an integrated scheme of development involving education, wage parity and changing the role of women. However, even though he felt this way, Walter, like McGilvray, admitted that the short-term effects of other components of any development scheme would ultimately be counterproductive without a stable population. One of these effects is value change, which, because it interreacts with the birth rate, perhaps should be introduced now.

It is generally accepted by population experts that "social and economic development that brings an increase in per capita income and a more equitable income distribution is probably also a necessary condition for a continuing reduction of rates in population growth."* The development agencies and voluntary agencies all subscribe to this view, and in the same issue of *Scientific American,* other population experts offered specific suggestions about how development works to affect decisions on limiting the number of children a family raises:

> Decisions leading to lower fertility can be regarded as originating in two types of individual desire. One is to seize opportunities that open up in the process of development. Examples include the drive to acquire new consumer goods (epitomized by the bicycle—motorcycle—automobile sequence), the costs of which tend to outstrip rising incomes; the desire to expand a privately owned enterprise by acquiring capital goods, the desire to provide a better education and upbringing to children already born, and the interest in upward social mobility. The change to success in such endeavors is often powerfully increased by restricting the size of one's family. The effect is reinforced by the decreasing economic benefits that parents derive from children as development progresses.
>
> A second psychological factor that pulls in the same direction is the pervasive disinclination to accept a lowering of one's accustomed standard of living. Both of these motives played a role in past fertility transitions and now exert a downward influence on fertility in many underdeveloped countries. Moreover, it is likely that the exposure to consumer goods and styles of living that conflict with a large family is more intensive now than it was in the past.†

Paul Demeny believes that these factors can have quite a strong impact on the birth rate, but even so, he recognizes

* Richard Revelle, "Food and Population," *Scientific American,* Vol. 231, No. 3 (September 1974).

† Paul Demeny, "The Populations of the Underdeveloped Countries," *ibid.*

that for the largest segments of the underdeveloped world, "development-induced changes in the perceived costs and benefits of children to parents are unlikely to be strong enough to elicit a similar reaction in the foreseeable future." Perhaps this type of "birth control" is not the answer.

In Lesotho there is evidence that people are beginning to reassess the value of having many children. That reassessment indicates that one of the processes that Demeny speaks of as following development is at work. In order to "take" in a non-Western people, development exploits two primary human motivations: envy (or greed) and shame. In order to want to develop, one has to be conscious of one's poverty, and the developer's task is thus to "teach the natives to want." However, development, if it is to work, also demands some resource which might be exploited for profit. Resources might be rich land, minerals or human energy. While a country devoid of what we decide are resources might exist blissfully ignorant of this lack, the country that wants the accouterments of development, but has nothing to sell in order to buy those accouterments, finds itself in a particularly abject position.

Lesotho and other similar Third World countries with poor human (because of the exigencies and effects of deteriorating ecology and migrant labor) and no existent mineral resources are now acquiring the appetites of development without the means to support them. It is frighteningly like the situation of the young man corrupted by a vision of luxury in Huysmans' *À Rebours*. There, a decadent aristocrat introduces a poor young man to incredible sensual pleasure in the hope that he will later turn to murder to support his unattainable expensive tastes.

One of the people who was very sensitive to the changing values in Lesotho was Sister Rose, head of the St. George's School of Nursing in Roma. Daniel and I drove up to visit her after speaking with Ivy Monoang. She was sensitive to these changes because she is a devout Catholic with strong antimaterialist feelings, and because she has spent decades in Lesotho and has seen changing attitudes as they happen. Sister Rose is a small, energetic woman. She speaks with great precision and orderliness, and when noting some failing or selfishness in Basuto men she would skewer Daniel with her piercing gaze and demand his acknowledgment of her accuracy. For the second time in one day Daniel was burdened with the sins of all Basuto and men in general, and I could not blame him if later he became a little reluctant to accompany me on my interviews.

Sister Rose said that she had direct experience with changing material values because she noticed a marked increase in the social rejection of children. "Where before children would be given to grandparents," she said, "now because of the demand for material goods, unwanted children are unacceptable costs," and it is hard to find someone to take them. Before, if a woman had an illegitimate child, it was handled discreetly. But, she said, increasingly "surprise" babies are abandoned, or if the husband returns home before the child is born, dispatched by a kick to the mother's stomach or by the husband's refusal to allow the mother to nurse it.

This is the type of value change that Mr. Demeny wrote about in *Scientific American*. However, as evident from Sister Rose's account, the "decisions affecting fertility" do not always have the surgical neatness that they have when presented analytically. Of course, access to contraceptive materials and abortion clinics might lessen the cruelty that follows this new cost-benefit analysis. Sister Rose noted that the "benefit" side of this new view of the value of children is also apparent in such frivolous ways as an increased fashion-consciousness among the Basuto. "When I came to Lesotho," she said, "children never talked about appearance or shoes, and those that didn't have shoes did not feel ashamed."

These new consumer values do not only affect fertility

decisions. Old people as well as children become economic
liabilities competing for the family income with consumer
goods, and once people become interested in doing things
to accumulate money, they begin to reappraise those communal responsibilities that involve helping their neighbors
for free. "When I first came, people were not paid to harvest
fields," said Sister Rose. "They would work on fields as
they were needed." The danger of monetizing communal
services was something the Basuto leader Moshesh warned
about a century ago. There are other ways besides affecting
fertility decisions that these changing values interreact with
population problems. Sister Rose dated money-consciousness among the Basuto to 1966—independence—when the
massive flow of aid started to come in. Still, she felt that
some of the mountain villages remained healthy. The
changing material values follow the roads, she said, and
many Basuto are not so far removed from their communal
roots that they cannot go back. Sister Rose wished they
would too. She did not think that the material benefits of development outweigh the social costs. "If I came back to
Lesotho," she said, "I would rather find it the way it was
then than the way it is now." She believed that the Basuto
were more dependable and loyal before. Because of her
feelings for the Basuto, it was particularly painful for Sister
Rose to see Basuto children lining the roads and screaming "Give me money" at passing expatriates.

For Lesotho the cry "Give me money!" has been particularly apt and particularly productive because, save for work
done in the South African mines, charity is the only way the
country has been able to get money. One thing this means
is that while money-consciousness might have some small
effect on the birth rate, the difficulties of accumulating
money in Lesotho produce a whole new set of burdens on
the country's minuscule resource base which will probably
dilute the gains from some future decline in the fertility

rate. This in turn means that while there is the prospect that some day people might be having fewer children in Lesotho, those children will be far more expensive for the nation to raise. For instance, as consumer values disrupt the extended family, they create orphans and homeless elders—a burden for the state.

Money hunger without opportunity has also led to a great increase in property crime—something else that is new to Lesotho—which burdens the country with police, prisons and court costs. Moreover, both the sense and substance of O. Henry's sarcastic remark that the poor tend to spend alms on trifles rather than giving it to the installment man applies with some amendment to Lesotho. One of the ambitions of the first Five-Year Plan was to increase cash crops with the idea that this would produce money for nutritional foods and for investment in improved seed and equipment. Voluntary-agency people throughout Africa complained to me that both money paid by voluntary agencies as wages and income produced by cash crops are largely spent on "luxury" items such as beer, clothing, cigarettes to satisfy new-found consumer appetites; in Lesotho's case it leaves the country via the pockets of Lebanese traders.

The emergence of consumer values and the monetizing of formerly free communal services means that the country now has to generate additional income merely to maintain the same standard of living and production, the difference being that that money leaves the country or the nation's productive sectors to satisfy the consumer tapeworm. Lesotho, where population pressures are already impoverishing the population, stands to find herself physically poorer with the advent of consumer tastes, and still poorer in spirit as well with the consciousness of her poverty and inability to satisfy her new insatiable appetites.

It is unlikely that any of the factors that experts feel normally halt population growth—decreasing infant mortality, changing perceptions of the value of children, fear of losing what living standard one has achieved, new freedoms and responsibilities for women, and the like—will prevent Lesotho's case of population poisoning from reaching a critical level. This means the future might well entail coercive measures to control the birth rate, a state of permanent relief, a "natural solution," political turmoil in Lesotho, in the South African mines, or in South Africa, or perhaps other unhappy eventualities. Such scenarios are at least as easy to argue as any of the wild-card scenarios for Lesotho's salvation such as revolution in South Africa, the discovery of oil, or the use of Lesotho as an export platform. But like the doctor who treats his patient for the flu because he doesn't know how to treat the patient's leukemia, the expatriate experts and voluntary agencies continue with their development projects carried on by a momentum generated in donor countries, and leave questions of population unmentioned and uncontrolled.

NINE

Image
and Reality

Given all that has been introduced about Lesotho, its background and its problems, perhaps it is the proper time to
contrast, against this background, the view of Lesotho taken
by CARE, a large voluntary agency with a reputation for
efficiency. There are actually three CARE views of Lesotho: the view of Lesotho which CARE presents to the
world, the view of Lesotho which CARE uses in planning
for the country, and the view of Lesotho and its problems
evident in CARE evaluations of its programs there. Altogether one swims through levels of increasing unreality
before one gets to the view evident in this quote from an
article about CARE in the New York *Daily News* Sunday
Magazine, May 13, 1973: "In tiny Lesotho, a kingdom of
about a million persons in Africa, CARE is being rewarded
for its patience as the little country takes giant strides forward . . . In less than five years, the natives have built over
1,000 earthen dams and planted over three million trees to
control what was once rampant soil erosion." Perhaps, then,
it is best to take the CARE view in stages.

The documents CARE had prepared on Lesotho and
which I had the opportunity to sift through included Prog-
gress Reports on emergency self-help assistance and Community Development, CARE Project Fact Sheets, a Project

Evaluation Report and the Post Report, and the draft Pre-Plan Paper, which, as of the summer of 1974, was the latest document CARE had prepared. I was assured that I had seen everything of importance prepared by the home office and by CARE Lesotho pertaining to programming there.

Not one of these documents discussed the nation's tribal heritage, the nation's communal and egalitarian traditions, the functions of village structure, or indeed, any of the questions which would be the first questions an anthropologist might ask if he wanted to determine the strengths and weaknesses of Basuto society, and from there, where it might be best to intervene.

Clearly, what one program head told me is true: "In planning individual projects, social consequences are not very important." When I asked Africa Programming chief Leo Pastore whether CARE consulted the anthropological literature, he replied, "Yes, at the [CARE] mission level. It's used for background." He went on to qualify this by saying that CARE men had no formal training in anthropology and that anthropological literature "really isn't used in program planning." It does not even show up in CARE background materials.

The CARE Project Fact Sheet comes closest to considering Basuto society when it discusses Moshesh's achievements and follows with, "As a High Commission Territory under Britain's system of indirect rule, the Basutos retained responsibility for their internal affairs, but the pressures of modernization eroded much of the traditional culture without a compensating growth of mass involvement in administration." I am not sure what this refers to, but if the author wants to imply that under the British, the chief system rigidified somewhat, he is correct (although there is still lively interest among the Basuto in reviving the pre-British consensual aspects of the chief system). But it is wrong to suggest that at the time of independence the Basuto were left without either traditions or modern bureaucratic structures. When I first spoke with Tom Bentley, then country chief for Lesotho, in 1972, he reflected this view that Basuto traditions were hopelessly eroded, and even went so far as to say that present-day Basuto have no strong cultural heritage. It is easy to see how one might draw that opinion about a country with a huge migrant labor force and overwhelmed by a hundred years of missionary propaganda. But at the time of independence, the land-tenure system was still healthy, the structure of village life was still largely traditional and communal (there is even today a strong subcurrent of ancestor worship in the mountains), and the great social changes that have accompanied the roads, the flood of foreign aid, and the projects of organizations like CARE were yet to come.

The CARE view gets more interesting as we enter the present. A 1969 Progress Report mentions "overcropping, overgrazing and perennial drought have caused erosion, crop failure, and loss of livestock," without ever mentioning overpopulation, which lies behind those symptoms. Later reports devote as much as a phrase to population pressures.

Much of the background information CARE offers seems derivative from the reports of others. For instance, the reports echo the Planning Office in citing land tenure as an impediment to agriculture, and the Pre-Plan Paper takes its cue from Comrudev in forming its attitude toward the Basuto village: ". . . over ninety percent of the population live in rural areas and many in isolated and scattered habitation without basic public services and which the Department of Community Development identify as being 'socially pathological and uneconomic to assist and develop.' " One can almost see a Comrudev official stamping his foot as, in frustration, he calls the Basuto village pathological, and perhaps the CARE man, better than I, can understand what it means for a village to be "socially pathological." The second part ("uneconomic to assist and develop") is easy to understand; it means, simply, that it is too difficult to help people so long as they are scattered in 7,100 villages, and things would be so much easier if they would congregate in larger towns—CARE and Comrudev are here begging for the curse of the rest of the Third World.

CARE's disinterest in Basuto society and its willingness to accept, unexamined, the opinions of others about the Basuto lead it to present some appallingly inappropriate statements about village life, and also make the agency a perfect accomplice in some of the ill-advised and perhaps ill-intentioned government schemes. Witness the description of village life offered prior to the Pre-Plan Paper in the CARE Project Fact Sheet: "However, most Basotho live in one of some 7,100 scattered villages having an average population of less than 150. The majority of these villages have none of the basic services normally required by a community, such as schools, clinics, water systems, electricity, markets, sanitation systems, post offices, and police posts." The question, of course, is: What is a normal community? The notion of a Basuto village needing electricity, a post office or a police post is patently absurd. There is nothing about the reasons for this scattering of small villages, the adaptation to the local ecology the scattering embodies, or how the villages deal with the problems we solve through the facilities mentioned. Having established the poverty and needs of the village, the Project Fact Sheet for 1971 goes on to detail how CARE intends to dovetail its activities with the Lesothan government's development scheme:

> Because funds are limited, the Government has recognized the need to concentrate its resources in approximately fifty villages which are considered to be potential centers of growth. It is hoped that this will stimulate the growth of these communities so that in time they will become planned urban or semi-urban centers. Five towns have been designated as "primary" growth centers, and another ten have been chosen as "secondary" centers. The responsibility for the development of these fifteen centers will be shared by

various Ministries of the Government. Approximately thirty-five communities have been designated as "tertiary" growth centers. It is here that CARE is concentrating its community development activities. Therefore, greatest priority will be given to requests for assistance in these communities.

With no countervailing information about the purposes of Lesotho's quasi-anarchical society, there was no reason why CARE should not throw its weight behind the government's intention to change the nation's very character. However, if CARE lacked anthropological appreciation of Lesotho, it might still question the "political" motives of the Five-Year Plan of a government that had seized power through a coup. In fact, this attention-grabbing aspect of the Lesothan political situation is not mentioned in even one of the documents I read. CARE does not see Lesotho as a nation, but rather as a never-never land where, as stated in the Pre-Plan Paper "the Basuto people are in a struggle against long odds, to build both a new nation and happier, more meaningful, more productive lives for themselves." One wonders how you program to give a people whose culture you ignore a more meaningful and happier life. In New York I asked Ray Rignall how you determine whether a Mosuto is living a more "meaningful life." He replied that evaluating this was "a question of indicators," looking at changes in postal savings, accessibility to medical services, and social mobility.

The omission of cultural considerations from background information and project reports, and the presence of economic jargon might be legacies of CARE's business bias and relief heritage. Starving people are all alike in one respect and that is that they need food, and beyond considerations like making sure that pork isn't sent to starving Moslems, the key problems are logistical. Similarly, a no-nonsense businessman would look at a Basuto village and see inadequate water supplies, poor roads, lack of post offices, etc., and in a can-do spirit see how those services might be provided or improved, and not worry about why the Basuto do things the way they do, or what the possible repercussions of providing those services might be. However, even if such considerations are absent from background reports, we might imagine that given CARE's reputation for efficiency, its evaluation of its projects would consider a project's total impact and appropriateness.

As noted earlier, CARE entered Lesotho on the heels of the emergency situation created by the recurrence of Lesotho's cyclical droughts in the late nineteen-sixties. It called its program then an Emergency Self-Help Assistance Program. CARE contributed tools for erosion-control dam building, for road and airstrip construction, and for tree planting—the projects the Sunday *News* article referred to. What the article didn't say was that the vast majority of the trees planted were cut down by the Basuto or trampled by livestock long before they matured, that almost none of the dams were built in the areas hardest hit by the drought, and that those that were built were scattered through the country without rhyme or reason.

For instance, the Five-Year Plan notes:

> Special attention will be paid to the co-ordination of soil conservation works and irrigation. In the past, protective dams, some of them very large, were constructed without considering the full utilization of the water. Out of approximately 800 existing dams only a few are utilized for irrigation . . . The construction of new dams without relating where possible to the immediate improvement of agricultural productivity is a wasteful practice, which the country cannot afford.

Actually, few of the dams are used for any of the purposes for which they were originally intended. In one evaluation I read, Tom Bentley, who was CARE chief in Lesotho during that program, brought out the insufficiencies of the dam-building program quite candidly. Bentley noted that people tended to draw out the work to prolong their food wages, that most of the dams were used for watering livestock, if at all, and that they would have been ultimately cheaper to build with paid labor. However, Bentley also felt that the program was justified because without food-for-work they would not have been built at all, and that part of the purpose of the program was to distribute food "without the onus of charity."

Bentley made a sincere effort to objectively appraise the dam program, but there were certain things he neglected to mention. Two Peace Corpsmen who worked for the Office of Community in the late nineteen-sixties said that not only did the Basuto not know what the dams were for, but the arrival of food-for-work dam projects had negative effects on nonwage community development projects already in progress. One of them said, "People would be working on a project for free, out of pride—gardens, water-supply systems and the like—then the government would come in offering food to build a road or a dam, and everybody would abandon the community development project." Both these men said that there was nothing self-help about the food-for-work projects because people only thought about the wages, and because they would abandon genuine self-help projects for the food. On these wages, and under the temptation to draw the work out, the Basuto would not take pride in what they did. (Both of these men intensely disliked the term "self-help" in any application and felt that such projects would be better termed "public works.")

The two Peace Corpsmen also said that the distribution of food wages caused some people not to plant seed, and drew other people needed for agricultural work from the fields. I bounced these criticisms off of Desmond Taylor of Comrudev. In defense of food-for-work, he said that there was evidence that the projects have not been getting as many

workers as they need during plowing and harvest time
(which is not to say that they do not draw people from the
fields), and that the projects would not be started at all without food. But he did admit that "food may foster a situation
where you don't get any voluntary effort without food." He
also acknowledged that many dams were misplaced, but
added, "every time you've stopped water from leaving the
country you've done something good."

CARE is missing something about Lesotho in its evaluations, something other people feel is important. Social or
agricultural disruptions were not discussed in the CARE
project evaluations I read. Tom Bentley and his successors
seemed more interested in questions like dollar value. For
instance, Bentley's evaluation of the dam-building project
dwelt at length on the costs of using food as wages in dam
building vesus what might have been accomplished with a
cash wage. A draft Pre-Plan Paper (preparatory to CARE's
new Multi-Year Plan system) sets forth evaluation procedures:

H. Evaluation:

   1. Targets:

      a. Indicators
        The indicator used to measure target achieve-
        ment will be the rate of construction of bridging
        and culverts scheduled to be built in each year's
        work plan.

      b. Methods
        Progress will be monitored through reference
        to regular field reports from technical teams and
        visitations. [I startled the first time I encountered
        this use of the word "visitation"—it gives you
        some idea of the home office's perceptions of its
        role that it cannot live with the word "visit." One

imagines a medium in Maseru beckoning a CARE
nabob and his appearing through raps on the
table.]

c. Requirements
No additional personnel, material or equipment
are needed to conduct the evaluation within the
framework of work activities.

2. Goals:

a. Indicators
Given local circumstances, it has proven difficult to select realistic and meaningful indicators
to measure the improvement in the social and economic conditions of the population to be affected
by this project. Those chosen are—change in
visitation patterns to these regions from education,
health inspectors, agriculture extension agents
and Community Development District Officers. It
is considered that increased visits at least suggest
a greater probability in effecting social changes.
—Changes in the number of participating
schools, amounts of commodities distributed
[suspiciously like the AID criteria of "numbers of
contraceptives delivered" that Mert Cregger was
disparaging], and delivery costs in the school
feeding program.
This indicator should demonstrate possible savings in freight rates and an increased facility to
move freight.
—Changes in economic activity at local trading
station both in terms of movement of consumer
items and purchase and shipment of wool,
mohair, and agricultural produce to markets. [I
thought that one purpose of the roads was to break
the stranglehold of local traders.]

b. Methods
Data concerning visitation patterns may be col-

lected from the appropriate district government offices relying on trip records.

Schools feeding information can be obtained from the Food Aid Program Office which is also CARE's counterpart in this project. CARE will be taken to discount such factors as changing AER figures and ration rates and disruptions in the pipe line because of external factors.

Trading store statistics, of course, will be much more difficult to secure; however, it is hoped that through personal representation the cooperation of traders in at least selected areas can be gained.

c. Requirements

This evaluation process can be conducted without special requirements, and within the framework of work activities.

What is clear from this evaluation method is that CARE's view of the success or failure of its projects is almost totally conditioned by crude economic considerations and almost totally blind to negative social repercussions. As Leo Pastore told me flatly, "CARE does not assess social consequences." An evaluation of a road project does not include destructive demographic changes like urban migration or ribbon development, nor would a study of trading-post statistics say anything about *who* was benefiting should the figures show an upswing.

There is of course the counterargument that these subtler effects might be noticed on "visitations." However, I have yet to meet a CARE man who was concerned with taking such effects into account in his evaluations; or, given the demands of the evaluation report, would go out of his way to find them. As any journalist knows, it is exceedingly difficult to discover such effects during a five-day "visitation" primarily devoted to discussing planning and logistics questions. Moreover, there is evidence that there is some degree of self-deception within CARE which would inhibit the accuracy of its evaluations. For instance, the Pre-Plan Paper on Lesotho notes that "CARE has had good results drawing on the self-help component in its programming efforts so far." But when I spoke with Tom Bentley on my return from Lesotho, he said that the biggest weakness of the CARE program was communication. "Although the government was aware of what they were doing, the villagers were not aware of what we were up to and why. There is so much foreign aid that the villager has no idea what it means."

In any case, most evaluations are not really read, except if they show some logistical flaw that might be corrected in future programming. One former CARE representative told me that when a new CARE man comes in, he has his own pet ideas and projects he wants to get started on, and is not inclined to spend his time worrying about what happened before his arrival.

Finally, some CARE men have the unfortunate habit of stretching dollars by listing dollar input in terms of the number of beneficiaries à la rural pacification in Vietnam. "Progress Report, PDPs [Partnership Development Programs] #27 and #80, CARE's Community Development Programs in Lesotho" lists various projects, a brief description of what is intended by the project, its costs and the number of beneficiaries. For example, "Dormitory Construction for Holy Names Secondary School: CARE provided construction materials. These materials will be utilized in an extension of a newly constructed dormitory for the addition of a kitchen, lavatory, and storage facility. $12,713 (5,000 beneficiaries)" or, for a more elaborate claim, "Gravelling Unit for Access Road Construction . . . $23,875 (350,000 beneficiaries)."

One of CARE's Project Evaluation Reports describes its food-for-work programs in Lesotho as of "unquestioned developmental value," and this is indeed true, but in a sense which CARE may not have intended. Because of the biases of its officers, its evaluation procedures and the exigencies of bureaucratic procedures, there are many effects of CARE projects of which CARE is unaware and hence cannot control. It is indeed possible that CARE might be helping to create the very emergency conditions it was set up to help relieve, and not be aware of it. CARE, which takes such pride in claiming that it is helping people to live "more meaningful" lives at the village level, is actually only seeing Lesotho as a set of very crude statistics, and in planning and evaluation is all but blind to certain realities of life at the village level.

This brings us to how CARE sees Lesotho in terms of how it presents its programs to the world, which is where the transformational properties at work in CARE become most interesting. For one thing, some problems apparent to CARE men in Lesotho are not passed on to CARE New York, either, because there is no procedure for passing on certain perceptions, or because they might look bad. Other things are actively transformed by CARE Lesotho before being presented to CARE New York. Thus what Tom Bentley singled out to me as a weakness—the lack of communication between CARE and the villages—disappeared. Instead the draft Pre-Plan Paper singled out self-help as a strength.

My first encounter with these transformational properties was on the question of "dovetailing into the Five-Year Plan of a developing nation" which first got me interested in Lesotho. This is what CARE officials told me I would find when they suggested that I go to Lesotho to check out a program which represented the "vanguard of the future." At that time, in 1972, Tom Bentley did nothing to disabuse me of that notion. However, later, after I had been to Lesotho, and it began to appear that dovetailing with the Five-Year Plan of a developing nation was an awfully lofty way of describing CARE's grab bag of programming, Bentley was more candid. He said, "I couldn't dovetail into their Five-

Year Plan, because the ministries themselves weren't dove-tailing into it. The Permanent Secretaries had nothing but scorn for the plan."

CARE New York could not but be aware of the failings of the first Five-Year Plan or of the dissension surrounding it, and Bentley admitted that there was a "lack of correlation [in the plan] to what was going on in Lesotho." Still, CARE's latest Pre-Plan Paper avows faith in both the wisdom and practicality of Lesothan planning:

> The national priorities are clearly stated in the Lesotho Five Year Plan which was prepared by the Central Planning and Development Office and formally endorsed by both the King and Prime Minister . . . while, naturally enough, problems of coordination and implementation have arisen, the above-cited priorities have remained stable since the preparation of the plan and it is not expected that the second Five Year Plan, presently in its initial stages of preparation, will vary significantly in relation to basic priorities.

Thus a document partially expatriate-written and largely expatriate-influenced is endorsed by CARE as a reflection of local priorities, and CARE reassures itself that it is tying its program to locally generated priorities—the hall of mirrors is complete.

It is easier to understand why CARE would dissemble in presenting its programs to me than it is to understand why it should deceive itself in its own documents. When I first arrived at CARE, I suppose few people believed that I would actually go to Lesotho to check up on what they were doing there. One official, astonished that CARE had suggested that I visit Lesotho, said in exasperation that "CARE must have been so carried away with its own publicity that they are starting to believe it, and can't any longer distinguish between what's real and what's for publicity."

Perhaps something similar is occurring between CARE Lesotho and the home office as well. A CARE official might well see the inappropriateness of a Five-Year Plan or that "dovetailing" with that Five-Year Plan is nothing more than so many words. He might also see that the villagers were indifferent to the development aspects of the projects he was administering. Eventually, however, it comes time to evaluate and plan for coming years. The CARE man then begins to think of this program in terms of other programs he has been involved in. True, the villagers don't seem to know what's going on, but on the other hand, CARE does have a strong relationship with the government, something which might have been a problem in another country in which this career man worked. True, the Five-Year Plan is out of touch with Lesothan reality, and has no real guidelines, but still, it gives a direction to programming efforts—that national coordination that is missing in so many other developing countries. Moreover, when it comes time to put your thoughts down on paper, people often feel compelled to foist some organizing principle upon what they are doing, if not to justify their activities to the home office, to justify them for themselves.

Many CARE overseas operatives like to describe themselves as activists—people who get things done and don't sit around "head shrinking" about whether or not what they are doing is right. Most of the day is spent supervising various projects in the pipe line, keeping the flow of commodities and materials running smoothly, and ironing out kinks in the program. It is not the kind of life that encourages or even allows the person involved to sit back and think about first principles.

I often got the impression that CARE men's doubts about the utility of what they were doing, or the effects of their projects, got snowed under by the very momentum of their work. Keeping an organization going is something real and challenging, and it is directly satisfying to efficiently

complete a project—much as, I am sure, it is directly satisfying to supervise the building of a missile system—and in
both cases I imagine the obligations and satisfactions of this
direct day-to-day involvement submerge nebulous, elusive
and not easily answered doubts.

Doubt gets eased out by expediency. Bill Schellestede,
CARE's chief in Liberia, said to me, "When we become involved in the game, we ask questions on a somewhat lower
philosophical level than you were asking [not whether
CARE should build schools] but 'is this the right kind of
school?' " But then there comes a time when a CARE man
has to put things in order and plan either because the home
office demands it or because a visiting journalist asks him
to. And if he is caught up in the running of things, he deals
with these outside problems the easiest way possible. Often
when I asked a CARE man a question, I got the feeling that
he was trying out his answer on me rather than giving me
the principles that governed his thoughts.

When I asked Leo Pastore about the high CARE station
costs in Lesotho as compared to the amount of money
CARE spent there, first he said, "Well, we're building infrastructure, expertise." A moment later he said, "We don't
spend money, because we are cautious." Picking him up on
this question of building infrastructure, I asked Pastore
how this ambition jived with CARE's former philosophy
articulated by deputy executive director Louis Samia of
only involving itself in "practical approach with tangible
project with identifiable goals." Pastore said that building
infrastructure did not represent different philosophy, but
was rather part of the in-country need. I had the impression that he was fishing for an answer.

By saying that CARE was building infrastructure, Pastore
left the impression that there was some intricate design
which connected the various aspects of CARE's school,
clinic, road-building and small-industry projects, and which
would somehow magnify the effect of CARE's low level of

funding. However, two of the principal considerations affecting the totality of CARE planning in Lesotho is what is available to give away and who walks in the CARE door with a proposal to take it—and not the needs determined by a minutely constructed series of interventions designed to improve the nation's infrastructure. What CARE does in Lesotho is not different from what CARE does in a host of other non-Western societies, and I could find little to indicate that CARE looked at Lesotho as anything other than one of a host of interchangeable non-Western societies.

If I had not gone to Lesotho, I would have derived an entirely different picture of the nature of Lesotho's problems and the nature of CARE's solutions than what became apparent once I visited the country. Of course, not every journalist who writes about CARE visits the projects the home office discusses, or has the inclination to probe if he does. And that is the reason articles get written about "tiny Lesotho" taking "giant strides," and "1,000 earthen dams" controlling "once rampant soil erosion."

At home in the United States, CARE has the reputation as an effective fund raiser. Abroad it has the reputation as an organization that milks its projects for public relations value. Larry Cooley, a UNDP (United Nations Development Program) expert on secondment to the Lesothan government, told me that CARE "gets a lot more publicity out of a lot less money than the big organizations [World Bank, AID] do." Jim Kelley, the local Catholic Relief Services chief, said that CARE and CRS once talked about doing a project together, with AID matching funds. "The CARE chief was constantly fretting about how to identify CARE inputs," said Kelley. "For my part, I couldn't give a rat's ass about identifying inputs." Former Peace Corpsman Dan Hogan told me that CARE refused to free an air compressor until a donation ceremony was worked out.

Bob McCullam, good logistics man that he is, looks at

public relations as another technical problem. On several occasions when we discussed visits to projects, he remarked that it would have been nice if I had arrived earlier when a government photographer went out to record some singing Basuto women wielding their CARE picks on a road project. It never occurred to him that I might not want to see a demonstration staged by the government. (By the way, these staged demonstrations give the impression that work proceeds at breakneck speed, when in actuality, women work at about the pace of a New York City civil servant, in order to draw out their food wages.)

The CARE overseas operations manual contains explicit instruction on how to write emotion-arousing donor reports and even contains sample statements about the CARE reception at the "local level." These reports should be written, according to CARE, to ensure the donor's emotional satisfaction, so that he will feel he has chosen the right organization and that as a result of his highly valued gift, he is a better person. Emphasis is placed upon the "tone" of these reports—the more personal the better. Judge the release on Lesotho entitled "The Road from Poverty to Self-Sufficiency" against CARE's operations-manual instructions:

THE ROAD FROM POVERTY TO SELF-SUFFICIENCY . . .

Poverty and Self-sufficiency are not towns but conditions. The people you see above [picture of people working with picks] are trying to go from one to the other. They are building a road because they want a chance to live and provide for themselves. Their country, Lesotho, in southern Africa, has many mountains, but few roads. A road that reached into the heart of the country would mean much in terms of national development and individual jobs.

They had strength and muscles, and they were prepared to sweat. What they did not have was tools. Last year they made a pact with CARE: "If you will provide us with the tools—we will prove what can be done with them." And they did. CARE sent wheelbarrows, picks and shovels to people who had little but their hands.

Tom Bentley, CARE Mission Chief, reported from Lesotho last Spring:

"In mid-March a bulldozer being run with CARE funds broke through to Thaba Tseka. Following in its tracks was the first vehicle ever to be seen in Thaba Tseka. It is almost impossible to describe the joy and pandemonium that greeted it . . . school was let out and 400 children came laughing and shouting to inspect the dusty vehicle. Church bells rang and nuns cried with joy. Even the men responsible for the road had difficulty deciding whether to grin or weep."

The tools CARE sent now are building other roads. They have also been used to plant 405,000 trees and build 88 earth dams—vital in the battle against rampant soil erosion that threatens food supply.

Each year throughout the world CARE feeds millions of hungry people, and helps them help themselves. If they will build, then CARE will supply the materials for schools and other needed facilities. Dig the trenches, and there can be pure water for the first time in generations. Share the cost, and CARE-Medico will heal the sick and teach modern medicine to local physicians and nurses.

How well does the Post Report satisfy operations-manual requirements? Does it make the donor "keenly aware that he or she showed excellent judgment in using CARE?" Does it provide emotional satisfaction for the donor? Extra-point question: What impression does the Post Report give the reader on CARE's impact on Lesotho's problems?

For some reason CARE seems to like to call attention to programs in which it has special problems. Like a man who cannot resist scratching a sore, CARE is continually bragging to reporters about programs of, at best, dubious value. It was this that bewildered the CARE official who told me that it was "incredibly stupid" for CARE to suggest that I go to Lesotho. Besides Lesotho, CARE also directed my attention to programs in Liberia and Bangladesh. I visited Liberia, which I will discuss later, but I will mention the Bangladesh program here, because the same Sunday *News* article which lauds the CARE Lesothan program also praises CARE's housing program in Bangladesh: ". . . ever since the Bangla Desh disaster [the 1970 cyclone that flattened the island of Bhola, and not the current famine] CARE has been battling broken bridges and ripped-up railroad tracks to construct from scratch 70 new villages—over 7,000 cyclone-proof homes. More homes will be built today. Perhaps a village will be completed."

Lou Samia had told me about this project in 1972. It was to be—familiar words—a "pilot project." The idea was that a "crash program to establish visibly what could be done in selected villages" would be followed up by the people themselves on a cooperative basis. Costs would be repaid into a revolving fund which would then be used toward financing new housing. CARE would provide the masons and carpenters for intricate work.

It occurred to me back then that there was little possibility of anything more than an infinitesimal percentage of Bangladesh's huge population ever occupying this new housing. Given this and a dauntlessly corrupt civil service, there was the likelihood that such pilot housing would become citadels from which the influential might look down on their neighbors. Samia agreed that this was a danger. Since then I have spoken with Bengalis familiar with the program who have said that this is what has happened in many cases. However, this is not the problem that convinced CARE to abandon this housing project in favor of building schools and institutional structures. What began to concern CARE was that cement, which was $27/ton for 10,000-ton quantities in Pakistan, rose to $100/ton in Bangladesh, making the housing far too expensive. All this, of course, is aside from the question of the envy-producing and socially disruptive effects of building this type of housing in villages of traditional organization and design—and also aside from the question of whether housing is the proper intervention in Bangladesh, which has the world's most pressing population problems.

The implication of the *News* article is that things are going swimmingly in Bangladesh, as swimmingly as they are going in Lesotho. Little questions about skyrocketing costs, political corruption or misplaced dams and wasted trees are all left unmentioned because they might deprive the donor of his emotional satisfaction of making his gift. In fact, in the closed circuit of donation, administration and report back to the donor, which keeps CARE men and people in the other voluntary agencies employed, the beneficiary is a nettlesome quantity, someone to be trotted out for picture-taking ceremonies. If CARE can transform a snafu into a triumph in terms of the public's impressions, then what happens to the beneficiary really does not matter at all.

It was curious that CARE directed my attention to three trouble spots—the Sasstown Road in Liberia, a one-year project that has taken over seven years to build; the Bangladesh pilot housing project; and the Lesothan program—sores CARE cannot resist scratching. Perhaps this analogy should not be tossed off so lightly. In the public relations world of CARE's information office, CARE is forthrightly helping Bengalis and Basuto on the road to self-sufficiency, but through the cracks in the façade of donor reports and evaluations seep disquieting reminders that something is askew in both these programs.

I suspect that CARE men intuitively know that what is askew in Lesotho, in Liberia and in Bangladesh is something more profound than an administrative miscalculation. Soiling the dream image of happy villages crying over air compressors are questions of nasty politics, local indifference, unexpected and uncontrollable spin-off—a packet of anxieties that darkly suggest that CARE is not what it thinks it is, or that it is losing touch with reality in the countries in which its operatives work. Perhaps then it is reassuring to have a journalist like the *News* reporter write about these trouble spots in bright, positive, reassuring tones. Then one can sit back and read about the good one is doing and keep those doubts at bay. There it is, right there in the *Daily News*, that's the real perspective, sure there are bugs in the program, but the bottom line is: "We are doing good." Read it right there in the *Daily News*.

TEN

A Sampling
of Projects

THABA KHUPA

A voluntary agency can sometimes be very opportunistic. Until three years ago, CIKs (Contributions in Kind from manufacturers) used to be a major source of CARE revenue. For instance, Dial used to give CARE a great amount of soap; Beechnut, Hines and Gerber used to donate baby food. Jack Cohen, head of procurement for CARE, said that since a change in the tax laws three years ago, such contributions have all but died. Formerly the law allowed a manufacturer to take the wholesale price of contributed goods as a tax deduction; now manufacturers can only deduct the cost of manufacturing, and as a result, drought has shriveled this stream of "generosity." Contributions of drugs have not fallen off, though; distributions are good advertising. CARE has received offers for many items that it has trouble distributing in the non-Western world, such as Kotex, or has turned down such items as lipstick from Revlon (CARE would have no trouble unloading lipstick, but it wouldn't have looked very good).

Back in 1972 when I was talking with Tom Bentley about CIKs, he remarked that a year earlier CARE had received an excellent donation of books which allowed them to start a library with 350 titles in every secondary school in Lesotho. The books were contributed by the publisher of this book, Random House. Because of Random House's largesse, every high school student in Lesotho has access to Carl Friedrich's study *The Philosophy of Hegel, The Symbolist Movement*, by Anna Balakian, *Drug Addiction: Physiological, Psychological and Sociological Aspects*, by D. P. Ausubel, as well as an interesting-sounding history of California, several works on Latin America, and many other intriguing if not forbidding titles which, presumably, will prepare the Basuto high school student to cope with the problems he will be facing.

Education is a hot issue in Lesotho, as it is in Africa and throughout the underdeveloped world. Often the experience has been that an academic education gives a student skills and expectations for which there is no outlet in a remote village or town. Alienated by knowledge from traditional ways, students drift toward the cities, emptying towns of needed manpower and overburdening the cities. In fact, I am sure that among the plethora of sociological titles which Random House contributed to Lesotho, there is some mention of the problems of education and urban migration to which Random House and CARE might well be contributing.

In each of the countries I visited, urban migration and alienated youth were regarded as a brewing problem. In Liberia, Peace Corpsman Sean Sullivan told me that young men and women would finish their education and then refuse to work. Leo Pastore noted the same problem when he said, "As soon as someone finishes junior high, he feels qualified for a high clerical position and he zaps right into Monrovia." Pastore went on to say that the classic example of such alienation was in Ceylon, which had a youth rebellion in 1972. The government quashed the revolt and still holds thousands in detention. It started because a large number of students who had benefited from Ceylon's program of free education found no opportunities once they had finished school. The government still does not know what to do with these people. Pastore had earlier been CARE's chief in Kenya, and he said that Kenya's solution to overeducation is to pass a law making migration to Nairobi illegal.

Education is but one of the forces that pries the young away from traditional ways of doing things and away from the villages, but it is perhaps the most powerful alienating force the young encounter. This force works in several ways. For one thing, education programs generally compete with traditional village organization because they are designed to prepare the young for something supposedly superior to the traditional way of life. In Iran, children would turn in scorn on their parents once education had given them a glimpse of the power of technology. Tradition is mute before reason. If the teacher is an outsider, the students note that he or she can't wait to leave town on weekends, or they notice the teacher's different style of dress or musical preferences, emblems of a more powerful world. A village can be a full and magical world until the villager is exposed to the wonders available beyond the hills, either through the curriculum or through the teacher, or through the villager's own deductions.

Some of the communities where CARE builds schools are aware of the threat posed to tradition by education, and resist school projects for that reason. In Kenya, for instance, the Masai have resisted school projects for the sophisticated reason that they pose a threat to Masai culture. Other peoples, such as the Turkhana, Borana and Somali, have also resisted school projects on more intuitive grounds. When I asked the CARE people how a project resisted by the locals could be termed a response to felt needs, they replied that school projects were coordinated through the government's community development division.

People have been educating the Basuto for a long time— in fact, since Moshesh enticed Eugene Casalis to come and teach his people. They are known for having the highest literacy rate in black Africa (although the figures are said to be misleading). However, planners have long complained about the useless academic cast to education in Lesotho. The Five-Year Plan notes: "The content of education is also of the traditional academic type and bears little relation to the development needs of the country." CARE, which is supposedly dovetailing its programs with the Five-Year Plan, made its contribution of books like *Renaissance Philosophy* two years after those words were written. I suspect that CARE's doubts about the utility of this CIK were swept away by its availability.

Between 1972 and 1974 CARE became aware of the problems that flow from academic education in places where there is no opportunity to profit from its benefits. CARE would have to become aware of this through the insistence of host governments, since CARE's own evaluative procedures describe a school project as successful with the physical completion of the structure. In Kenya the government is now building village polytechnics which it hopes will absorb the great numbers of primary school graduates and give them vocational skills which are needed in the villages. In Liberia the government is now making a similar effort through its rural primary school program. However, curriculum is but one vector of the forces unleashed through schools which impel the young to the cities.

In Lesotho, CARE is still devoting the majority of its budget to school construction, but it has also contributed to the Thaba Khupa Farm Institute, which is founded on presumptions inimical to those which would encourage school construction. Thaba Khupa also has ambitions counter to those of the country's first Five-Year Plan. While CARE's involvement is minimal—a $1,977 contribution for oxen and oxen equipment—that it is involved in Thaba Khupa at all shows the "scattershot" pattern (as an expatriate who worked in CARE put it) to its programming. The Thaba Khupa project is also worth considering because its planners devoted both energy and ingenuity in attempting to construct the program so that it would not be undermined by the repercussions that make other education programs counterproductive. The institute is designed to provide follow-up education for students who complete primary education but who are either unable or ill-equipped to continue academically. It is designed to prepare the students for better subsistence farming in the remote villages from which they are drawn, and it is intended to make sure that the students return to those villages once they have completed the two-year program. Its training program presumes that the students will have access to nothing more sophisticated than oxen upon their return to village life, and it tries not to make its facilities any more comfortable than the ones to which the students will have to return. The institute is sponsored by Sodapax, the developing arm of the Lesothan Christian Council, as well as a host of aid organizations, including AID, CARE and Save the Children Fund. The students, who receive "a certain amount of religious instruction," are drawn from outlying areas. Upon the urging of Bob McCullam I visited Thaba Khupa, and later I spoke with the Sodapax people in Maseru.

I went out to Thaba Khupa with Kent Black, the Peace Corpsman on secondment to CARE whom I had met on my second day in Maseru. Thaba Khupa is part of the district surrounding Thaba Bosiu, and it is situated amid the huge World Bank and AID sponsored Thaba Bosiu Rural Development Project. In 1971 Principal Chieftainess Makhuabane allocated 62 hectares (one hectare = 2.5 acres) to the institute, and a local committee was appointed to caretake the site and supervise the food-aid labor building roads and conservation works in the area. In 1972 when Keith Morriss, the principal of the institute, arrived, he was not sure what the institute should teach. In planning his curriculum, the distribution of wealth was his main consideration. He was afraid of disrupting the even spread of money in the villages to the point where jealousies might erupt. What he wanted to do was give farmers the techniques so that they might better support their families, so they might grow a slight surplus for export, and so they might provide employment for the growing numbers of landless—possibly on a barter basis.

The first year, students were taught basic techniques, the second year the students were given a house, some "broilers," and 1/10th hectare on which to grow what they could. The students kept all but 12.5 percent of what they grew on their own, and these earnings were banked toward what implements they would need later on. Also, before the students came to Thaba Khupa, their parents obtained a guarantee from the local chief that land would be available on their return home.

Keith Morriss introduced me to John Durant, the chief husbandrist, who took me around the institute. Durant is a rangy, soft-spoken Englishman with previous experience working in Uganda and Nigeria on agricultural projects. He learned on those projects that one of the most difficult things is to get students to use training as it is intended. "If you take a student out of a village and put him or her in comfortable housing," he said, "are they prepared to then go back to a smoky mud hut"? The answer in Nigeria turned out to be no, and the government was eventually forced to turn the training center into a government plantation. At Thaba Khupa, said Durant, they are going back to building rondevaals as housing after a dalliance with concrete and zinc. They discovered that besides being at odds with traditional design, the concrete-and-zinc structures were hot in the summer and cold in the winter. Durant said that the program also calls for two years of intermittent supervision after the students return to their villages, and that a principal purpose of that follow-up was to make sure that the students established themselves in their home villages rather than trying to market their new skills in more favored areas.

Thaba Khupa is an impressive, seemingly well-thought-out operation. Cyril Rodgers, of the University of Botswana, Lesotho and Swaziland, described it aptly as "an interpretation of Julius Nyerere's 'Education for Self-Reliance.'" Durant took me through poultry sheds made of thatch and fieldstone joined with mortar, to a chicken-killing shed (chickens are killed by hand by snapping the neck) contracted to a local man to keep the money in Lesotho. We walked past a Food Aid Dam they have adapted for trickle irrigation (a pumpless method that gives good water penetration), past cabbage, raspberry and strawberry fields, past an integrated fish-farming project where ducks inhabit a pond and their droppings feed carp. Finally we walked by a lot where kitchen swill supports pigs (Durant feels that in Lesotho people make far less productive use of waste materials than do other peoples in Africa).

They seemed to have thought of everything: the scheme is designed to work within land tenure, it is supposed to impart skills for a type of agriculture the poorest Basuto can afford, and it was thought through with an eye to dampening the social repercussions that dog other projects.

Thaba Khupa's ambitions fell pretty much in line with the judgment on priorities offered independently by soil expert Bob McKee over at the Agricultural Research Station. He discovered that by plowing and mixing duplex soils (breaking up the hard pan beneath the thin layer of topsoil), he could both slow erosion, by breaking up the pan and increasing absorption, and at the same time increase output by between 30 and 1200 percent. This as opposed to 5 percent increases he achieved through fertilizers, that sacred cow of agricultural intensification schemes. At Thaba Khupa they are using oxen plows with this ambition in mind. But as with every project in Lesotho, behind this façade of self-assurance troubles lurk. There is the problem of how the students will market their produce from villages far from population centers. McKee also says that even should Basuto get their produce to market, he is not sanguine about their chances of getting a fair price through dickering with South Africans.

McKee said that when a Mosuto replaced a white in negotiating the sale of produce down south, the Mosuto got "eaten alive" by the South African he dealt with. The Thaba Khupa Farm Institute is considering the idea of starting its own label for produce which would cope with that problem and provide a means for standardizing the quality and marketing the product.

Back in Maseru I spoke with A. A. Kikine of Sodapax about the project. Mr. Kikine, an elderly Mosuto, has seen enough of expatriate aid to adopt a wait-and-see attitude toward the institute, which his organization is sponsoring. He is optimistic because he feels that vocational training is what the country needs instead of the academic expertise that might come from studying the Renaissance, and he believes the institute is important because it represents an example of ecumenical cooperation in a country where the churches have been one of the most divisive political forces. However, he said, there is widespread dissatisfaction with the presence of expatriate experts. Expatriates come on contract with the idea of training an "understudy" counterpart to eventually replace them. "When the contract expires," said Kikine, "the expatriate says that the counterpart is not prepared to take over." Kikine feels that expatriates make little effort to train counterparts. He noted that Keith Morriss at Thaba Khupa had no counterpart, and that John Durant has, but that Durant's counterpart is an old college chum.

From visiting Kikine I went next door to Geoffrey Marsh's office, an expatriate affiliated with the All Africa Council of Churches. Kikine said he was watching him very closely to see whether Marsh trained a Mosuto to take over his functions.

Marsh, a pleasant, liberal, old-time Africa hand, discussed

the Thaba Khupa project as an island of common sense in a country drifting toward chaos. He said that the Sodapax aim to keep people in the villages and increase their productivity there runs precisely counter to the intention of the government (enthusiastically endorsed by CARE) to get more people into urban areas.

The planners of Thaba Khupa made an effort to debug the institute of the subtle problems that render so many projects useless. Thaba Khupa was to benefit from Durant's experience in Nigeria, where the students, once trained, refused to return home. But perhaps the very presence of expatriates and their alien designs is the toxin which infects the student with the Western desires and makes the idea of returning to the home village intolerable. Because even as Morriss, Kikine, Durant and Marsh were telling me of the institute's designs, the students were talking among themselves of petitioning the Principal Chieftainess for land to start a settlement of their own, a sensible idea from their point of view, but an idea which would, in the words of Jim Kelley, "invalidate the whole concept of Thaba Khupa."

Given that even those planners who attempt to anticipate social repercussions find things out of their control, perhaps it lessens the indictment against CARE for not attempting to control these factors in its other projects. CARE itself could never have devoted the time to try to frame a project with the effort put into designing the Thaba Khupa Farm Institute. As Felix Ashinhurst, CARE's chief in Kenya, put it, "The problem is that we are operational so we can only put a limited amount of time on project development." Moreover, CARE in some cases interprets positively some of the indications of social change that projects like Thaba Khupa attempt to dampen. For instance, in the Evaluation section of the Pre-Plan Paper for Liberia, one of the "Indicators" given for the Sasstown Road, which CARE has been building for over seven years, reads: "Determine the number of zinc-roofed buildings along the road site as opposed to thatch-roofed buildings before the road is completed. Then measure any change in these conditions on a yearly basis for a maximum of five years after the road's completion." Here CARE is foisting a positive interpretation upon what is in Lesotho a curse—ribbon development. I visited the Sasstown Road before going to Lesotho, and because CARE places such faith in road building as an all-purpose panacea, it is worth detouring briefly to Liberia to explore CARE's attitude toward ribbon development before reviewing that phenomenon in Lesotho.

RIBBON DEVELOPMENT

Liberia is a mess of a country. Long dominated by foreign rubber and mineral interests like Firestone Rubber; with a corrupt government élite, a capital that is a mélange of slums, gas stations, half completed and already crumbling government buildings; a presidential palace that looks like a Patricia Murphy restaurant, Liberia might be a model for Evelyn Waugh's *Black Mischief*. Its's a country where Firestone could lease a million acres of rubber land for ninety-nine years at $1/acre for the term. The fallow land supposedly is to be made available to farmers, but it is taken by politicians as it becomes available. It's a country where unofficial sources claim 60 percent of government revenue comes from the registration of oil tankers as a flag of convenience. And it is a country where to innocently believe that it is possible to help people and stay above politics is to make your organization a pawn of Liberia's corrupt élite. A case in point: LAMCO, a European conglomerate, has extensively deforested areas of Liberia, and by law has the choice of either reforesting these areas itself or contributing money to the Department of Forestry through the Ministry of Agriculture. Because of the degree of corruption in Liberia, money contributed to Agriculture would probably never make it to Forestry. (Liberia is so corrupt that Americans never receive their magazine subscriptions; *Newsweek* and *Time* are pilfered at the post office and sold on the street. One American told me that the only subscription he actually received was *The New Yorker*, which the Liberians obviously felt had a low resale value.) So LAMCO, not wanting to reforest denuded areas, asked CARE to administer its reforestation funds. CARE gets something off the top (standard is 15 percent) and keeps the books and acts as paymaster in the LAMCO reforestation program. The reforestation project illustrates the hollowness of the claim that CARE is responding to "felt needs at the village level." The villagers, according to Bob Kirmse of CARE, all want the forests cut down for farm area, not replanted, and only work on the projects because the wages are cash. However, some voluntary-agency people connected with Liberia are more concerned with this relationship's political implications. They feel that by acting as a conduit through which LAMCO might dissolve its obligation, CARE is letting the Liberian government off the hook. If CARE did not step in, the government would be forced to address its own problems of corruption. Without CARE LAMCO might force the issue by merely putting its compensatory funds in escrow. Third World politics make even seemingly simple programs like reforestation a lot more complicated than the "we are doing good" tag line would suggest.

The project that drew me to Liberia was the Sasstown Road. As of the summer of 1974, seven years after work began the Sasstown Road was still incomplete. Sasstown, about four hundred miles southeast of Monrovia, is the "seaport" of a remote, "primitive" part of Liberia. Before the road, a network of footpaths wound beneath the jungle canopy and connected a web of villages and towns. Some of the larger towns had small airstrips.

The purpose of the road is to allow people to get rice, cocoa, coffee and palm oil to markets more easily than they might trekking along a footpath. A five-day journey on foot is a three-hour journey by truck. CARE also believes that "without roads these areas cannot be tied into the national economy and assist in the overall development of the nation . . . people living in the interior are not able to take advantage of the services made available by the National Government, such as medical, educational and agricultural programs designed for rural areas."

I flew down to the Sasstown Road with Terry Jeggle, the man CARE has installed on the scene to make sure the road is completed. We chartered a Cessna 185 from a charter service run by Lebanese, who in general dominate the trading life of the nation. A Lebanese man assured us that the Portuguese pilot had flown in the war, but he did not specify which war. Our route called for the pilot to fly down the coast and land, if possible, at Sasstown, then fly up to Kanneakan, in the interior, where he would pick us up after we completed our drive down the road, and then fly us home through the interior. This sounded simple enough, except that the vagaries of the weather made it uncertain whether we might be able to *see* the airstrip where we were supposed to land. Returning through the interior precluded the possibility of a forced landing anywhere short of Monrovia, should we have trouble.

Liberia is not a beautiful country. The ocean is steely and forbidding, the long beaches down the coast are often limned with oil; Sasstown is ugly and poor, not poor the way a village is poor, but poor the way a town is poor when it tries to emulate a model it cannot afford. As luck would have it, when we arrived there the clouds had broken momentarily and we could corkscrew hastily down through this evanescent window. We were greeted by Jeggle's surprised foreman and work force, who relaxed upon learning that the purpose of his unexpected return was to show me the road.

Jeggle, referred to in pidgin as Big Boss Man, is a blond

rugged-looking person. He seems to have a good rapport with his men and is concerned with the effect the road will have on the lives of the Liberians in the area. Once when driving on the road he encountered an old man who immediately began a vituperative denunciation of the project in pidgin. The old man claimed that the road would bring in outsiders who would take over. He liked things the way they were. Jeggle replied, "I hear you, old man" (meaning "I follow you." Jeggle was not being impolite, a senior citizen in pidgin is an "old man"), and then said that the road would also bring in doctors and open up markets. He says he left the old man partially mollified.

To a degree the old man's fears have proved accurate. In Kanneakan, where there used to be no stores, there are now six: four owned by Lebanese and two by natives. Within the CARE evaluation ("determine the number of stores and buying centers along the road site before the road is completed. Then measure any change on a yearly basis . . .") these Lebanese-owned stores would count as a positive development rather than as the realization of an old man's fears. There are also indications that besides Lebanese, politicians from Monrovia are grabbing the choice land along the road to develop it for their own purposes.

The road is a laterite strip, what in the United States would be called a third-class dirt road. It has some steep embankments, slick spots, and amusing dips and curves. Between stops Jeggle drove at his standard pace—homicidal—which besides forging a common bond between the Liberian foreman and myself, gave the trip a luminescent intensity.

When we left Sasstown, new growth and canopy began converging on either side of the road. A farm in this area— it is a rough, uneven clearing—would go unnoticed by an American farmer. After one harvest the fragile soil is exhausted and the farm is returned to the jungle; in a few years it is a patch of scrub and trees slightly lower than the rest of the canopy. In the meantime the farmer has cut a new tract. An ecology like this demands a constant supply of rotting vegetation to put nutrients into the soil and moisture into the air. If the canopy is cut to the degree that this cycle is interrupted (much of the topsoil can run off in the rains), a jungle can turn into desert.

Along the way we stopped in one or two small villages. Klicken, which lies just off the old part of the Sasstown Road, is a series of thatched rondevaals spaced and bordered by cow-cropped lawns. Old men and women looked at us with mild curiosity. Soon we had a squad of children following us around. From the village a series of paths radiated into the jungle, leading to the various farms cut that year. The village was quite peaceful and comfortable. It was unclear whether or not the people here knew that they were poor. They were learning, though. Some of the children asked me for money, and one or two people had abandoned the rondevaal and the village to set up concrete-block and zinc-roofed huts by the road.

In the village of Parakihan it was the same thing: the village off on the hill and a few renegade concrete-block and zinc-roofed homes by the road. This phenomenon is the beginning of what is called ribbon development, and it too is positively interpreted in the CARE evaluation indicators. But what happens when people abandon the village and its culture? As far as CARE's evaluation is concerned, tribal organization might collapse, the young might all migrate to Monrovia, and Lebanese and Liberian élite might completely take over the commerce of the area, but the project might still be considered a success.

Before making the last leg of the trip to Kanneakan, we stopped for a brief moment at Jeggle's house. It was nice, with a large, comfortably furnished porch, spacious rooms, and its own generator for electricity. A guard/caretaker looked after things in Jeggle's absence. It was the only house with electricity in the vicinity.

At Kanneakan, to our consternation, we found the pilot drinking wine with two Portuguese who worked for a lumber firm. His mood had brightened considerably since the trip down, but our spirits dampened as we tried to estimate how many drinks had preceded the generous portion now in his glass. A look at the crazily tilted airstrip did nothing to lift my spirits either, but at least I reassured myself that whatever lay ahead, it was probably safer than driving back down the Sasstown Road with Jeggle at the wheel.

Back in Monrovia, Bill Schellestede invited me to a party that night which was to commemorate the departure of Ira Given, the assistant director and a long-time CARE operative who had been one of the original Peace Corpsmen pictured on the cover of *Newsweek* back in 1961 when it all started. Schellestede was one of two Harvard graduates whose CARE biographies I had sifted through back in New York. He is young, athletic (he was once a world-class swimmer), and perhaps it was his touch which accounted for some of the surprising statements in the Liberia Pre-Plan Paper. For instance: "Indeed Liberia seems a classic example of the failure of the aggregate or Keynesian economic approach to development. That approach has led the nation from near stagnation at the close of World War II to an impressive pace of economic activity with a GDP of about $400 million in 1969. That growth and development has not 'trickled' down to the bulk of the population."

Schellestede also showed himself to be sensitive to counterproductive social repercussions, but these senstivities were overwhelmed, as they are in so many cases, by an activist impatience. At his party that night Schellestede remarked that "if charity means spending thousands to have eight Indians write eight-hundred-page studies on building low-cost housing when the Liberian government won't release the land, I say I would rather piss up the lives of natives in the bush."

Eventually the conversation turned to the Sasstown Road,

and it soon became clear that although these doubts did not show up in Pre-Plan Papers or the like, the worth and effects of the Sasstown Road were the cause of great concern to CARE men in Liberia. The man who seemed most seriously concerned with the cultural effects of the road was Patrick Harrington, a man with no extraordinary credentials in anthropology or much of an educational background at all, for that matter. Many of the expatriates I ran across in Africa might articulately describe the decay of a tribal authority system and even perceive their own role in that process, but would continue what they were doing, explaining that "it's my job," or falling into one or another defenses of the expatriate expert.

Patrick was still trying to determine whether his role was good or bad, and I had the feeling that if he decided that what he was contributing to Liberia was not worth the costs, then he would get out. When discussing whether the appearance of zinc-roofed, concrete-block structures indicated a positive or negative development, Patrick noted that thatching and mudding of rondevaals is a community effort, and wondered whether zinc roofing spelled the end of this community reinforcing service.

On the other hand, Ira Given, who had spent fourteen years in the non-Western world, seemed to have no doubts about the value of the cultures CARE was disrupting. He was a blocky, Marine-type figure, and as the evening and the alcohol flowed on, he became increasingly belligerent. I must have struck some nerve, because he seemed to think that I was not asking questions but taking a position. On one occasion he said, "It's easy for you to defend their way of life because you don't have to live it," thus articulating a judgment I was to come across again and again, delivered with varying sophistication. Other people would say, "Yes, tribal life is self-sufficient, but at a miserable level of sufficiency," ignoring that these cultures might offer compensatory nonmaterial satisfactions.

As the conversation proceeded we pinpointed what the

principal questions or doubts about the Sasstown Road
were. To begin with: Why build it there in the first place?
Did the road benefit the number of people it was supposed
to? In towns like Gekan, had it "interrupted the culture"?
Gekan had one of the last talking drums in the area. Now
people send messages down the road. CARE men also
questioned the criteria used to get involved in the project,
for they felt that not enough attention was paid to the logistics of building the road in a remote part of the country, nor
to the difficulties of working with Liberia's extraordinary
government. The road turned out to be enormously more
expensive than it was supposed to be, costing about $6,500/
mile. And finally, CARE people regretted that the project
had involved CARE's reputation to such a degree that
they had to finish the road, even though it had initially begun as a single-year project.

Patrick had mentioned the "talking" drum, and he expressed regret that the road would spell its doom. At this
point Ira, who had become increasingly belligerent said,
"Yeah, that's easy for you to say. But you're not the guy that
has to beat that drum."

Those CARE men involved with road building in Lesotho have none of the doubts about the effects of roads that
were evident in my conversations in Liberia. After all, the
World Food Program which supplies the food wages cited
the project to build access tracks in the mountains as its out-
standing effort a couple of years ago. Still, ribbon development is far more evident in Lesotho than in Liberia. Comrudev official Desmond Taylor and Bob Phillips administer
and oversee the use of the graveling units and bulldozers
that CARE donates for use on the road projects. I spoke to
them both about the road projects in Lesotho and about the
effect they were having on the nation's communal traditions.

Phillips, who spent most of his time in the mountains
issuing the food donated and seeing that work gets done for

it, felt quite positively about the access tracks. He offered the standard arguments that the roads make it cheaper to get goods and services into remote areas, that they break the stranglehold of the large traders (so far, though, there is little evidence that the traders' power is diminishing), and allow entree to social, agricultural and police services. On this last point Phillips did admit that the tracks make patrolling that much easier, and that patrolling seemed to be a principal consideration behind the government's zeal for the tracks.

Taylor was more concerned with side effects like ribbon development and urban migration, as well as with the problem of the upkeep of community development projects if outside money dries up. Upkeep is a key practical question aside from assessing the social impact of projects, because many people question whether Lesotho will be able to afford the development she is being given if the country loses its charisma for foreign donors. For instance, the village water-supply systems that CARE and other organizations have sponsored demand a few thousand rand input per unit, and, says Taylor, the maintenance problems are considerable even for simple wind pumps. The roads which regularly wash out under Lesotho's hard rains also demand extensive maintenance, and Lesotho cannot even maintain the existing road network. With certain of these projects, the villagers could go back to traditional ways if there is a problem of future funding, but other projects make such a return to tradition very difficult and raise the specter of mass migration to Maseru or Leribe if things turn worse in the future.

Once villagers abandon their villages for concrete huts strung out along the roads, the communal structures that compensate for poverty disappear, and as noted earlier, the changing values that lead the villager to abandon the village also erode the supportive functions of the extended family. In the next crunch the Mosuto is going to find himself standing alone, without his neighbors and friends to help him. Taylor feels that the Basuto who abandon the village for the roads are making a conscious choice. Jealousies have begun to spring up between villages that benefit from food and those that don't. The road has a direct detrimental effect on communal life. It presents the immediate temptation of abandoning the close world of the village for the opportunities associated with roads that have been bred into the villagers by legions of expatriates and government officials. With the road, the villager no longer has to live that traditional way of life which no one seems to want to defend.

Ribbon development and roads attack communal traditions in less direct ways as well. Many chiefs have been succumbing to the temptation of selling choice sites along roads in direct contravention of land tenure. This is especially true around Maseru. The Basuto were originally a seminomadic people, which is why they were content to have shifting tenure over fields. The chiefs kept a record in their heads of who had been given what. Now as the capital investment in certain parcels of land increases, the leaseholder wants something more ironclad than the chief's memory to ensure his rights, and the chiefs in turn are beginning to see potential profits in selected leaseholds.

It is ironic that one of the effects of ribbon development has been to compound the problems of development. In moving to sites along the lowland roads, Basuto are often cutting into precious agricultural land which Lesotho can ill afford to lose. This forces more people to cultivate marginal mountain lands, which increases erosion, which further diminishes the amount of arable land. Taylor also felt that ribbon development will create increasingly severe problems as the traditional village structure breaks up, because "you can't help people along a road as you can help a village unit." Like the parasite which destroys its host, development destroys the community it is supposed to benefit.

While Taylor and I were talking, John Murphy stuck his

head into the Comrudev office, grinned mischievously, and said, "When you two are finished head shrinking, I'd like to speak to the boss." Murphy was head of the World Food Program for Lesotho, which donates the food used for wages to build the roads. I met him later at the Holiday Inn. Murphy, alias "Panic Stations" Murphy, had no illusions about accomplishing good. He took terrific pains to make sure that WFP food got to where it was supposed to go, and he had nothing but scorn for what it accomplished once it reached its destination. "What gets me," he said that night, "is that Europeans and Americans fostering community development projects abroad have no sense of community at home. In fact, what they are doing is exporting the poison that destroys whatever sense of community these people have."

Murphy was right, of course. Community development really means shedding the sense of communal responsibility that dampens initiative and striking out on one's own. Community development might as well be a code word for "beggar thy neighbor"—a curious attitude to foster in the name of charity. What CARE and the other organizations seem to be attempting to do is to replace a communal system in which charity does not exist because it is a way of life, with a system that makes charity a necessity.

BUILDINGS

Besides roads and schools, CARE builds clinics. One day Bob McCullam asked me if I would like to ride out with him to check up on the Nakong clinic, a "self-help" project purportedly generated by the local development committee. McCullam, Kent Black and I set off in McCullam's four-wheel-drive Ford. It was a cold, clear day. After whistling along Lesotho's one highway north from Maseru, we turned off toward the Maluti foothills. Soon we had to turn from the secondary dirt road we had been riding on and found ourselves wending our way along mountain tracks. The tracks were rough indeed. The jeep had to ford streams and traverse long expanses of rock. Along the way we passed a bus which was in no better condition than the road.

The clinic itself was modeled on the voguish concrete-block and zinc-roof configuration that is all the rage in poorer countries. The site commanded a spectacular view of rugged valleys and foothills. If you looked hard, several camouflaged villages materialized out of the russet background. The villages here were still orthodox in both organization and architecture. We visited one which had an enormous *pitso* tree and a well-constructed horse corral in the center. Some of the rondevaals were half stone, half mud, and all were decorated with the bold red and blue Basuto designs painted on the mud. The rondevaals and the village were immaculate. There were few men around, but lots of children who would run up, saying "Give me money." The clinic was the first European-style building in the immediate area.

On the day we arrived there were several women making and stacking bricks. I asked the Basuto contractor from Comrudev whether today's was the average turnout. No, he said, the turnout to help complete building the clinic recently had been very low, only about three or four a day and sometimes no one at all. It was a matter to be brought up with Mrs. Moshoeshoe (no relation of the king), who headed the local development committee.

The clinic was designed by an architect named David Robinson. When we returned to Maseru I spoke with him about the subtler effects of his design on the surrounding area. He was a lean, soft-spoken and serious-minded man, and he said right off that the design for the Nakong clinic was "lousy." He noted that concrete exteriors repress the native spirit of design. Robinson said that the Basuto originally built rondevaals because of the availability of bendable poplar poles and thatch, both of which are becoming increasingly scarce. Cultivation is beginning to impinge on lowland areas where this reed grows. Still Robinson feels that it is critically important for a Western design to endorse local design and materials, and for this reason he was designing a clinic for Mokhotlong which would have traditional thatched roof and stone and mud walls.

The entrance to the traditional hut is an elegant portico, sometimes peaked and sometimes semicircular. The interior walls and floors are plastered with a mixture of clay and soft manure which makes a very smooth surface and is easily decorated. Exterior and interior walls and floors are covered with bold geometric designs done in bright blues, reds, and browns. The designs make the hut an exceedingly cheerful place to visit. The interiors are furnished with skins and rugs. The family might have three huts, one for sleeping, one for cooking, and one for meeting. As Robinson pointed out, there is something quite marvelous about the efficient thermal properties of the thatched rondevaal, which retains heat in winter and remains cool in summer. This sharply contrasts with the thermal properties of the zinc-roofed, concrete-block houses which have been replacing traditional design.

There is one point about native design that is consistently lost on well-meaning expatriates who lobby for the more durable concrete-and-zinc design, and that, bluntly put, is that the thatching, decorating and constant remortaring required to maintain the hut serve vital functions: they bond the person to his house, they bond the community together, and perhaps most important, they give people something to do which tests both engineering skills and artistic imagination. The expatriate never seems to realize that seemingly unnecessary or "backbreaking" tasks are what keep a lonely village alive. The concrete design sunders the bond between the individual and the community, it stifles the artis-

tic imagination and releases the family from many chores—
or rituals—that keep village life from becoming intolerably
boring. Freed from obligations to tradition, the young find
few reasons to remain in the villages, and less and less do.

In order to prevail with such a design, Robinson and
others like him often have to answer local demands that
they build Western-style block-and-zinc structures and
prove that local design is better. This is true throughout
Africa. European-design structures are associated with the
power and prestige of European civilization, and, says
Robinson, these considerations often outweigh mere matters of comfort, practicality and economy. Leo Pastore says
that in Kenya, one Masai village insisted on a Western-style
schoolhouse, even though they knew that a school could be
built more economically in traditional beehive-like design.

As in the case of the villager forsaking his village to live
by the road, there is, in addition to the desire to associate
oneself with the magic of "modern civilization," a rejection
of traditional tribal life in the selection of these ugly block-
and-zinc designs.

One can imagine that a village might be reluctant to have
a school in traditional rondevaal style because they have invested the school and its square appearance with totemic
importance. It is desired or feared precisely because it is
not Masai, or Basuto, or Turkhana. For the elders it represents a threat to traditional authority; for the young and
those infected with Western desires, it is a pathway to "development," something far more powerful than the world of
the village. Why have a school in Masai design? Young
Masai don't need a school to mature as Masai. What magic
could a school have if it was just another beehive? Perhaps
there is no clearer symbol of the irreconcilable antipathy
between development and "traditional" non-Western ways
than the reluctance of the villager to build a school or clinic
or new house in traditional native design. If the villager
sees his choice as *either* the old ways or the new, how can

those in development speak of "improving life within the traditional village framework." I recall one conversation with a Kikuyu in Kenya that underscored this point. When speaking about the Masai, or about other tribesmen, he would scornfully refer to them as being "fifteen years behind the Kikuyu [who are in the driver's seat in Kenya] in civilization," or "thirty years behind us in education." There was no question for this man of going back or of even preserving what remained of the old ways.

If the Nakong clinic was finished, there was still some question about whether it will be equipped and staffed. This came out during a conversation over at World Food Program headquarters next door to CARE in Maseru. (The World Food Program office causes some talk in Maseru because it appears to be segregated, the counterparts and staff occupy one half of the building, while the expatriates have their half. This was not the intention of this setup.) The WFP is involved in this through a clinic-oriented feeding program. I was talking with David Morton and Matilda Van Der Wiel about Nakong. Matilda Van Der Wiel was a UN volunteer nutritionist and home-economics instructor. She did an excellent imitation of John Murphy (as does almost everyone in Maseru). David Morton was the second in command at the World Food Program.

Mrs. Van Der Wiel told me that the World Food Program sponsored an Institutional Feeding Program which was supposed to free money that the government could then use for capital expenditures. However, Matilda said that the government was not contributing the money it would have spent on Institutional Feeding to the fund for capital expenditures. In effect, then, rather than using donated food to finance capital expenditures, the Lesothan government was using the World Food Program as a source of revenue to cover operating expenses—the type of pillaging of the capital budget which has caused so much consternation in New York City.

David Morton raised the possibility that the money would still be there in the Ministry of Health to be used regardless of whether it was contributed to the fund. Matilda asked, "What if they reduced the [Health] budget proportionately?" (The agreement called for the Lesothan government to make scaled contributions to the fund of 20,000 to 60,000 rand over three years.) So we trooped into John Murphy's office to check this out.

Murphy looked up with a gleeful smile and went to his files to get the figures. Murphy is not above reorganizing postal services and railways if he finds it necessary to move his food, and when he came to Lesotho he had ferreted out all the government budget statistics relevant to World Food Program projects in Lesotho. In fact, the figures in Murphy's "Working Statistical Documents" were the *only* compilation available that brought figures out of their cubbyholes in the various ministries, out of donor and voluntary-agency files, and out of every other conceivable source and presented a comprehensive picture of what was being spent on education and health in Lesotho.

Murphy noted his source on every document, and he proudly told me that not only do the other agencies use his figures, but that the Lesothan Ministry of Health relied on them as well. And so with some respect we turned to the document that gave the Ministry of Health and Social Welfare budgets for fiscal years 1968–72, and there it was photocopied in black-and-white. With the inauguration of the World Food Program agreement, the Lesothan government had cut its budget for "Drugs & Dressings Provisions" by over half from 82,500 rand in 1968–69 to 40,500 rand in 1969–70.

Murphy noted with a cynic's satisfaction that the agreement specified that the budget not be reduced. Actually the government had intended to reduce the budget in proportion to the WFP's contribution all along. Coming to Lesotho, Murphy encountered a man from the Ministry of

Health (this was before the agreement had been put into effect). The man said, "Boy, did you guys screw us up! We wrote a decrease into the budget eighteen months ago, and we're still waiting for the food." As I was leaving, Matilda remarked that once the food is delivered, much of it is taken by the nurses for their own use and sometimes for sale. David Morton looked decidedly unhappy with the anarchistic satisfaction his colleague and superior took in revealing this information to a journalist.

One day I arranged to have a drink with Harry Johnson, the local USAID representative attached to the American embassy. Harry is a cheerful, intelligent, blond-haired man who seemed to have very clear perceptions about Lesotho and its problems. We talked a bit at the Maseru Country Club bar, and eventually the conversation turned to how one might look at aid and the whole nexus of development expertise as a type of welfare system for American academics, in which the real beneficiaries are not the recipient nations but the people sent over to "help" the recipient nations. Johnson was describing how universities and agencies stack overhead on their people (universities and agencies are compensated for the loan of their personnel) until a $30,000 year expert might end up costing AID $75,000. The $75,000 might be listed as aid to some poor country, but virtually all of it returns to the United States. At one point Johnson mentioned that AID was considering supporting a group in Lesotho called Modular Systems Pty. Limited, and that he had suggested CARE as an affiliation to administer the grant. He noted that for this service CARE would get 15 percent off the top of the roughly $300,000 grant. "You've been introduced to the game of leeches," he remarked cheerily as he turned back to his drink. Ultimately, CARE decided not to get involved with this project, but the project history is still worth considering for the number of organizations it entangled.

I was interested in Modular Systems because I had run into various people connected with it around Maseru. One of them, Warren Van Hoose, an architect and former Peace Corpsman, recalled in dress, speech, comportment and life style the early days of the hippie era in San Francisco. Habits of speech and dress acquired before leaving the United States seem to linger far longer with expatriates than they might had the expatriate stayed home. People I have met who left America during the beatnik era still remained beatniks by outward signs; hippies remained hippies. In any case, this big friendly bear had told me a couple of things about Modular Systems during one or two chance meetings. It seemed like an unlikely alliance—CARE's roundheads and these cavalier ex-Peace Corpsmen. What Modular Systems intended to do was to set up a Basuto-owned construction company with three main purposes: to design and build with an eye to local flavor the many office and housing facilities that are currently designed abroad and contracted to foreigners: to build low cost housing; and to train Basuto managers and artisans. Their proposal noted that about 85 percent of all foreign aid to Lesotho "is spent on the construction of facilities essential to the country's infrastructure," and that most of this money leaves the country because there are no Basuto companies to take it. They see Modular Systems as a way of keeping more of this foreign aid in the country. They also speak of exploring "alternative sources" which might heat and power homes in oil-less Lesotho.

The word "modular" refers to a system of architectural design and construction in which a structure is built from standardized and cost-controlled units which simplifies the design and construction process at all levels. When I spoke to Ray Rignall in New York he claimed that CARE's interest in becoming involved in Modular Systems centered around the possibility of building modular food-storage buildings and not merely "laundering AID money" and taking its share off the top. Modular Systems is one of those projects in Lesotho that everybody is getting involved with: the Peace Corps is paying the salaries of two of the key people, OXFAM and CARE gave grants before CARE agreed to administer the AID Operational Program Grant, even the Lesothan government has donated money and services. Modular Systems dovetailed perfectly with CARE's desire to get involved with small industries. The board of directors of the project included some of the most respected men in Lesotho. In short, everybody seemed to think this project was a winner. Almost everybody.

I spoke to one organization in New York which had been approached to administer funds for Modular Systems and its parent, the Architecture and Construction Society of Lesotho (ACSL). On the basis of a long interview with an officer of Modular Systems, this organization decided that they did not want to associate their name with ACSL and Modular Systems. Their objections were threefold and somewhat surprising, given the objectives stated in the ACSL proposal and the people involved. First, they felt that the expatriate fees and perquisites mentioned in different parts of the proposal were quite large when stacked up. "You had to keep your finger in three different pages of the proposal to add up what they were getting," said the head of this organization. Second, even though there was considerable counterpart training at the lower levels, they felt that there was little movement by the top people toward replacing themselves with counterparts. Finally, this organization pointed out that the housing proposed was not low-cost, but in terms of Lesotho, high-income housing.

With regard to the question of fees, I am told that other organizations, including AID, brought up this question, and that the proposal has since been modified to adjust this disproportion. Moreover, AID has also modified its willingness to support this project. Apparently AID has now agreed to pay the Americans' salaries if the Canadian development agencies supply the other expenses which will make Modular Systems operational. CARE had reached the point of draft agreement with AID and Modular Systems, but subsequently withdrew when the AID money became uncertain. This uncertainty was the principal reason for CARE's cold feet.

It was their reservation about the expatriates' intentions to replace themselves with counterparts that I found the most surprising. This was because the proposal stresses over and over again the idea that the purpose of the ACSL and Modular Systems is to create Basuto-owned enterprises. For instance, in detailing the responsibilities of the ACSL director, the first thing listed is his responsibility to "train a Mosutho counterpart who will eventually take over the directorship of the ACSL." The same is true for the ACSL environmental planner, research engineer and sociologist, although in the case of the ACSL architect, training a counterpart is the last responsibility mentioned. While this might be listed as a responsibility, the agency pointed out to me that no timetable was given for the replacement of top management. The head of this agency said, "I pressed them quite hard on this point and was not satisfied with their answers."

This is true, with two significant exceptions. While there is no mention of when the director, architect and environmental planner will be replaced, the proposal does present a vague schedule for the Africanization of two positions which were unfilled at the time of the proposal—those of research engineer and sociologist. With regard to the research engineer the proposal states: "It is assumed that a 'counterpart' Mosotho engineer can be employed and trained to assume the duties of the expatriate engineer within this two year period." Similarly for the sociologist: "as with the engineer, a sociologist will be initially recruited for a two year period. It is assumed that a Mosutho sociologist can be recruited from the University of Bots-

wana, Lesotho, and Swaziland in the near future." Perhaps
it is easier to talk about replacing expatriates whom you
have not yet hired. No such statements are made about the
positions filled by the expatriates who were the initial
framers of the proposal, and from the salary schedule presented it is clear that they intend to be around at least until
fiscal year 1979–80.

Before I went to Lesotho, former Peace Corpsman Dave
Massey said, "Look for the expatriate who replaces himself
with a Mosotho." While in Lesotho, I came across no one
who had performed that basic service, and now there was
doubt cast upon a proposal specifically designed to satisfy
that failing.

There is no question that the "case study" house presented in the proposal is not low-cost; at the writing of the
proposal such a house would cost over $12,000, which
would place it beyond the reach of all but high-level civil
servants and expatriates. Admittedly, the case-study two-
bedroom house was not intended to be a low-cost house,
but even if it were one-sixth the price, it could not be called
low-cost in a country where the average per capita income
is about $90. In contrast, a small voluntary agency is build-
ing housing for squatters in Bogotá, and their simple housing costs between $200 and $400 a unit.

Apparently, Modular Systems is now trying to devise
lower-cost housing in an effort to save its project. It ac-
knowledges that the rural Basuto take care of their own village housing needs, and that Modular Systems hopes to fill
urban needs. The proposal sees little virtue in the existing
land-tenure system (the proposal describes land tenure as
"peculiar"), and hence has no qualms about adding stress to
that system by building permanent city dwellings. In a society as recently urbanized as Lesotho—at independence,
Maseru was still a small town—the costs of urbanization and
its amicability with traditional social organization should be
considered before one decides to intervene as land devel-

oper. However, the proposal which speaks of planning with a local bias does not examine in any fashion the forces at work urbanizing Lesotho. Instead it accepts this process as a *fait accompli*, and adds its weight to the burdens on the nation's communal traditions. Of course in other countries, those in South America with long-standing favelas, for instance, one might muster persuasive arguments to intervene in housing. But in Lesotho, its nascent urban areas are not past the point of no return.

There is also some question of how well the modular approach can be adapted to local design as the proposal claims to intend. There is a group of European architects who are trying to fit African design to the needs of building larger structures, and they reportedly feel that the modular approach is unsuitable for this type of undertaking. There is certainly nothing that would distinguish as Basuto the case-study house presented in the proposal. Rather, it might have been designed in London or Kansas City.

Finally, should this project be successful, there are delicate questions of its effect on income distribution. We often cluck about the gap between rich and poor in poor countries and how a small élite benefits from "development" while the benefits fail to "trickle down" to the populace. And we sometimes wonder where these élites come from. Well, in many cases we create them. And we are creating an élite in Lesotho. For the most part, to be a chief in Lesotho is to live little better than a villager. Although a cabinet minister earns enough to spur resentment among non-Maseru Basuto, he still earns less than half the salary of the UN expert who may be working for him on secondment. However, with the training of managers, accountants, and the like, and the setting up of various private enterprises such as the proposal envisions, there is the likelihood that disproportions of wealth will become ever more common.

Given the nation's communal traditions, some people believe that state farming and state-run enterprises might be a way of saving the land-tenure system and increasing income and health within the nation's communal traditions. Desmond Taylor said that some Basuto were beginning to talk about these alternatives. If successful, though, the Modular Systems project would commit the Basuto to a type of development that would surely lead to gross inequities in the distribution of wealth. I was a little surprised that the framers of the proposal had not considered this, because some of them seemed to endorse the communal aspirations of the hippie era.

One of the goals of the proposal is to train Basuto for skilled jobs and start enterprises which might offer an alternative to going to work in the mines "under the humiliating apartheid system." (Actually, although the Basuto have no love for apartheid, going to work in the mines has taken on the status of a rite of initiation—a means by which a young Basuto proves his manhood and his fitness to take a wife and receive land.) If the ACSL project is successful to the point where it would spawn serious inequities in income distribution, the project might also present such an alternative. Unfortunately, the more likely result is the opposite—that rather than opening opportunities for remunerative labor at home, trained laborers will go to South Africa to seek better pay there. Desmond Taylor noted that job reservation (the holding of jobs exclusively for whites) is diminishing in South Africa, and that as jobs open up, qualified people are leaving Lesotho. He said that six people from the printer's office left in this way to get better jobs under the "humiliating system of apartheid." The significant thing is that these six people *had* jobs in Lesotho. With regard to ACSL, one of the original board members, Tim Tahani, now works in Washington for the World Bank.

The ACSL project which CARE at first supported and subsequently soured on embodies a view of Lesotho which is strikingly dissimilar to that underlying the Thaba Khupa project. While Thaba Khupa seeks to prepare students to better make a living within the communal system and land tenure within the traditional agricultural framework, the

ACSL scheme seeks to inculcate managerial and artisan skills suitable for Western, free-enterprise development in the cities. ACSL fits within the urbanizing ambitions of the first Five-Year Plan; Thaba Khupa sees its role as exactly counter to that goal. The only thing the two projects have in common is that they are both supported by a plethora of organizations besides CARE, and that they both might be plagued with similar problems.

CARE programming in Lesotho is a mixed bag, the goals of the MYP notwithstanding. It does in Lesotho many of the things—builds roads, schools, water systems—that it does throughout the non-Western world, talk about in-country focus to the contrary.

Perhaps more than in other countries, CARE is entangled with other agencies and donors in the funding and administration of projects, but these entanglements serve to illustrate the similar orientation of different agencies helping Lesotho. It is true that some agencies disparage the approach of other agencies, but in Lesotho, flooded as it is with foreign aid, one might imagine that to the Basuto, the different expatriate philosophies and programs would seem interchangeable in broad terms and bewildering in their particulars. Different experts might be pushing soft fruits or trickle irrigation, or soil mixing, cash crops or catchments, but all are similar in that they are aliens pushing alien ideas. It is no accident that none of these ideas fit the nation's communal traditions.

Expatriates in Lesotho find themselves beleaguered by problems similar to those which hound the do-gooder throughout Africa. As a result of expatriate interference, Lesotho finds itself increasingly bedeviled by problems which bedevil developing countries throughout the world. This similarity of effect indicates that something is overriding the intentions of the planners. The expatriates themselves all have a nagging sense that something is out of control. However, often this sense of unease is muted by the manifest benefits of living overseas.

ELEVEN

From Hair Shirts to Maids

The CARE public relations mill works wonders—similar to those evident in its ability to make Lesotho's future seem bright—when it goes to work on the life style of its operatives overseas. CARE's reputation for making the most of each penny, the run-down former brewery it occupies in New York, the shabby clothes, descriptions of its "harried staff"—all connote a life given over to monastic deprivation and self-sacrifice. Here's the description the *Daily News* reporter gives of the headquarters in New York: "Even the most eagle-eyed of observers would have a time trying to find even the most minute frill in the organization's 'world headquarters' . . . No fancy offices, no luxurious rugs, not even badly needed coats of paint can be found." Overseas the picture is a little different.

On my first day in Lesotho I had lunch with CARE's assistant director, Bob McCullam, and his wife Marion at their home in Maseru West. CARE had built the house for the McCullams in this former preserve of British administrators; it is a modern split-level structure. The living room opens onto a large veranda on one end, while the other abuts a massive stone fireplace. That fireplace and adjoining wall separate the living room from the dining room and kitchen area, where the cook and Marion prepare sumptuous meals. A maid helps Marion keep the house in order, while outside a gardener helps improve the landscaping. The house might sell in the United States for $70,000.

The McCullams belong to the Maseru Country Club, and they were the first voluntary-agency people to join. It used to be that Americans shied away from joining the club because of its colonial associations and mostly white membership. Increasingly, however, voluntary-agency and aid personnel are dropping their pretenses of poverty. Throughout Africa, wives now chat about the availability and efficiency of servants and the condition of the tennis courts.

Besides golf and meals at the country club, Bob occasionally amuses himself duck hunting, while Marion, a busy and social woman, has church organizations and a singing group to fill her day. Marion told me that on their first overseas assignment she had been hesitant about hiring servants, but that over the years she had overcome her inhibitions on the matter, and with each new assignment, she remarked, her staff gets larger.

Singling out the CARE life style might be interpreted as unfair, especially since every expatriate seems to live well. However, the waspish community of people who are in Maseru to help the Basuto would repeatedly refer to CARE personnel as examples of a level of affluence not in accord with the unstated dictates of a "people to people" program. Several times I was asked "Have you seen their houses over there?" (in Maseru West), and the head of one voluntary agency remarked that "[CARE people] could have been a little more modest in their life styles—you know, complaints about servant problems from wives, or about trouble getting electricity for their pools."

The McCullams took me to lunch a few times at the Maseru Country Club, a luxury which one might argue is an economy because the fare was substantial and very inexpensive. Other Maseru expatriates dine at the Holiday

Inn or at the Basuto-owned hotel by the airport. The club-house itself is quite nice, constructed out of native stone with a comfortable, dark, woody bar, although the cricket field and golf course looked a little ratty, probably because it was winter. McCullam had taken up golf since coming to Lesotho, a sport you'd imagine a voluntary-agency representative would have to give up upon going abroad. But to his credit, McCullam did not quite fit the Maseru Country Club image—he seemed uncomfortable, as though going there was something he shouldn't be doing. There were a few Basuto members, including the king. I think, though, that it would be a safe bet to say that far more Basuto worked there in menial capacity than belonged there as members.

The country club also had tennis courts, and the king apparently often comes down to the country club to play squash. McCullam, conscientious host that he was, scouted up some tennis and squash opponents for me. One of them, Mike Hobson, the chief mine recruiter, had been a fairly successful district-level tennis player in South Africa; in Lesotho he was about the best in the country. Actually, one of the startling things an American has to get used to in Lesotho is the idea that being the national champion or being on the national team or the Olympic team means something a little different than it does in the United States. On Sundays there is a continually rotating men's doubles game going on at the Holiday Inn which congenially mixes both guests and local players. One might be playing someone who looked particularly athletic (though not in tennis), and find that he is being groomed for Lesotho's Olympic track team, and that his partner is the nation's best soccer forward.

The first question that comes to mind is who, in this penny-pinching organization, pays for such amenities as the CARE overseas officials enjoy. The answer helps explain why CARE goes so aggressively after public relations and the donor dollar. In most cases, the local government of whatever country CARE operates in picks up CARE's local administrative costs, and these costs are not an insubstantial amount. CARE claims that it stretches monies so that each dollar contributed buys over $7 in goods and services, and this makes its ratio of administrative costs to remittances very low, but in so saying, CARE is transforming a weakness into a strength. The 1974 total budget was $123,419,-051. CARE listed administrative costs of $5,088,942—an incredible 3 percent of the total budget. Auditors start getting nervous when administrative costs creep up over 20 percent, so in this respect CARE looks very, very good. However, of that 123 million dollars, the great preponderance was in the form of PL 480 commodities and ocean-freight reimbursements. Voluntary contributions amounted to only $20 million, but even this figure is misleading because it includes state donations of civil-defense biscuits worth some $8 million. Cash income from the public, then, was only about $12.2 million, or less than 10 percent of CARE's total budget. When judged against cash income, that $5 million in administrative costs begins to loom a little larger; however, there is still more to come. Not included in this reckoning are overseas costs of $6,389,506 which were recovered from host country contributions. True, this money is donated by the host countries, but it is still money spent on administrative costs. Thus a charitable organization supported by $12.2 million in cash contributions has total administrative costs of $11.4 million. That is indeed alchemy.

Perhaps this is why CARE is so aggressive in going after public donations. They are necessary to maintain the pretense that CARE is a private voluntary agency. Should such donations fall too precipitously, the U.S. government might be forced to think twice about using the organization as a sluice for PL 480, and a lot of people would be out of jobs. Moreover, the cash that is donated is needed for development projects as well as for administrative costs, and any constriction in the inflow of donations would be magnified disproportionately because of double burdens placed on those unpredictable donations.

In countries like Lesotho, where CARE does not have a PL 480 Food for Peace program, CARE's ratio of expenditures to administrative costs is almost the same as the almost one-to-one ratio described above, and this, along with CARE's immodest life style, causes consternation among the expatriate community in Lesotho. CARE's commitments for 1972–74 amounted to $142,108.72, the better part of it for school construction. During that same period, CARE's local administrative expenses will run about $102,-000, and this figure does not include payments of $330 a month on the two CARE houses (which CARE argues are recoverable costs), nor such government contributions as rent, light, heat, telephone, vehicle operating expenses, a drawing account of about $3,000 for vehicle maintenance, a cleaning lady for the offices and a messenger. The Lesothan government also agreed to absorb about half the $102,000 figure.

Because in most countries the host government absorbs all CARE's administrative costs, CARE feels that Lesotho is getting a good deal in only having to supply half these costs. However, because CARE's level of expenditure is so low in comparison with these costs, many expatriates felt that the Lesothan government was being robbed. One official, Jonathan Jenness of the Planning Office, described CARE as a "chickenshit outfit that spends as much as it donates." Larry Cooley described CARE as "an embarrassment; they don't do jack shit. As of last year they were two years behind in their spending. They seem to be quite narrow in what they do and don't program nearly as much as they should in response to felt needs." He added that CARE got a lot more publicity out of a lot less money than the big organizations (AID, the World Bank, etc.) do. I should add here that with the new Multi-Year Plan approach, CARE hopes to increase the level of funding in the near future.

Besides criticizing CARE's disproportionate administrative costs, some voluntary-agency people feel that the CARE life style, as Jim Kelley put it, "isolates them from Basuto society quite a bit." My own feeling is that this criticism is fair but that it applies to nearly every expatriate I encountered in Maseru, save perhaps a few Peace Corpsmen. It is, however, an interesting question: How can you claim to be part of a people-to-people program if the Basuto you see the most of are your servants? The question is more complicated than it appears on the surface. I discussed this, and the hostility that CARE aroused among other expatriates, when I returned to the United States.

Leo Pastore claimed that the bad attitude toward CARE in Lesotho stemmed from envy over the fact that other agencies do not get government counterpart funds, and because other agencies do not have the good relationship with host governments that CARE has. When I asked him about the almost one-to-one administrative-to-expenditure ratio, he replied with his remarks about building infrastructure and being cautious.

Pastore looks a little like Mario Procaccino, and he is a very likable man. He replied to my questions not with resentment, but in an equable manner which should have made his answers more convincing than it did. We discussed the question of whether or not having servants and maintaining a higher standard of living than the people you should be helping places an insuperable barrier between expatriate and native. Pastore replied, as so many expatriates reply, that by hiring servants, CARE representatives are helping the local economy, and that in Ceylon, with severe unemployment problems, expatriates were criticized for not hiring more domestics. He also said that "we have to treat and work with counterparts at the ministerial level, and we have to entertain fairly frequently," and that this required that the CARE representative have something more than a hovel.

This raises a knotty problem. If you look at one way, it is easy to understand that it would be insulting not to satisfy the dignity of the offices of government officials just because they come from a poor and powerless nation. It is annoying to come across Americans who out of some sense of solidarity with the poor might wear a T-shirt to a meeting with a Lesothan cabinet member when you know damn well that if they were meeting with an American cabinet member, they would wear a jacket and tie. On the other hand, CARE operates in the non-Western world at the invitation of host governments, and one wonders why, once invited to come to Lesotho or Libera, CARE should be doing any entertaining of cabinet ministers at all, especially in a people-to-people program. The host governments supposedly know that CARE is trying to stretch its resources to reach the poor, and should not be offended if the CARE homes are not lavish.

One could make the argument that government officials *should* be offended if they attend soirees where the only representatives of the supposed beneficiary group are servants. Finally, if this argument applies abroad, why should it not apply in New York and militate for better offices, where, often, Third World ministers and ambassadors make their first contact with CARE? The answer, I imagine, is that in New York the offices serve as part of a smoke screen of self-denial that masks the comforts that CARE men overseas enjoy.

The whole argument about entertaining host officials seems to be another example of after-the-fact reasoning and justification. The indications I got were that most of the entertaining CARE people do involve expatriates. CARE has a reputation for not liking to mingle with the locals. A former CARE chief in Costa Rica gave a New Year's party once (so another CARE man told me). He invited over two hundred peole, but not one of the guests was a Costa Rican.

Simply put, CARE people do not like to live like the natives they work with. For the most part they have bourgeois ambitions and bourgeois standards. Said Leo Pastore, "I was a Peace Corps volunteer. I couldn't stay overseas if I thought I was going to live that way forever. I have a family to raise. Sure it was great to wear the hair shirt for a while, but I wouldn't want to raise my children that way."

Pastore's reluctance goes right to the heart of CARE's attitude toward the cultures in which they work. It's difficult enough to gain a sympathetic perspective of such cultures if you are sequestered in a white enclave in one of the semi-Western cities that dot the Third World, but if that detachment is conditioned by distaste for village life, then there is no connection which might make the CARE man care what happens to the integrity of village life. The CARE man cannot be concerned with the preservation of a culture, because he does not see anything worth saving. No one notices this disapproval more quickly than the villager himself.

It's not just CARE men. John Hurst said that he suspected that the giant Thaba Bosiu project was located close to Maseru because the experts would rather commute out from town than be forced to live out in the bush. Hurst noted that the Leribe Pilot Agricultural Scheme had two types of housing: nice dwellings for the expatriate experts, but apartments for Basuto counterparts which were unfortunately similar in color and design to black hostels in South Africa.

Still, to argue that this hermetic, bourgeois life style reflects a dismissive attitude toward Basuto and other cultures is not to argue that virtue resides in donning the hair shirt. For one thing, many people dismiss the effectiveness of the Peace Corps ("Should all people live like Peace Corps volunteers?" said Pastore. "Do you think the Peace Corps gets a lot done?") More to the point, the Peace Corpsman is also there to "help people to help themselves" to repair the inadequacies of non-Western ways, and his or her presence is with few exceptions a living and constant reminder of the inferiority of the "old ways" of doing things. Aside from the implied censure of the beneficiary's way of life, the key aspect of Pastore's remark "Sure it's great to wear the hair shirt for a while, but I wouldn't want to raise my children that way" is the suggestion that at some point immediate self-interest begins to drive a wedge between the voluntary-agency representative and his concern for the beneficiary. Self-sacrifice is gradually corrupted by concern for the creature comforts of home and by the realization that one has to choose a career; something begun with a sense of mission becomes a job; concern for the dignity of the beneficiary is supplanted by annoyance over petty indignities suffered abroad and by pleasure over the "forbidden" luxuries (such as servants) available there.

I remember one incident that happened in Liberia. This was at a dinner party given by the CARE chief Bill Schellestede. The dinner, prepared by Schellestede's Korean wife was delicious, and she smoothly supervised her native servants as they served drinks. Schellestede's modest house is across the street from the emergency entrance to a hospital. Sometime during dinner we heard a car drive up and begin blowing its horn. I asked what was going on. Someone remarked that the driver was trying to get someone's attention to unlock the emergency entrance. Someone else cracked a joke about the petitioner's chances of ever getting someone to unlock that gate. Eventually we resumed our conversation and all but forgot that horn blowing insistently in the background. No one showed the slightest curiosity about what the emergency was.

TWELVE

The Expats

As a group, expatriates ranged from freewheeling buccaneers who took full advantage of the freedom permitted one who lives outside the strictures of his society to those who overseas became intensely domestic and conservative and carried with them the trappings of home. Some expatriates seemed to partake of the morality of journalists and businessmen and enjoyed the temporary freedom from marital responsibilities. Others were monkish. Dissimilar personalities who might have shunned one another at home seemed to get along in the enforced proximity of an expatriate community.

Although the expats reflected many conflicting life styles, they shared a common alienation—if not spiritual, at least geographical. Whether they embraced or sublimated that alienation, the expats still carried with them powerful emanations of the societies they had left.

JOHN MURPHY

David Morton and I were sitting in his office at the World Food Program complex. Drivers and volunteers passed through intermittently. John Murphy, the head of the WFP, lurked in his own office through a passageway, separated from Morton by his own secretary. Nobody at the World Food Program seemed particularly happy. Murphy was leaving in a day or two to attempt to unsnag the logistical foul-up preventing WFP food from getting from Lagos, Nigeria, to the Sahel. Murphy's departure meant Morton's getting used to a new boss, and a new style. The WFP driver had reportedly been in tears earlier over the news of the departure of the Big Boss Man.

Lately Murphy had been spending his time briefing his replacement as WFP adviser, a former CARE man named James Kehm. The briefing seemed to have turned into a type of psychological terrorism for Murphy's own amusement. Morton said that he often passed Murphy and Kehm rushing from place to place, Murphy with a mischievous gleam in his eye and Kehm looking bewildered and increasingly regretful. Without blinking, Murphy had multiplied the distance to the nearest shopping and schools by a factor of ten, and what few charms Maseru possessed instantly vanished and were replaced with descriptions of crime and racial discord which occasionally punctuate Maseru's soul-shriveling boredom.

Morton was not altogether displeased with Murphy's antics. He idly speculated how he might follow up Murphy's act. He envisaged a project-planning session in which he, Murphy and Kehm would sit down to come up with new ideas. Morton would then take a pistol from his desk and casually say "Why not clinics there, there, and there," as he plugged the map of World Food Program projects stapled to his far wall. "That should do the trick," he mused. If Kehm refused the assignment, Morton might run the program as he liked. But no, Morton resigned himself to a new boss.

That night I ran into Kehm at the casino. He was talking about refusing this assignment and he looked thoroughly depressed. "I'll give it another day or two," he said as he wandered off to the roulette table.

Morton's sadness over Murphy's departure was in part inspired by Murphy's consummate bureaucratic expertise. When dealing with headquarters in Rome, Murphy would always hold a little something back from his reports, so that when they inevitably pounced upon some figure, he might utterly silence them with a deft rebuttal. For instance, when filling out a form which demanded how many miles per year World Food Program people used official vehicles for personal use, Murphy cautioned Morton not to say zero, but to give some figure or other. Then when headquarters came back screaming, demanding an explanation for this personal use of official vehicles, Murphy advised Morton to explain that the figure represented the cumulative mileage between project sites and lodgings, an entirely legitimate claim. Headquarters was sufficiently chastened, and the local WFP office came out with a better reputation than they would have, had they offered this explanation in the first place. The same thing happened with the work/food ration on projects in Lesotho. Again Murphy sent in the figures without any footnotes. When the beagles pounced on the fact that Nigerians accomplished much more work for food contributed than did the Basuto, Murphy again took the wind out of their sails by explaining that in Lesotho the work was done by women, some of whom were encumbered with infants.

When Murphy came into a country he did more than organize the program; he organized whatever government services he needed and were found wanting upon his arrival. In Lesotho's case it was the post office. Morton said that Murphy was constantly down at the post office haranguing and waving his arms in Murphy fashion. When, as was often the case, the plane could not land because of the weather, Murphy would drive to Bloemfontein, a town in South Africa, to haul the mail back by truck. One Friday the plane came in late. Murphy asked that his mail be sorted by seven o'clock Saturday morning. The clerks, figuring that

Murphy would only be getting mail from the United Kingdom, only sorted those bags. So when Murphy received a
letter from Australia on Monday, he went storming down to
the post office. They claimed that it had come in on the train
and was sorted at six o'clock that morning. "No, it didn't,"
Murphy bellowed, "it came in on the plane on Friday, but
you didn't think I'd be getting mail from Australia, did
you?"

Murphy also followed the football pools. He used to tell
Morton, "If I win, I'll not even send you a telegram; I'll buy
whatever clothes I need in Europe." He listened to the
results on the BBC picked up and rebroadcast in Lesotho
by a U.S. donated transmitter. The technicians at Radio
Lesotho did not keep very close watch on the frequency,
and the signal would drift as the scores were read. This
drove Murphy wild, and he would regularly call up and demand that they watch the signal. Once he got the football
results on short wave, and he called up the radio station.
When they answered he held the radio to the telephone and
said, "Look, I've got it better than you have."

One gets the impression that could Murphy exchange
places with Sisyphus, he would be supremely fulfilled. He
thrived on clogged "pipe lines," Third World bureaucracies
and drifting radio signals. When something broke down
that he could repair, he was ecstatic. He turned prodigious
energy to the most humble tasks, and if something was too
easy, he manufactured complexities. Like leaving. When
arranging for the transport of his luggage through to Nigeria,
he repeatedly went over the schedule of ports of call with
the shipping agent until one had the feeling that he was not
shipping household effects but arranging an itinerary for his
ailing grandmother.

Murphy left Lesotho with some regret, but with no hopes
for the country's future. He, like many other expatriates,
derived particular glee from examining the implications of
some of the periodic statements Basuto politicians would

make about bringing the miners home, or starting Basuto's own currency, or about the day when South Africa will be run by blacks. On this last point he noted, "If Lesotho wasn't surrounded by South Africa, it wouldn't exist. Imagine an Amin next door." Here I think Murphy is mistaken. I cannot imagine anyone wanting to invade and take control of Lesotho.

If South Africa allows independence to the Bantu homeland, the Transkei, Lesotho hypothetically will have an "African" corridor to the sea (and in the optimistic eyes of some Basuto, additional lands for Lesotho's exploding population). Murphy dismissed this as a pipe dream as well. The "port" which would be Lesotho's outlet is, said Murphy, no port at all—it's shallow and blocked by a sand bar. Moreover, he added, the Xhosas and Basuto have been fighting since before the arrival of the first *voortrekker*.

The idea of Lesotho's beginning its own currency gave Murphy particular pleasure. If Lesotho had its own currency, collapse would come through a fantastic increase in the cost of living, since it is hard to imagine on what terms anyone would accept Lesotho currency, and through the costs of preventing smuggling (given Lesotho's porous border with South Africa) and controlling an inevitable black market. The conversation turned to what the currency might be called. Someone suggested that the basic unit be called the donga in honor of the huge eroded gullies which are the landscape's most obtrusive feature, and someone else suggested that the coinage be called the molapo in honor of the relative of Chief Jonathan who proposed that Lesotho should have its own currency. There might be 100 molapos to the donga.

Murphy's belief was that in the doubtful event that Lesotho survives, its future must be agricultural. This prediction neatly completed the set of predictions I had received from other expatriates. Tom Bentley had said that "any future had to be industrial," and Jonathan Jenness held hopes that Lesotho might save itself by exporting trading expertise like Lebanon.

Clearly, for Murphy the game was the thing. He was an operative, and his scorn for what development accomplishes matched the scorn the soldier feels for the strategist. Once I asked him why, if he felt such contempt for the ultimate worth of development, he still worked for the World Food Program. "Well, that's what it comes down to, doesn't it?" he said. "If we all sat around head shrinking all day, none of us would do anything, would we?"

DAVID MORTON

Morton was one of the sizable community of expatriates who find their ties to Lesotho strengthened by the fact that he married locally, although he did not marry a Basuto. His wife Naomi is what the South Africans delicately classify as a colored, the daughter of a famed doctor from Thaba Nchu and an Englishwoman. Naomi's sister Dottie married John Hurst, and another sister married Albert Mohale, Lesotho's first ambassador in Washington. Their brother, who goes by the name James Dorothy, is an artist, and his paintings and murals, of questionable but consistent realization, seemed to bedizen every official structure and private residence in Maseru. With such family connections as well as a web of friendships with other long-term expatriates, Morton was well plugged in to life in Maseru, so much so that his job with the World Food Program was more like a nine-to-five job than an assignment.

There had been a lot of crime recently in Maseru—that rising money-consciousness of which one expatriate approved semifacetiously—and in consequence many of the expatriates had taken to keeping guns around the house. Actually, some of the crime was attributed to blacks from Johannesburg who found Maseru's unsophisticated police force easy to evade. Whites with money and property were the natural targets, and revenge seemed to play almost as much a part in Maseru's latest crime wave as acquisitiveness. Several expatriates were gratuitously stabbed. In fact, a volunteer who lived a few doors down from where I was staying had been severely wounded by a gang attack just prior to my arrival. With this preamble I was not in the slightest hesitant about borrowing a pistol to keep beside my bed the day after someone tried to break into my digs.

Morton and Hurst kept guns for duck hunting and protection, and often went target shooting for amusement. I remember one time I came over to Morton's for dinner after playing squash. As I relaxed with a beer I idly picked through a stack of magazines. There was a copy of *Vogue.* The model on the cover had a neat bullet hole through her right temple. Several more deceased dotted the pages of the magazine. Underneath was a World Food Program publication with several "bloated belly gets the buck" type pictures. Each child had been neatly dispatched.

Although closely tied to Lesotho, Morton had few illusions about its prospects. He observed that a "don't care attitude" in the civil service, which is a legacy of the 1970 coup, was holding back the economy considerably, but felt that even if the government worked perfectly, the future for Lesotho was at best a state of permanent relief.

Morton and I spoke on several occasions about why Lesotho should be developed at all. In the developed world Lesotho can only be a basket case. As a quasi-anarchic collection of native villages, at least the Basuto might have some freedom and traditional satisfactions—if the country could come to grips with its exploding population. Morton said that the momentum of development was political.

Before my eyes Morton would often shift from critic to advocate of development. One minute he might be telling me that he saw a world depression coming and that "when I ride out into the country and see a Basuto in his kraal,

I think that the world economy could utterly collapse and he would not be hurt." Then a minute later he might speak with some enthusiasm about some scheme of development which would tie that Basuto into the world economy. I asked Morton why he helped to undermine the autonomy of that Basuto off in his kraal if he saw the coming collapse of the Western economy. He replied, "It's my job."

SEAN SULLIVAN

Sullivan is a rangy, moody American in his mid-thirties. He is director of training for the Peace Corps for Lesotho, Botswana and Swaziland, and his feeling about the whole thing is that "Africa would be better off if every expatriate packed up and went home." He advanced this opinion when I met up with him one day at a home near the American embassy on the Kingsway. His feelings about development are somewhat like Murphy's. "Look at what's happened in the United States since the industrial revolution in terms of society and the destruction of the environment," he said, "and this tiny place [with 5% of the world's population] the United States with all its problems is saying be like us. To me it seems like suicide; perhaps there are resources to support five or six hundred million people at this level [the U.S. standard of living], but not the whole world."

As noted earlier in this book, Sullivan distrusts the motivations of the African leaders who push for development, the Westernized leaders, embarrassed by their own traditions. Finally Sullivan has come to dislike the judgment on non-Western cultures implicit in development. "If someone felt that this society was just as good as a Western one, you wouldn't begin a project," he said.

One thing that has been said about the Peace Corps is that the most prominent beneficiaries are the young Americans who are sent abroad and gain exposure to other cultures. Indeed the most prominent beneficiaries of most voluntary agencies, aid organizations and foundations are the people who operate them. But what of the cultures who must suffer the presence of Peace Corpsmen until they gain insight into their workings? Sometimes, as in the case of Sean Sullivan, insight into the workings of a non-Western society coincides with the judgment that one's role in that society has been inimical.

ROBERT McKEE

McKee was a soft-spoken, early-middle-aged scientist from England. He was a pedologist and soil physicist working at the Lesothan Agricultural Research Station, and he was supported by the British Overseas Development Administration (now called Ministry of Overseas Development). He spent part of his time trying to get policy decisions so that he could even begin research, then he sifted through forgotten papers and reports to see what had been done so that he would not waste energy duplicating the forgotten efforts of the past. A good portion of his time was taken up by fighting to prevent the ill-advised generalization of the crop research findings of half-thought-out pilot projects scattered through the country.

Ultimately though, for all the energy McKee put into his work, he felt the situation was hopeless. As an agricultural expert he was acutely aware of the potential for agriculture in Lesotho, and of the direct and indirect constraints that population growth and other factors place on the realization of that potential.

Lesotho's potential is to feed somewhat fewer people than the present population. The general figure for Lesotho asserts that there are about a million acres of arable land, of which one third is "marginal." McKee says that attempts were made to plant wheat, beans and peas in some "marginal" lowlands, and that not one was harvested. Moreover, even with agricultural wild cards such as irrigation or the possibility of bringing water over the Maluti Mountains to open new areas to agriculture, self-sufficiency is a dream. At present there are a thousand acres under irrigation in all of Lesotho, and the potential for irrigation is only thirty thousand acres. A massive project like damming the Oxbow River and diverting water over the Maulti Mountains might open the possibility of increasing production by one-third, but it would still leave Lesotho short of its own needs. McKee stated flatly that "it is impossible for Lesotho to feed itself now or in the future, with or without population checked."

Still McKee continued, but unlike some of the other expatriates he did not see his work contributing to Lesotho's future problems. It is somewhat easier to persevere against what one sees as an ultimately hopeless situation if one feels that one might contribute in a small local way toward lessening some of the worse agricultural abuses and problems.

McKee tried as best he could to adapt his research to the realities of Lesotho. His testimony brought to earth some of the dreamier scenarios that come spilling out of the Planing Office. He felt that such goals as improving agriculture to make it an occupation competitive with working in the South African mines were "folly"; it was inconceivable that agriculture might ever reach the point where it could be competitive with the South African wage scale. Similarly, he felt that pushing for sophisticated cash crops like asparagus was unrealistic because it was so difficult to control their stalk size when one was collecting the vegetable from small village scale plots. "I can't even control beans given the lack of machinery, diseases and the like," he said, "so how can they [the Thaba Bosiu project] hope to control sophisticated crops like asparagus?" McKee also

eschewed fertilizers as requiring expenditures which the
Basuto cannot afford for a relatively small increase in production.

McKee's own priorities included researching the growing
of vegetables and soft fruits, increasing yields and decreasing erosion causing run-off by the mixing of duplex soils
(plowing so that the thin layer of topsoil gets mixed with the
clay hard pan underneath) and the training of counterparts.
McKee disliked the arrogant tendency of expatriates to look
at Lesotho as a laboratory, and he felt that projects fail because of that tendency. "There used to be a professional
group who made overseas work their life," said McKee.
"Now people are here for far shorter terms, and they come
with this tone of arrogance: 'We in the West got man on the
moon, so therefore we know how to plant maize.' This idea
that you take our ideas and plunk them down everywhere
is wrong."

VICTOR BURKE

Victor Burke is project manager of the huge, controversial
Thaba Bosiu Rural Development Project. It is controversial
not only because of its approach to development but also
because in hiring Basuto at greatly increased salaries it has,
in the words of one expatriate, been "bleeding the ministries dry." With a $10.5 million funding over the next six
years and a project area that encompasses seventeen thousand families it is also the largest development undertaking in Lesotho.

Although the planners of Thaba Bosiu made some initial
missteps—McKee was aghast that a project this big might
proceed without an agronomist on its staff—it has also attempted to be cautious and considerate of Basuto traditions.
For instance, Thaba Bosiu was meant to work within land
tenure, and the initial findings astonished those legions of

developers who would throw land tenure out the window. It is also the first big project to have a full-time sociologist on staff to monitor the effects of its endeavors.

The project's goals, says Burke, are "to secure better the subsistence of the seventeen thousand farmers in the area"; to increase income from crops; and improve the conservation of Lesotho's dwindling agricultural resources. In pursuit of these goals the project is specifically trying to improve the "infrastructure" of the area (build roads and the like); furnish instruction "in improved agricultural methods"; provide the area with a supply system, marketing system and also make credit available; and finally, make funds available for sending locals overseas for training.

To give an idea of what the project seeks to do, Burke compared it with Thaba Khupa, which lies within the Thaba Bosiu project area. "Thaba Khupa," said Burke, "is endeavoring to give a few people intensive training. In contrast, Thaba Bosiu is not interested in creating a few stars, but in improving the general level of investment." Like Thaba Khupa, though, Thaba Bosiu is assuming that the Basuto will be poor and have limited access to credit for some time. According to Burke, the project eschews mechanization in favor of oxen.

I spoke with Victor Burke twice, once briefly at the house of his resident sociologist, Susan Burke, and another time at Thaba Bosiu headquarters in Maseru. Burke is tall and good-looking, and like most of the British expatriates, soft-spoken. If I might be permitted an outrageous generalization, there seemed to be national characteristics to the expatriates I met in Africa. The British were as a rule soft-spoken and reacted to questions about development work as though you were treading on a delicate and painfully sensitive area. They would often discuss projects in an arch way, as though they were amazed at the questioner's lack of tact in bringing up such matters. The American technical experts, as opposed to the American volunteers, were much more kinetic and aggressive. They threw around jargon and talked about "dicey" problems. The American volunteers were a mixed bag, ranging from immature and abrasive men and women, out to right the wrongs of American imperialism and embrace the Third World, to modest, hard-working teachers and technicians.

Burke, in the British mold, at first discussed Thaba Bosiu in veiled, defensive terms. Later he was far more open. Burke was also somewhat like a publicist, which I suppose is what a good project manager should be in dealing with outsiders. He mentioned that a lot of other agencies are "jumping in to Thaba Bosiu" because of its efficient administrative setup, and because with its separate project authority they don't have to deal with Lesotho's ministries. As Modular Systems was at first blush, Thaba Bosiu offers the attraction of jumping aboard a winner and a handy vehicle for investment whereby an agency might get money into Lesotho quickly.

However, this expensive administrative apparatus is the source of some discussion in the expatriate community, centering around the question of whether Lesotho will be able to afford to keep it going at the end of the six-year project term when the funding ends and—purportedly—the expatriate experts will have pulled out. Burke divided the project's activities into two categories: (1) simple: the marketing system and the distribution of farm supplies— activities which Burke said were at present within the capabilities of the local staff; and (2) investigational (complex): "activities concerned with breaking very complicated social constraints and integrating new style of agriculture." Burke felt that there might be some problem carrying on complex activities because "what we are trying to do is change these people's way of life." The complex activities involved a livestock, crop and soil conservation network which depends on specialized skills. Burke also believed maintenance of the project's infrastructure might put a strain on the government's department of public works.

Burke eschewed questions of whether Lesotho as a whole has a future. "My only hope," he said, "is to improve things. I have no long-term goals—only trying to enable people to grow better crops for staple food. You can't go wrong trying to satisfy simple local needs." Unless perhaps satisfying simple needs leads one to "complex" solutions that involve "changing these people's way of life."

HY HELMAN

The two Israelis I encountered struck me by their intensity and the utter clarity of their approach to development. If they might be wrong-headed, at least they knew exactly where they were going and what they wanted to accomplish.

Hy Helman is the type of person who reminds you why Israel in twenty-five years has managed to acquire most of the benefits of Western technology, along with most of the problems. He's a knife-sharp economist and seems to share an economist's biases about such imperfect "soft" sciences as sociology and anthropology. He is head of planning and evaluation for Thaba Bosiu and as such rules Susan Burke, the resident sociologist.

Susan Burke came into the project with an economic training, having done her Ph.D. on the influence of economic variables on household organization. Under Helman's influence it appeared that her functions would be even more economic and less anthropological or sociological. Her job was to gather baseline data on agricultural practices and household composition. The Planning and Evaluation Unit wanted a crude picture of the life of 350 randomly selected households so that they might monitor change as it occurred.

I was told that Helman and Susan Burke had had some disagreements over her functions. Burke wanted to continue monitoring social repercussions, while Helman argued that she collected "useful data." Helman described "useful data" as production figures and the like, figures which might tell them how their crop and livestock projects are working. The impression was that Helman would like to subordinate Susan Burke's sociological functions to the economic "needs" of the project.

This was precisely opposite to the impression of Ms. Burke's functions given to me in conversation with Harry Johnson, the Lesothan USAID representative. When Harry Johnson mentioned Susan Burke it was to suggest that for the first time a sociologist was to be present to supplement the limited view an economic perspective provides with information on social constraints which might affect the realization of certain goals, as well as information on social repercussions which might flow from the project. This seemed an eminently sensible move to make, since a lack of such a perspective left experts throughout the Third World saddled with failed projects and economically unexplainable side effects. However, if Ms. Burke's functions were circumscribed by economic considerations, then that perspective was lost.

Helman, apparently, did not feel that the loss of that perspective would be debilitating, although he was aware of, and even eloquent, in discussing the pattern of failure of previous projects in Lesotho. He was brimming with confidence. "Nobody knows about one successful project in Lesotho," he said to me. "We want to be the one that succeeds." Helman did not believe that lack of attention to cultural considerations had subverted the goals of past projects as much as a lack of interest in accomplishing tangible results. The pattern, said Helman, had been to write reports on Lesotho's problems and to start pilot projects. Reports demand that someone read and implement them, and pilot projects demand that the Basuto and expatriates see that what you did was good. He cited a 1965 report which projected greatly increased fertilizer use by 1970; by 1970 fertilizer use had in fact declined. "By writing the report," said Helman, "they thought that production and use would improve."

Helman was previously connected with the Leribe Pilot Agricultural Scheme, and he included it in the past pattern of failure. "Leribe is the equivalent of our core area where we try our more complex activities," he said, "but they started with the complex things." Because the project pushed so quickly for results, they had a high overhead, and because it was a pilot project and not a development project, the expenses of that project were pointless unless Leribe's findings were implemented. On the other hand, Helman claimed that Thaba Bosiu has such a large area that "we can implement our findings," whereas Leribe only has a small amount of land.

One finding of Leribe's which Thaba Bosiu was attempting to implement had to do with the growing of asparagus for export—the finding that McKee at the Agricultural Research Station has been trying to nip in the bud because of the problems of standardizing a crop like asparagus and because the soil around Leribe happened to be particularly well suited to asparagus. McKee felt that it would be dangerous to generalize from that experiment that the same success might be enjoyed elsewhere in Lesotho. In defense, Burke and Helman said that the decision to try to grow asparagus was made on the basis of reports submitted by a UN horticulturist and that asparagus was never written into the original proposal (read: the project can be dropped if it doesn't work out, with no loss of prestige on the part of Thaba Bosiu). Moreover, Burke and Helman claimed that the experience elsewhere in Africa suggests that such crops can be grown on a small-farmer basis.

Discussing development with people like Hy Helman is a little like what it must have been to discuss Vietnam with Robert McNamara back in the days when he cited statistics that he did not have at his fingertips. You don't really know what lies behind that confidence.

Neither Helman nor Burke could offer any overwhelming

evidence that Thaba Bosiu would be any more successful than the scores of projects that preceded this giant effort. The best technicians and bureaucrats in Lesotho were fleeing the ministries for the high salaries offered at Thaba Bosiu. Who could expect them to return later to Lesotho's decaying bureaucracy or even to Lesotho if they had the chance to use their skills elsewhere at higher pay? But who could blame Thaba Bosiu for wanting to get the best men and for wanting to side-step the ministries?

JIM KELLEY

Jim Kelley headed the Lesothan office of Catholic Relief Services. He appeared to be in his mid-thirties. He is dark-haired, candid and articulate. He cheerfully viewed Lesotho's situation as ultimately hopeless, and just as cheerfully wrote off foreign aid to Lesotho as useless if not harmful. "The wildest idea," he said, "would be to close down all international assistance and divvy it [the money] out. The country is increasingly being fucked over by this flood of aid. Lesotho can't absorb all the money that's coming in." This appraisal had a personal note; three of Kelley's Basuto assistants had recently turned in their resignations to go work on the Thaba Bosiu project. Kelley stated flatly that the "country is not economically viable. The best thing," said Kelley, "that could happen is for majority rule to come about in the Republic. If not, they [the Basuto] are always going to have to live in a depressed economy."

Because Kelley's feelings about Lesotho's prospects and the worth of foreign aid were so clearly negative, the usual question occurred concerning what, then, Kelley was doing in Lesotho. Kelley's response was that his beliefs about foreign aid and Lesotho's future translated into several things he would not do, and had also led him to devise a strategy of assistance which he felt would be the most useful for the Basuto. For one thing, Kelley dismissed school projects as "throwing money down a rathole," given that schools in Lesotho generally only outfit students for unemployment and alienation. Nor did Kelley feel that the movement toward producing cash crops for export has merit. According to Kelley, such crops as asparagus and cherries are "nutritionally valueless." Moreover, he doubted that any additional income produced from such export crops would go toward purchasing nutritional foods or farm equipment. "Do you think people will take their money and buy nutritional foods?" he asked. "Bullshit, they will buy cigarettes, fancy clothes and beer." Kelley felt that Lesotho will never be self-sufficient in food, and he was trying to set up a bulk-buying project so that when it comes time for Basuto to purchase their inevitable food imports, they "might buy the best instead of garbage."

CRS provides a substantial amount of food toward the Mountain Access Tracks, which also involves the World Food Program and CARE. Another pet project of Kelley's has been supporting health education for preschool infants and their mothers in seventy clinics. Kelley took great pains to stress that "CRS is acutely aware of how population growth wipes out economic gains. What CRS people do in the field," he continued, "doesn't always relate to what headquarters in New York thinks should be going on." However, although Kelley stressed CRS's local commitment to family planning, other people involved with family planning in Lesotho mentioned that while CRS is somewhat more involved than CARE in family planning, their involvement is less than the commitment Kelley conveyed.

The descriptions of the types of projects the different expatriates are involved in have been abbreviated, in part because most of these projects fall into a genre that have been previously discussed, and in part because, taken as a composite, they offer a globally negative assessment of any effort to help Lesotho to help itself. Virtually to a man, the expatriate experts and volunteers I spoke with in Lesotho had nothing but scorn for all the previous efforts at development in Lesotho. With the exception of those who felt that Lesotho and Africa would be better off if all expatriates packed up and went home, the expatriates would suggest some failure of judgment or vision which had caused all previous efforts to founder, and then suggest how their own approach had taken that critical problem into account. The problem is one person's miracle solution turned out to be part of another person's assessment of what was wrong with development in Lesotho.

There is a considerable amount of backbiting in Maseru, but I do not feel that backbiting alone explains this pattern of negativity. For one thing, the most generous and fair-minded expatriates offered no less harsh estimates of the pattern of expatriate assistance than the more mean-spirited and jealous members of that community. For another, the failure of past expatriate efforts was manifest in Lesotho's declining fortunes and snowballing problems to all but the most self-deluded individuals. Rather, I think that the "we're going to be the one that succeeds" syndrome is the way the expatriate who comes to doubt the worth of his contribution to the non-Western world justifies his continued enjoyment of the fruits of the expatriate life. If one can believe that development fails or screws up a culture because the developers simply were not cagey or subtle enough in their approach, then that belief serves as an effective smoke screen, diverting one's introspection from more fundamental questions about what development is all about and what one's role in that process is.

Often expatriates will be avowed defenders of the cultures which they suspect development projects are helping to destroy. They might have enlisted in the cause of development because such work offered a paying way to get away from the consumer society at home. Others believe in carrying the American way of life beyond where the pavement ends, but are perplexed to see their best-laid plans undermined and sidetracked as though some poltergeist were dogging their efforts. Many expatriates have a change of heart during their time overseas that turns them from one of these postures to the other. Common to all of these people, save perhaps a few missionaries and some of the more robotlike World Bank experts, is a sense of malaise that things in Lesotho and in the non-Western world are not going according to the script, that events are out of control, and that what they are doing in some way figures in why they can neither escape or re-create the society that sent them overseas.

One of the last people I spoke with in Lesotho was Ambassador Bohlen, who represents United States interests in Lesotho, Botswana and Swaziland. He deals with the sense that the non-Western world is out of control by saying that "development is a destabilizing influence, anyway," and that consequently one has to expect some disorder to attend the changes that comprise development. "You can't stop progress," he said. Bohlen utters that cliché with great confidence. For many expatriates, that inevitability is the cause of claustrophobic fear.

The question is what progress is, that irresistible tide that enlists both the charitable organization and the multinational corporation in its advance; and specifically, what is there in the nature of self-help which indicates what purpose it is really serving. If the expatriates seemed to present a spectrum of opinions on Lesotho's prospects and problems, there are still overriding communalities to their different approaches, communalities which give a coherence to the momentum of development, and explain why the effects of development projects are similar despite the different sensibilities of those involved in that work.

III

Who Is Helping Who?

THIRTEEN

Vicious Circles

From the first, [says a CARE document entitled "Overview of CARE Programming Goals and Strategy"] we have tried to make food and self-help work together. We have used self-help and technical assistance to reinforce and strengthen food and nutrition programs. We have tried to use food not only to feed the hungry and treat malnutrition, but as an impetus to development. We have called these programs different names at different times: Food Plus Programs, Integrated Programming Agglutinative Programming, etc., but common to them all is our intention to deal with the developmental processes as a whole, rather than pursue a fragmentary approach that would result in isolated, unrelated activities.

This lofty intention grew out of CARE's frustrating experience of approaching development in isolated villages, on a fragmentary, ad hoc basis. CARE found the impact of this approach minimal and in 1966 came up with something called the PDP (Partnership Development Program), which it felt integrated local development efforts into national programs. Now CARE has recently instituted the MYP (Multi-Year Planning) system to augment the PDP. CARE believes that this system allows for more effective self-help planning by putting it on a long-term basis. Thus within the last fifteen years, the concept of self-help at CARE has evolved from local ad hoc efforts to multi-year national contracts.

One impetus behind this evolution has been frustration. CARE discovered that its various projects in villages throughout the non-Western world tended to have very little impact with regard to improving local "living standards." In fact, despite twenty-five years of intensive efforts directed toward self-help in the "underdeveloped" world by donors and private agencies such as CARE, a convincing case could be made that on the whole, *real* standards of living have fallen, even though hundreds of millions of people have been brought into the world economy.

Merle Curti, author of *History of American Philanthropy Abroad,* describes the ostensible aims of development in the postwar period in this way: "On the official level, technical aid first proposed as a major enterprise in the Point Four program rested on two main considerations. The first was the humanitarian and democratic desire to help non-industrialized countries develop potential resources and improve standards of living within a framework of political freedom. The second was the effort in the Cold War to prevent the spread of communism and to win the support of the still uncommitted nations." The tentative results of this effort might be summarized as follows: where development has "taken" in the underdeveloped world, as in the cases of Brazil, Korea and the Philippines, it has been at the expense of political freedom; often in these same cases and many others like Colombia, Liberia and Kenya, where there are rich natural resources, the dividends of development accrue only to the power élite, leaving the populace no better off and in many cases worse off than before development. Per capita food production has been level or dropping, and in many countries the percentage of income devoted to food has been increasing. The cold war scorecard is even worse, of course; twenty-five years of development has given those uncommitted nations a commitment—almost to a nation, the Third World opposes the United States on questions of policy that come up before the UN. It is little wonder, then, that CARE and every other agency concerned with development should feel frustrated. Why should people hate us for trying to help? Do they not want to help themselves, or perhaps, is the problem in the nature of self-help itself?

Self-help: helping people to help themselves. That, according to CARE's promotional material, is what CARE is all about. Or as that father in one television ad remarks to his inquisitive daughter, "Maybe if we all care enough, someday these people will be able to stand on their own two feet." The image of helping the baby to walk, guiding its first steps so that eventually it can walk by itself. Or the image of the sergeant prodding the cowering recruit into battle, making a man out of him, getting him to stand on his own two feet. Self-help is the umbrella term CARE uses to describe its development work. From what I can tell, CARE was using the term "self-help" as early as 1950 when it first tested the waters for development work. I still have trouble with the phrase. If it is meant to lessen the implications of dependency that surround foreign assistance, it fails. Rather, it clumsily but effectively calls attention to such dependency by implying that without the element of outside assistance contained in the phrase "helping people to help themselves," the beneficiary could not help himself. On the other hand, if it is meant to reassure the donor that his money is not being given carte blanche to lazy, backward natives, it succeeds, because the phrase summons stirring recollections of the notion of "white man's burden." I have other troubles with the phrase as well.

"Helping people to help themselves" is another way of saying "helping people to change themselves," especially if such help requires the intervention of "experts" from outside the culture in which the change is to occur. Presumably the Tuaregs of the sub-Sahara region need no help to outfit themselves for their nomadic life, or at least no help that a non-Tuareg ignorant of their language and customs might give them. The self-help which outsiders have offered the Tuaregs has to do with settling them, weaning them from their nomadic ways, educating their young—in short, helping them to do things that will help them to become something other than Tuaregs, as their culture defines the Tuaregs.

CARE is quite aware of this aspect of self-help and makes no bones about advertising its desire to change the people with whom it works:

> The poverty and isolation of the village, induced in part by lack of knowledge and by traditional ways of perceiving the world, cannot be changed by temporary infusions of external aid, by "model demonstrations" of progressive farming, or by exhortation to modernize. There is no quick route, no developmental gimmick that will result either in the alteration of traditional modes of thought and values regarding the possibility and desirability of change, or to long-term betterment in the lives of people caught in a vicious circle of poverty, ill health, ignorance and low productivity.*

The author of this CARE paper, Ralph Montee, makes the same point at greater length in another document which outlines CARE's approach to local development:

> . . . it [is] difficult for villagers to accept the notion that they are capable of helping themselves; that with effort and newly learned skills some of their most pressing problems can begin to yield to solutions. *The villager does not accept naturally the idea that nature can be modified by human efforts* [my italics]. He must have the direct experience of having done just that, even if on only a small scale, before belief becomes a reality. In short, men and women must be able to accomplish things for themselves before the attitude that they can accomplish things for themselves becomes accepted in their view of themselves and the world.

* "Toward a Reassessment of Development Priorities," CARE Program Department Position Paper for the ICVA General Conference, 1971.

Both these quotes identify the villager's traditions and ways of perceiving the world as the enemies, the impediments of development, and note, with some pique, the difficulties of weaning natives from their beliefs. The closest CARE comes to accepting that "traditions" might have something to do with a way of life is in a position paper, again by Ralph Montee, of CARE's programming department. Although this paper, entitled "Activating Resources for Development at the Local Level," sees "underdevelopment" as a system, it only sees the "native way of life" as underdevelopment. The "native way of life" is described as a system only to stress its imperviousness to ad hoc efforts to develop it, and not to identify anything in that way of life which might serve positive purposes in the lives of the "underdeveloped." In a popular device used to describe underdevelopment, a vicious circle, Montee amplifies even further the notion of tradition as the enemy of development:

Causative Circle II—Institutional Arrangements
and Psychological Obstacles to Development

A. *The Attitudinal and Psychological Circle:*

The general lack of institutions and attitudes positive to development exemplified by *traditional religious and cultural beliefs and values resistant to change*—reinforcing the *reliance on traditional methods that perpetuate low productivity and frustrate the introduction of improved techniques* —also engendering a *lack of problem solving orientation and confidence that situations can be changed*—which is magnified by *low levels of technical skill and general literacy*— predisposing toward *minimal risk taking on a base of limited capital resources*—interacting with a *lack of awareness of both local and outside resources*—maintaining *low levels of productivity and social development* acting to *perpetuate institutions and attitudes that are negative to development.*

This position paper is an important indicator of CARE's thinking, and we shall have cause to return to other sections of the argument it sets up. What is striking about the above quote is that it occurs in a position paper that pretends to be an enlightened reassessment of development priorities. In the paper Montee quotes Eugene Black, former head of the World Bank, who noted how we inflate the differences between Western and non-Western countries through our inflated GNP—is a $2.50 haircut in the United States ten times as valuable as a 25-cent haircut in India? Montee notes how many transactions that contribute to our GNP are not monetized in poor countries; he also shows that activities resulting in traffic jams and pollution which detract from the quality of life contribute to our GNP; he tries to show how misdirected development efforts have been and how inappropriate Western economic models are for attacking problems in the "underdeveloped" world. How could a paper be sensitive to the inappropriateness of foisting Western models of economic analysis on the non-Western world and yet be insensitive, or worse, blind to what the non-Western world is? Montee was a Peace Corpsman, and his perceptions of development are more complex than those of the pragmatic, former businessmen who have made CARE what it is. But in one curious respect, Montee and CARE's businessmen seem to share a common blind spot.

From its first line, CARE's "Attitudinal and Psychological Circle" pits development *against* the villager's cultural milieu: "The general lack of institutions and attitudes positive to development *exemplified* [emphasis mine] by traditional religious and cultural beliefs and values resistant to change . . ." This line should disabuse any illusions about CARE's attitude toward non-Western cultures, and perhaps it begins to shed light on why efforts to help people make us more enemies than friends. Some villager might resent that the cultural accretions of generations might be dismissed as an impediment to development, and no matter how subtly the do-gooder tries to insinuate himself into "village" life, ultimately the villagers will intuit the do-gooder's attitude toward their way of life. Especially if, as in CARE's case, an important "development task" is seen to be "the restructuring of attitudes and institutions to make them positive for development."

Something else about self-help should be evident from these quotes, something which is related in corollary fashion to CARE's attitude toward *native* traditions. All the above-mentioned quotes, and all other CARE position papers or documents I have read, see the context of self-help as an undifferentiated lump called the "underdeveloped" world. CARE has an all-purpose development strategy which it applies to local development in hundreds of different cultures in South America, in Africa, in the Middle East, in the Caribbean and in Asia. All cultural differences, strengths and weaknesses are ignored in the CARE development strategy; in its terms, the long-lived, healthy Abkhazians have the same problem and the same aspirations as the starving Bengals. It's not just that local traditions are an impediment to development, it's that once you've seen one non-Western culture you've seen them all. Moreover, this reductionist tendency is not a unique CARE predilection, but a vogue shared by virtually all professionals in the field of development. It is in part cultural chauvinism which allows the self-help professional to treat the entire non-Western world as an undifferentiated lump. À la Montee, I might invent a vicious circle which details how this chauvinism suffuses every aspect of charitable programming in a self-reinforcing way:

Causative Circle I—Self-reinforcing Aspects of Charities' Blanket Approach to Non-Western Cultures

A.   The Attitudinal and Psychological Circle:

Urge to upgrade the lives of non-Western peoples, coupled with need for practical programs with identifiable goals, causes do-gooders to ignore differences between cultures and instead concentrate on assumed common aspirations and methods of realizing these aspirations, which leads to development of all-purpose development strategy that treats all cultures alike, which leads to an all-purpose method of implementation that, coupled with "activist" nature of field personnel, leads to a rotational system of employing overseas operatives every two years, which discourages expatriates from learning culture, language and peculiarities of "villagers," which further reinforces blanket approach to non-Western peoples.

CARE has of course an image of the typical village in which it becomes involved in self-help, but for the most part the non-Western way of life is described negatively, in terms of what the particular society lacks. For instance, CARE's Fact Sheet on Lesotho states: ". . . most Basuto live in one of some 7,100 scattered villages having an average population of less than 150. The majority of these villages have none of the basic services normally required by a community, such as schools, clinics, water systems, electricity, markets, sanitation systems, post offices, and police posts." This is what CARE's self-help programs have in part tried to provide. Yet, given CARE's dismissive attitude toward the virtues of non-Western cultures, I was led to wonder whether some of the services CARE found lacking were in fact supplied in forms CARE did not recognize, and whether others reflected wants of the people, or what CARE felt they should have, and what purposes other services such as police posts might serve. Did the fact that Basuto villages lacked police posts mean that criminals roamed the street of a village of 150 souls, terrorizing the Basuto at will? My suspicions were aroused because virtually every fact sheet I read described whatever culture CARE was trying to help in terms of the same basic lacks, and, to reiterate, these common lacks and common remedies indicated that CARE regarded each culture as having the same aspirations. From the Fact Sheet on Lesotho you might get the idea that the Basuto village aspired to be a rural town in the Midwestern United States.

In one of the quotes I mentioned earlier, there is a particularly telling clue to what CARE hopes to help the non-Western village to become. Citing tradition as an impediment to development, the paper claims: "The villager does not accept naturally the idea that nature can be modified by human efforts." In this quote, and in CARE's description of what thinking it feels is positive to development, we find the essence of what self-help really means.

But to tease out this essence requires some startling digressions into the nature of primitive ritual and into human prehistory. It is necessary to understand how we are different from the people we are trying to help in order to show what we are helping them to become, and why we are helping them at all.

FOURTEEN

Charity and the Consumer Mind

"The villager does not accept naturally the idea that nature can be modified by human efforts." He must be shown this by the men from voluntary agencies, he must be helped to experience this delicious original sin, before he might imagine such proscribed manipulations on his own. The CARE documents offer us no help as to why the villager does not accept naturally the idea that nature can be modified by human efforts, nor do the documents specify which villagers suffer such limitations. But, no matter, in this particular blanket characterization I feel that CARE perhaps has stumbled on a legitimate point of distinction that helps shed light on the differences between non-Western and Western (particularly American) cultures.

The term "non-Western" encompasses a vast number of cultures, and many would argue that the extremes of "achievement" reflected in non-Western cultures are as great as the differences between Western and non-Western cultures; that, for instance, the contrast between Mayan or dynastic Chinese culture and Tasaday culture is as great as the difference between American and any non-Western culture. Certainly, even within Africa there are immense differences between the culture and technology of the hunting and gathering Pygmies and Bushmen, and that of the pastoral Bantu peoples who conquered them. However, the great theocratic civilizations, the Stone Age Tasaday and the Bantu nations are all tradition-bound in a way in which Western man is not, and this communality offers a point of approach by which one might contrast consuming (Western) and conserving (non-Western) cultures.

To describe non-Western cultures as conserving is not to imply that only consuming cultures are capable of environmental rape. Many a non-Western culture has polluted and denuded its environment with a thoroughness that would leave even the most rapacious Western developer lost in admiration. (However, many such cultures have disappeared as a result of their profligacy.) Arab shepherds played an important role in the southward march of the Sahara. Certain tribes among the Plains Indians of the American West herded buffalo to their death in canyons with huge attendant waste. Other tribes wasted nothing. Some paleontologists argue that the southward march of the ancestors of these Plains Indians led to the destruction of innumerable Ice Age species that populated the Americas, and eventually to a drastic reduction in human numbers. If this is the case, then we might consider the aboriginal peoples that whites first encountered in North America to represent some natural solution to their forebears' prodigality.

Whether or not this occurred in North America, this same phenomenon has occurred elsewhere and it contains a number of instructive Darwinian lessons: cultures or species that encourage ecologically maladaptive practices, either hunting, pastoral or otherwise—eventually eliminate themselves, and sometimes they do so as a function of their earlier short-term successes. Cultures that engage in seemingly wasteful practices often maintain a conserving relationship with their environment because other factors act to limit the amount of damage they might inflict. For instance, the Plains Indians never seriously threatened the buffalo herds, because infant mortality and warfare curbed their numbers to the degree that they might never overtax the restorative powers of the herds. On the other hand, a few thousand white men brought the buffalo to the brink of extinction in a few short years.

By surface appearance, the Maring tribesmen in New Guinea might be the most profligate group of all. They cultivate by using slash-and-burn techniques, to clear new patches of forest each year. Every decade or so they slaughter almost their entire herd of pigs, and then follow this slaughter with bloody warfare among different clans. Agronomists believe, correctly, that uncontrolled slash-and-burn agriculture is the most wasteful of resources of all types of agriculture. Given their extravagant gluttony, their profligate agriculture and their periodic wars, one might expect that the Maring would denude the land around them, or have otherwise killed themselves off. To the contrary, although their numbers rise and fall, over time the Maring population has remained fairly stable. Although they practice slash-and-burn, certain forces seem to control where they cut their plots so that no one area gets denuded. Nor is the overall integrity of the jungle canopy drastically altered as an intricate weave of warfare and ancestor worship conspires to make sacred previously cultivated areas until they might reconstitute their cover. This is the argument offered by anthropologist Marvin Harris in his book *Cows, Pigs, Wars, and Witches: The Riddles of Culture*, where he tries to show how this bizarre pattern of warfare and gluttony acts to control human numbers and to prevent the Maring from exceeding the carrying capacity of the environment.

It is this total pattern that is the Maring culture. If you asked a tribesman why he did not plant or cut in a particular area for a decade, he would not say that it was because the flora of that area needed a breather; he would reply that he did not plant there because he feared retribution from the ancestors of a foe. In the case of the Maring, environmental harmony is maintained by the force of tradition and religious law. It would be easy for the outsider to fail to see that this was the intent of many strange aspects of Maring life, and certainly this intent was not framed consciously by the Maring themselves. What their culture represents is the solution to a number of enduring social and environmental problems.

To the man from a voluntary agency, Maring culture might appear irrational, and hostile to development, but to the Maring it is a way of life, and to the perceptive outsider it is a coherent system. It would be very easy to throw this system into disequilibrium. For instance, merely by lowering the infant-mortality rate, one might bring to the surface the inimical properties of slash-and-burn and ritualized warfare. The *idea* of the culture is to shape Maring behavior in the way most advantageous for their survival, and it does so by exploiting archetypal appetites and fears. The way of life is not something idly followed by dimly conscious savages. To be effective, a culture must capitalize to the fullest on the human capacity for joy, for terror, for pity. To threaten a culture is to threaten to take the meaning out of the lives of the people who live under its thrall.

A natural question should arise here, and that is, If these people are not consciously solving their environmental problems, then who is making these decisions and then disguising the decisions even from the Maring? Since it is the authority of religion and tradition that organizes Maring behavior, the first answer is that the Maring are making these decisions collectively. Down through the tribe's history, some agent has been observing the fortuitous and recurring events in the tribal life, and selectively encouraging actions and delusions that might favorably affect the survival of the group. That agent is the seamless entity of the Maring and his culture. The two adapt together as a single organism, much in the way modern ethologists are coming to believe that the overall pattern of adaptation is for the organism and environment to adapt together—that there is some principle of environmental integrity, some gestalt, which influences the selective histories of an organism in an ecosystem. Recently British scientists discovered that insects evolving at sea level contributed methane gas necessary for the earth's protective shield in the upper atmosphere. Similarly, a culture might selectively reinforce individual behaviors most advantageous for a group's survival.

The tool of flexibility, the means by which Maring culture remains responsive to change, and assimilates change without overwhelming the reconstitutive powers of the culture, lies in a relationship between reason and the unconscious. It is a relationship in which the unconscious has the controlling hand. It is a relationship in which change and discovery are fit into perceptual patterns, into a gestalt prepared by the Maring's experience and reinforced with the power of myth. Reason operates, to be sure, as hosts of frustrated anthropologists have discovered when they tried to disabuse animistic peoples of some of their notions. For instance, in his classic study of the Trobriand islanders Bronislaw Malinowski noted that the Trobrianders held to the notion that intercourse had nothing to do with childbearing, and with patience and logic turned away arguments to the contrary offered by Malinowski and a succession of intellectually well-armed scientists. We mislead ourselves if we believe that modern American culture has any more imagination, humor or intensity than any of the thousands of cultures we have displaced. Still, there is a critical difference between these so-called primitive cultures and our culture, and it accounts for the reason we have displaced competing cultures.

Reason did not evolve to allow us to read a newspaper; it evolved under emergency conditions to permit us the flexibility to adapt and survive. From the first, nature considered reason a dangerous tool, and we might see this judgment in the strict controls that govern the use of reason in many human cultures—and in other species; and from the first, there has been a war for control of behavior between that evolutionary marvel, the "new brain," that pretender world of symbols and logic, and what we might here call the "traditional," the world of our inherited behavioral vocabulary, the genetically encoded lessons of survival.

Our surrogate world of symbols and logic evolved to allow us to adapt our behavior faster than normal selective processes of revision permitted. I describe it as a surrogate world because it is a set of principles and attributes which was abstracted from immediate sensory experience but enshrined in the new brain as a blackboard upon which propositions for survival might be worked out, and which has come to compete in man with our old brain for authority over behavior.

However, as this new, pretender brain brought more and more behavior into its ambit and increasingly encroached on the territory of the old brain, new risks arose which threatened not just evolving man but the creatures around him as well. Nature takes generations to work out propositions, and as has been noted, short-term success often can spell long-term self-extinction as well as environmental havoc. And so, as our new brain became more anatomically independent of the authority of the old brain in forming its propositions, nature increasingly exercised dampening influence on the use of this power through the power of myth and religion. Nature has always used pleasure, pain, fear and joy to encourage correct behavior, and we might suppose that as conscious decision making became increasingly more important in the lives of men, so did the importance of myth increase as a means by which man might have access to these enduring emotions, or by which they might have access to him. When we tremble or soar before the power of myth we are possessed by the power of nature, we are feeling the power of our old brain.

In a functioning ecosystem, reason operates in the thrall

of tradition and myth, and as all businesslike adults know from memories of childhood, the pleasures of such harmony are not inconsiderable. Nature tries to protect us from ourselves, sometimes, as in the case of the Maring, without letting us know its real intent. Marvin Harris describes the complicated Maring cycle of pig raising, infanticide, feast, warfare and field rotation, as "a clever 'trick' on the part of the ancestors to get the Maring to breed pigs and men instead of women, in order to protect the forest."

This is the arrangement of the conserving, "tradition-bound" peoples—flexibility within strictly defined limits. But what about the contrasting and ever burgeoning consumers?

In the consumer, the religious and psychological restraints nature imposed to temper the use of reason have begun to break down. What was intended to be a surrogate reality, a blackboard on which man might work out strategies for survival, has come to compete with the real world for our attention. In early man, and still in primitive man, there are connections between symbols and their visceral referents; however, as civilization advances, so do these connections become attentuated. I believe that for rational man, these connections have snapped. In fact, in some cultural niches the reified world of symbols and logic has come to be regarded as the real world, while the un-displaced, animal world of emotions and reflexes is derogated as chaotic and savage.

The movement of human evolution has seen authority over man's behavior move progressively forward as the new brain grew and brought increasingly more behavior into its province. Displacement is the time frame that made necessary the construction of man's separate reality of symbols and logic. Without displacement there can be no self-consciousness. As displacement attenuated the connection between our thought processes and the immediate natural continuum, it made necessary the development of the per-

sonality and such constructs as the ego to negotiate between
the developing world of the forebrain and the world of the
old brain. Our ancestral memory of usurping nature's authority (shared by all agricultural peoples) is embodied in
that mythical constant called original sin; and as we usurp
more of the old brain's authority and retreat further into our
surrogate world, so does our unrequited need for the natural
integrated solace and meaning provided by nature surface
in that malaise called alienation. We might also understand
the philosophical problem of the mind/body dualism in
terms of the competition between the new and old brains.
In short, we can explain much of modern man's behavior
and many of his problems in terms of an ever widening gulf
between the world of displacement and the world of our
evolutionary behavioral heritage. Time (displacement permits our sense of time) has become malignant for man; this
malignancy is the product of cultural evolution. Here it is
interesting to note that many expatriates claimed that one
thing we have to change is the "natives'" sense of time,
that they lack the ability to plan far ahead and live according to a rigid schedule.

The impetus behind this gradual usurpation has been a
series of evolutionary pressures somewhat akin to the self-
reinforcing cycles Montee uses to describe underdevelopment. We might see that even with strict unconscious controls, displacement and analysis require disruption of the
"natural" mechanisms that keep man in touch with and re-
acting to his immediate environment. Reason by its nature
is pitted against our repertoire of inherited responses.
When analysis enhances survival value, normal selective
pressures will favor those organisms equipped for such
flexibility. As the flexibility of man increased, the disruptions of his inherited responses increased proportionately.
Once disrupted, these mechanisms would gradually lose
effectiveness to cope with the problems evolving man
faced. This would in turn increase pressures to bring more

behavior under rational scrutiny and into the realm of those
behaviors culturally imparted, and in turn would further
break down our noncultural pattern of responses. In this regard, some people believe that ESP reflects a fine attune-
ment to nature which antedates the earliest religion and
which is present in animals, but which has atrophied in
man under the erosive power of reason. This pattern of
usurpation continues today, only now the need for flexibility threatens even those cultural restraints which replaced
our more direct biological restraints.

One of the most important events laying the groundwork
for the development of the "consuming" peoples was
monotheism. Viewed in terms of this competition between
new brain and old brain, monotheism indicated a rupturing
of polytheistic bonds which fettered reason and kept our
minds attuned to nature, and the construction of an *abstract*
paradigm founded in the ideals of the new brain, and by
which man should judge his behavior. This adaptation permits radically greater flexibility of response than that permitted the polytheistic native. When polytheism allows nature to control man through a host of gods, monotheism
reduces nature to so much raw material, placed at man's dis-
posal by God, who, coincidentally, is a look-alike for man.
The Bible dramatically summarizes the alienating pressures of displacement by having man evicted from the Gar-
den of Eden. Once evicted, man is separated from nature by
an insuperable void. No longer can he communicate with
his fellow creatures (as he could before the Fall), but now
he might exploit them as a resource necessary for his survival. Monotheism granted them that license, and it also set
the stage for an attempt by the new brain to become, in effect, self-governing.

Models of human autonomy express the ambition of our
rational self for victory over time and nature, the ambition to
live in our head. The idea of free will, of choosing one's destiny, reflects a flexibility that derives its authority from the

ideals of reason rather than the necessities of nature. Both serve as elements of a paradigm of order constructed out of the needs and attributes of our rational surrogate world and designed to replace the paradigm of nature. The construction of this new paradigm did not merely tolerate ignorance of nature, it demanded such ignorance. Only in willful blindness of the world around could this paradigm keep our attention focused inward, and only with such willful insensitivity might we exploit the world as what Arnold Toynbee calls "unsacrosanct raw material." Actually it was no coincidence that God came to look like man.

Christianity permits an even greater flexibility than that offered by the moral license of the Old Testament. Christ serves as a psychic sponge, absorbing the sins of man, a service which takes considerable responsibility off the individual. One is permitted to sin and then redeem oneself through confession or through acts of charity. The Maring tribesman does not plant in the sacrificed area for fear of the immediate retribution of the ancestors. The Christian, on the other hand, need not fear retribution for sin until after death, and in the meantime he might redeem all but the grossest transgressions through *token* placatory gestures. This procedure provides a psychic window between act and responsibility for an act which, from an anthropological point of view, might be seen to *encourage* transgression rather than prevent it.

Within this view, charity serves the same purpose— encouraging transgression. For instance, a robber baron might spend his life raping the earth and exploiting his fellow man, and then through a series of gestures token in comparison to his earlier pillage, he might redeem himself and claim, as did Andrew Carnegie, that he accumulated wealth solely to benefit his brethren. Clearly, then, moving responsibility for one's actions from immediacy back to some distant afterlife permits the individual much greater flexibility than that permitted by the Old Testament's touchy and ever vigilant God. Within the framework of displacement, Christianity is saying, *Act*, nature cannot get you until you die.

Incidentally, within Christian mythology, the devil is cloaked with the attributes of the senses and immediate earthly delights—the devil is nature. The anthropologist Margaret Murray makes this point when she attempts to show how Christianity, as the usurping religion, follows the pattern of nascent religious movements in casting the role of the old religion as evil. Religious movements by their very nature are intolerant, especially so in the case of Christianity, where the battle between the usurper and the old religion is as profound as evolutionary necessity. Ms. Murray claims that in outfitting the devil with horns, Christianity is identifying its most feared foe with the fertility idols of its predecessor pantheistic religions. In so doing, Christianity, the usurper, is identifying nature—the sponsor of pantheistic religions—as the authority it intends to replace. Such Christian devices as the "Puritan ethic" indicate the displaced world attempting to keep our animal heritage at bay.

In these respects there are tremendous differences between the set of mind of the Westerner and the set of mind fostered by the so-called primitive religions. For "primitive" man, the forces that maintain his cultural continuity are sufficiently rigid so that if his cultural capacity for change is overtaxed, the tribe might drive itself into extinction. Western man, however, is far more flexible—adaptable —on the short term. Consequently, we pay our dues on the longer term, and as we are discovering, for higher stakes. Although the consumer draws on many of the characteristics of this model of Christianity, the consumer demands a flexibility beyond even the relative freedom permitted by Christianity. The limitations of the mind's attempt to become self-governing become apparent in the consumer.

A consumer frame of mind refers to a particular relationship between an individual or group and the world. A consumer, as the word implies, expresses himself in acts. If humanness lies in the ideas of usurpation and natural advantage, then the consumer is so far the furthest extension of that idea. Being a consumer is not a matter of choice, it is a construction of mind that determines choices, and as its inexorable spread around the globe suggests, the consumer construction of mind is *immanent* in nearly all of us. But it is the United States that has contributed the furthest development of this cast of mind.

A German writer once characterized America as Europe's sin. It's an apt metaphor because America has been the refuge for Europe's economically and religiously oppressed peoples. We were founded and populated by people with rightful scorn for oppressive traditions. Neither did the settlers and immigrants have aboriginal love for the land of the continent they claimed, stole and appropriated as their own. The land was there to be used, and it was inexhaustibly rich. Unburdened by tradition and encouraged by a harshly practical Puritan ethic, we relied on reason in framing many of the rules governing our relationship with the land and our mutual responsibilities. To be sure, many European traditions came to be transplanted, but when we were creating a new government and instituting change, reason was less restrained by tradition, a common religious base or conserving love of land than it was at any time before.

The rejection of tradition and the desire to reform society along rational lines gave us a type of freedom, but it contained latent costs as well. We have always been a country where a man is said to be able to rise to the limits of his abilities, and we have always also been a nation with a corresponding mobile, even rootless population. In making much of freedom of choice and in our scorn for the rigid classes and traditions of European society, we also threw out a significant stabilizing factor; we threw out a type of society which sanctioned and gave meaning to menial but essential work.

Over the years it has become more difficult for an American to take a profound pride in his work unless he is at the top of whatever it is he does. Christianity may hold that the meek hold the deed to the earth, but in a supposedly free and enterprising society, that is small comfort to the man who doesn't make it and spends his life serving those who did. The emphasis on quantity rather than quality in production—itself a product of consumer forces—has gradually suffocated the satisfactions available through craftsmanship. In this way freedom produces a set of anxieties for the average person, and the very nature of that freedom walls him or her from the religious solace available in other cultures. Without an honorable living or the solace of religion, many of us turn outward for our identity. We look outward and attempt to find satisfaction in material possessions and in a higher identity and purpose in the fact of being Americans. Our religion is the American standard of living.

It is in the need to substitute material possessions for religious solace that the consumer lives, at least in terms of his relationship to his environment and culture. The Maring might work out anxieties and tensions through a dance or ritual, but the consumer, walled off from such outlets, attempts to deal with anxieties and fears by placating that manipulatory side of our nature which has usurped the role of the unconscious. Instead of placating the gods, we, through a purchase, placate technology.

Unrestrained by tradition, that manipulatory side assured us of survival early in American history. With survival assured, we turned our technological prowess toward the provision of creature comforts. The nature of this process has been the attempt to use technology to take the element of chance out of survival and out of pleasure; to regularize the environment around us so that our needs (as we perceived them) might be satisfied in as orderly a fashion as possible. Rather than adapt to the environment, we would use technology to adapt the environment to us. At least that is how we see it. Tree farming takes the vicissitudes out of lumbering; aquaculture makes fishing more convenient. Through air conditioning, deodorant sprays, chemical taste substitutes and the like, we've extended the war to the senses—so much so that food manufacturers have discovered that many people have come to prefer artificial tastes to the natural flavors the chemicals were supposed to duplicate. Now with scientists turning their eye toward weather control and genetic engineering, it appears that the battle to standardize the world is almost won, that we will have human navel oranges growing up in a global hothouse. What to the ancient Greeks was an ambition to live among order in a refuge from change, with control over our destiny, seems to have become a manifest possibility.

Social critics and science-fiction writers have been droning on and on, endlessly, about the encroachments of technology. However, what has been missed, or ignored, is the mechanism of the consumer mind that impels us to take apart the world and put it back together again according to rational principles, as well as the flaw in that mechanism which will prevent the consumer from ever accomplishing its goal.

The new brain is a type of prosthetic device which originally filled the gap between the exigencies of survival and our physical failings. Its genius lies in its ability to translate psychic energy into physical advantage. With the consumer, the authority of the new brain has reached the point where it can translate religious needs into material appetites. These new appetites create tasks for the new brain to fulfill. Since they reflect the new brain's ambition to construct for humanity an orderly environment safe from change, safe from nature, the solution to these tasks further expands the new brain's hegemony over our behavior and our habitat. This entire cycle is dependent on the *purchase*. The purchase fuels the processes of capital formation; it commits resources and mobilizes competitive technologies. It is not the utility of whatever is purchased that is important in a consumer society, just the fact that something is purchased at all. In a consumer society, a Frisbee can become more important than a farm. The rational goal of convenience and competitive pressures produce demands for logistic and productive processes with tremendous attendant waste—the search for a technology to produce a cheap plastic container might be terrifically inefficient in terms of the use of resources in comparison with alternative technologies, but still economically viable, given the vicissitudes of the market.

Since the system is geared to thrive on *frequent* purchases, ideas of planned obsolescence and disposable, one-use items come into play. This forces the consumer to purchase new plastic containers time and again, which places additional stress on the supply of raw materials. In this way a purchase-oriented consumer economy tends to exhaust resources and thus constantly search for new sources of supply. In addition, competitive forces place a premium on growth and mass production if the enterprise is to have competitive prices and access to resources, which in turn creates pressures for new markets. For this reason, corporate America has until just recently liked the population explosion because it offers the potential of an ever expanding number of purchasers.

This brings up the question, crucial to understanding a consumer society, of what motivates the consumer to allocate his resources in a particular pattern of purchases. Aside from particular examples of the way products are marketed to exploit fears and desires, a telling indicator of the consumer mechanism is the broad and powerful element of faddism in a consumer society. Faddism is evident both in giant cultural spasms such as the rock-music scene of the late nineteen-sixties and in little tremors such as the Silly Putty fad. The same process is at work in the constantly shifting assignations of value which different groups within society unconsciously confer on people and objects.

Such assignments of value can seem absurd to people outside the cultural niche where they are made. An artist told me of an exhibit where a lady patron offered to buy a simple work fashioned out of string. The price was high, about $1,000. The artist accepted the woman's check, then crumbled the string work into a ball and handed the lady her new acquisition.

The forces at work transforming a ball of crumbled string into an object of value, and the massive transformations by which the rock-music scene took on the appearance of a world movement, both reveal the temporary focusing of some energy loose in society. The fad fulfills by expressing some previously pent-up energy. Nor is the consumer a passive part of the fad. Rather, he is a medium through which outlaw energy might be expressed. The energy behind the fad is outlaw because it comes from that mythic side of life disenfranchised by an increasingly rational culture. The genius of the consumer mechanism is that the consumer mind both disenfranchises the irrational side of life, and then taps that same emergy for profit when that repressed energy breaks through society's rational façade.

The mention of the word "outlaw" is a good point to deal with the argument that the consumer society is on the way out. No sooner does one mention the encroachments of technology, processed foods and the aridity of modern life than the clamor begins: natural foods, communes, the movement back to the land, all indicate that our way of life is changing. I agree, but with a major qualification. I feel that the rebellion of the late nineteen-sixties was proleptic, that instead of indicating that things were changing, it signaled changes that would occur sometime in the future. It was like a first warning that humanity's obeisance to the dictates of reason is not limitless. The counterculture represented a guerrilla sortie from the collective unconscious, and the strongest evidence of the superficiality of the revolution is that the revolutionaries have made great consumers. The phenomenon of the late nineteen-sixties seems rather to underline the extreme flexibility and subtlety of the consumer mechanism. The re-enchantment with nature and revulsion with technology of recent years were a counterreaction to the increasing spiritual suffocation of the consumer, but it was a counterreaction that the consumer society could manage. Take the rock-music scene, for instance.

Rock was outlaw music, and originally its celebrants reveled in violation of the norm. Now, paradoxically, rock is fading in the embrace of the establishment that originally called it outlaw. And now it is evident that the rock scene never really posed a threat to American society nor promised a new culture. Even before it expressed itself politically, it had been subtly harnessed by a corporate superstructure that is ever vigilant for eruptions of that outlaw energy (known to business as consumer interest) which it might cap as a source of profit.

In its earlier vitality, the rock scene supported an enormous industry. But the disaffections, repressed needs and anxieties in the young that supplied the rock scene's life energy are also basic to the consumer personality. The record industry skillfully exploited the consumer aspects of rock. The music that first offered a promise of liberation soon became a need—something to be consumed. Now no sooner does a musician who inspires "consumer interest" emerge than he is strip-mined for "product" to feed a rootless mass of rock consumers.

It is because of the consumer mentality that underlies faddism's shifting tastes and the huge attendant waste of resources diverted to satisfy these tastes that such apparently innocent developments as a heightened fashion-consciousness among the Basuto seem so frightening. These material appetites, the consumer society's "religion," are what charity is bringing to the non-Western world.

Because that corporate superstructure is amoral—it can mine the revolution as well as it can mine the establishment

—it can, to a degree, co-opt these anti-consumer eruptions for its own purposes. However, there are limitations to the effectiveness of this controlling mechanism. Because it exploits collective emotions, the workings of this mechanism demand that the consumer make his commercial decisions in something akin to a state of possession—that is, the mechanism demands the temporary ascendance of unreason over reason. This is a particularly dangerous game to play because that same denied irrational side of life which erupts through consumer interest also subverts a rational society in the form of paranoia, and militates for ever more elaborate and dangerous systems of defense.

The very nature of the consumer society fixes a limit to its own growth because in the end there will be no resources left to exploit. But most important, the ambition of the consumer society is ultimately futile. Consciousness is a thin mosaic floating on and nourished by the infinite well of energy and image that is the unconscious. The unconscious is the source of all meaning and mystery; it is both literally and figuratively our umbilical connection with the immediate world. In that it contains the evolutionary history of man, it is our organic path back to the origins of the universe. By its very nature, reason cannot assimilate the whole picture. The most awesomely mixed-up priority of all lies in the idea that reason or consciousness can control its very source.

What should be clear from this is the profound differences between the way consuming and conserving societies confront environmental problems. The critical differences are flexibility and the consumer mechanism. The corporate instrument that permits the functioning of a consumer society is that mystical concept called *management*. By no coincidence CARE's and other voluntary agencies' fondest hope is to give "underdeveloped countries" the management skills necessary so that they might help themselves.

Management is really nothing more than the set of organizational principles necessary to exploit some resource and then market it. It requires people with certain skills, but as Charles Reich has pointed out, in a well-ordered corporate structure, people do not run the corporation, they *tend* it. More than skills, then, management demands a reservoir of a particular type of person, people who are willing to subordinate their ambitions and idiosyncrasies to the needs of the corporation, people with self-control and that old Puritan ability to postpone personal gratification on the short term in the hopes of long-term dividends—in other words, people who are capable of fitting the rational mold foisted on behavior in a consumer society.

Not surprisingly, such people are difficult to find in the non-Western world. Throughout my trip to Africa, aid experts and technical assistants would tell me that our most valuable assistance to the non-Western world was not money but management, or that what this or that country needed was not capital goods but the management skills, the human resources to exploit what resources they had. With management you can turn any country into a consumer society. CARE's documents had told me that management skills were what they hoped to inculcate through self-help. Using this tool, we have constructed for ourselves a society which with 5 percent of the world's population uses 30 percent of the world's resources to solve the same basic human problems the Maring solve through ritual.

Ralph Montee's opus, "Activating Resources for Development at the Local Level," cites a UN paper which details the role of management in self-help programming:

> In terms of economic content, it has been true that most community development programs have stressed the improvement of sectoral economic activities such as agriculture and cottage industries and handicrafts. But they have given little attention to the generic aspects of growth which must be nurtured at the local level. Community development

programs have generally not stressed the development of management abilities and other human skills essential to effective participation in the economic aspects of development, i.e., developing habits of saving, planning productive investments, ability to undertake cost benefit analysis of economic performance, promoting awareness of how cooperative efforts can improve the individual's lot, etc.

Montee then notes that a bureaucracy is not enough, that it is necessary to develop the human resources to make the bureaucracy function,

> ... the acceptance of the goal of strengthening the capacity of man as a productive agent, investor, innovator and developer, [increases] his capability to participate effectively in economic activity and contribute to social development.

Given such goals for non-Western peoples, there is little wonder then that self-help programming treats the non-Western world like an undifferentiated lump. Management is neutral, and, so the theory goes, with proper management any culture can develop into a consumer society. Moreover, given the contrasts between a Western consuming society, and a characteristically conserving non-Western culture, CARE and other voluntary agencies are right: certain cultural attitudes are impediments to development. If a voluntary agency's desire is to equip peoples to become consuming societies, it is better to ignore the peculiarities of non-Western cultures.

In recent years there has been a resurgence of interest in "indigenous cultures," and soul-searching among aid organizations and voluntary agencies about the ultimate value of the type of development we are exporting. I encountered a lot of such "head shrinking," as one colorful World Food Program official called it, during my trip through Africa. In fact, many of the Peace Corpsmen and voluntary-agency people who are working overseas have opted for the expatriate life out of disappointment with the rewards of the consumer society. Many of these people reflected the outward trappings of the counterculture with all its anti-consumer totems and taboos. But once again the subtlety of the consumer society comes through. I found it radically ironic that many of these disaffected consumers were working to create the society overseas that they had rejected at home. Apart from the internal motivations that might cause the do-gooder to advance abroad a type of society he has superficially repudiated, it should be clear from the foregoing characterization of consuming and conserving cultures that the two are profoundly incompatible, and that this incompatibility makes fanciful blendings of the old ways and the new unlikely.

Earlier in discussing some of the introspective influences on the charitable impulse, I raised the issue of the prose-lytizing aspects of charity. In seeking converts, who is the religious or economic missionary trying to help—himself or the heathen? The common aspirations implicit in CARE's and other voluntary agencies' all-purpose development strategy further highlight this question about the charitable impulse. To put the question another way, Can an organization really be interested in helping foreign cultures if its self-help programs treat all cultures alike? When CARE and similar agencies are pushing management rather than food, it is a good point to speculate on some possible functions of charity in a consumer society. At least there seem to be indications that something other than pure altruism is at work.

FIFTEEN

Charity and Poverty

CARE and other voluntary agencies such as Catholic Relief Services and American Friends Service Committee do not look at themselves as agencies whose mission is to expand the frontiers of the consuming society. They see themselves as organizations helping countries to better their standard of living. It is also true that even today, due to the exigencies of PL 480, much of CARE's budget is directed toward child feeding. A number of its "development" projects are so small-scale that they would hardly seem to fit into any larger scheme of development. Still, CARE's position papers detail CARE's ambitions, regardless of how successful the agency is in fulfilling them. It is strange that an organization founded to feed starving refugees is now using its resources to encourage development of the human resources and management infrastructure that might better suit the needs of multinational corporations than they do the needs of a small village.

During my retracing of CARE's early history I offered some suggestions about the different forces conspiring to keep CARE in business and aggrandize the ambitions of its programs. Now is the proper time to reiterate some of those suggestions and elaborate on them in terms of how organizations such as CARE seem to fit into a consumer society.

Earlier I noted that CARE had characteristics of both a business and a bureaucracy. At first, run as a business and blessed with fantastic growth, CARE endured as a product of its own vitality. In the early nineteen-fifties, as that vitality (in the form of contributions) began to ebb and it came to rely on government contributions more and more to fill in for dwindling private contributions, CARE began to look and act more and more like a bureaucracy, specifically like those quasi-private corporations such as Lockheed that exist on the government dole. Why didn't CARE disappear when its initial chore was accomplished? For one thing, as Bloomstein notes in his *History of CARE*, early on in its history the agency became aware that there was in the United States an urge to give, which was in itself a pressing need, and which CARE requited. CARE recognized that as much as it might ease the suffering of the displaced, it was also servicing some anxiety in the American public. More-over, it became clear that that need in the American public would endure (though at reduced levels) even when the temporary crisis caused by the war was brought under control.

For those businessmen who came to CARE on loan from their companies, CARE offered a type of glamour unavail-able to a middle-management type from Sears, Roebuck. CARE offered an exalted position, a sense of urgent mis-sion, and the opportunity that one was doing something *good* efficiently. CARE's early success quite clearly bred into its workers an optimism born of legitimate achieve-ment, and similarly, the rewards of staying with the volun-tary agency glowed in comparison with the prospect of re-turning to the gray world of ledgers and triplicate order forms. Overseas the CARE man was a hero. Foreign post-ings offered a sense of adventure and accomplishment (and amenities and a life style that few could afford at home). In the home office there were confabs with high government officials, and the opportunity to *run* a businesslike organization and not just muddle around in the middle ranks. The whole process might be called "falling into a career in voluntary work," and it is something that continues today.

CARE's current major source of manpower is the Peace Corps, which also feeds a number of other voluntary agencies and development organizations. There is incredible cross-fertilization of manpower throughout those agencies concerned with development overseas. In one country an expatriate might work in turn for several agencies, finding new funding when one source dries up. In other cases, expatriates might move from agency to agency to change countries or projects, or for a host of other reasons. This "old boy" network exists because there are a certain number of Americans who, once having tasted the rewards of such work overseas, find themselves addicted. Regardless of the success or failure of particular strategies and projects, there are people for whom the work itself is a means to their own ends.

Ask a knowledgeable person to characterize an organization that endures twenty years beyond its original mandate and whose employees are attracted as much by personal considerations as they are by interest in the organization's mission, and that person is likely to say that you have just described a bureaucracy. CARE has followed a classic bureaucratic evolution.

I have a theory about bureaucracies—namely, that bureaucracies are not intended to solve problems, but to appear to ease the anxiety that a problem exists which is not being solved. The bureaucracy functions like a psychic sponge, soaking up potentially destructive energy. If crime is a problem, we form an anti-crime commission and the nation collectively breathes a sigh of relief; the same thing is true of pollution, highway safety or reading standards. The wild proliferation of special prosecutors reflects our current anxiety about political corruption, as well as the failure of the traditional bureaucratic controls on corruption.

Like any organism, the first instinct of bureaucracy is to ensure its perpetuation. And one thing which is death to a bureaucracy is to wrap up its mission without having more pressing problems to deal with. To ensure their perpetuation, bureaucracies evolve. For instance, when J. Edgar Hoover believed that he had cracked organized crime, there were Communists and radicals to keep his men busy. Ironically, organized crime flourished after Hoover's premature notice of its demise, and now a host of special commissions, congressional committees, and task forces are dealing with our renewed anxieties—the same anxieties which the FBI was set up to relieve.

This adds another element to this pattern of bureaucratic evolution which might be summarized as follows: (1) an agency is set up in response to an urgent need which other institutions cannot accommodate; (2) through time the agency loses its temporary character, it takes on a life of its own, and the specific need it was formed to serve broadens and deepens; (3) efforts to meet the need become more long-term, sophisticated, grandiose, and conversely less urgent, immediate and direct until (4) another agency is formed to meet the immediate need no longer serviced by what is now a bureaucracy. In this way we stack agency on agency, each supposedly dealing with some particular problem. Of course, not all such agencies survive; witness police review boards which reflected anxieties about police methods in the late nineteen-sixties. But any bureaucracy is hard to kill. Why, for instance, do we still have draft boards now that we no longer have a draft?

It should be easy to see how CARE fits within this pattern. The temporary need that spurred its creation was the refugee crisis following the end of World War II. Before the end of that mission became apparent, CARE began to attend to the enduring nature of underdevelopment and broadened its mandate from Europe to Everywhere. Once into self-help, a second process of evolution pressured

CARE into more and more sophisticated and long-term planning, until now CARE officials actively disparage refugee relief and food programs as a "Band-Aid" approach to world problems.

It is also easy to see how CARE functions as a psychic pacifier, absorbing money directed at the anxiety that those hollow-eyed infants who stare from the pages of magazines are not being helped. The hushed reverence with which CARE is treated by the press further suggests that CARE is as important to Americans as it is to those being helped.

Despite its bureaucratization, CARE has remained a relatively trim organization. If its programs are becoming grander, they are still for the most part unmarred by the gross flaccidity characteristic of other agencies. This is because, even though the federal government may supply 85 percent of CARE's budget, CARE still has to go to donors to get part of its operating costs.

However, this brings us to a critical point, because it is not the administrative sleekness that is important in CARE's case, but rather what CARE's programs are really designed to accomplish, and what the effects, intentional and unintentional, of CARE's programs are.

CARE has evolved from an organization that gave food to starving Europeans to an organization that sees its value in promoting international development among people who are not starving. This has led to some ironic situations: for instance, with Bangladesh facing overwhelming population and food problems, CARE is there bogged down in a "pilot project" providing durable housing, while other organizations attempt to cope with that beleaguered country's immediate problems.

Some of the selective pressures in CARE's bureaucratic evolution have been mentioned and are obvious. CARE officials talk about the need for a more profound approach to making people self-sufficient or of the frustration of giving food to people without dealing with the "root causes of poverty"—the "job is done but the work is not finished" syndrome. Self-image might have something to do with this evolution as well. Just as someone might rather think of himself as a sanitary engineer than a garbage man, so might a voluntary-agency official prefer the image as "expert in international development" to that of a distributor of food, especially if the official comes from the business community. Anybody can hand out food. To look at it another way, when a former businessman sees the seemingly chaotic "underdeveloped" world, it would take immense self-control to *just* hand out food without interfering in the lives of the recipients. Once into such interference with their lives, it is easy to see how a frustrating resistance to simple solutions might lead to ever grander programs.

Then there were the encouragements and pressures of the United States government, hinting that CARE should broaden its administrative ambit and then paving the road into the non-Western world with candy. There was also the tenor of the times. The success of the Marshall Plan in raising Europe phoenixlike from its own ashes bred the confidence that such miracles might be performed elsewhere, even in places without Europe's unique susceptibility to development. However, I do not think that these forces together—the desire to stay in business, a brash optimistic urge to take on world poverty, the desire for an enhanced self-image, impatience with unreliable natives, and official encouragement—sufficiently explain CARE's move into development to let the matter rest.

My reluctance has to do with my suspicions about the functions of charity in a consumer society. In the chapter which considered self-help projects in terms of a consumer society, I noted that Christianity, by not promising immediate punishment for transgressions but rather offering redemption for sin through token acts of contrition or beneficence, might be seen to be encouraging sin. By creating a "gap" between act and responsibility, Christianity in effect winks and lets us get away with things which we shouldn't do, but which enhance our prosperity. The agent within this mechanism, which makes the whole process of wealth gathering all right, is charity. Charity's original meaning—"you shall love your neighbor as yourself"— would seem to argue for a prior restraint which might prohibit the accumulation of embarrassing riches upon which the practice of today's charity depends. However, what charity has come to mean is a beneficent act which, because of its redemptive nature, encourages a lot of behavior other than loving your neighbor as yourself. If you can buy your way into grace on the installment plan, why earn your way day by day? During the Middle Ages, many noblemen tried to buy their way into heaven in one fell swoop. Big-time sinners were able to purchase indulgences from the Church through, among other things, contributions to a cathedral. For those who found themselves in more straitened circumstances, small cash emoluments, passed sometimes not so surreptitiously under the table, might bring, if not a plenary indulgence, at least a few days off in purgatory.

Traditionally we might think of the redemptive charitable act as something wholly separate from the acquisitive side of the donor's life. This is usually just appearance. The container companies, whose detritus litter the countryside, sponsor clean-up campaigns while at the same time fighting legislation which would limit the production of nonreturnable containers. Thus the container companies disarm their critics without really addressing the criticism. The classic example of redemptive giving might be that of Alfred Nobel, who made a fortune in explosives and then established a prize dedicated to encouraging world peace.

A natural question is whether CARE, supposedly dependent on small contributions, fits within this same syndrome of redemptive giving. Is the small donor motivated by the same forces that impel the tycoon? Actually CARE is not so dependent on the small donor as one might think. The U.S.

government, of course, provides better than 85 percent of CARE's budget. Among the private donors, an élite 2 percent provides one third of the money CARE gets from the public, according to Gordon Haskell, CARE's chief fund raiser. Still, there are half a million people who gave small amounts to CARE last year, much of it designated for victims of the year's disasters—the Sahelian drought, the Honduran hurricane, etc. These contributions were elicited through television ads and fund-raising campaigns, and there is not the slightest question that these contributions were elicited by playing on the affluent American's reservoir of guilt. Who among us do not feel at least a momentary pang when we see the face of a starving child on the cover of a CARE brochure, or looking out at us from the television set. We sense that our affluence is in some way connected to the child's plight, and guilt obscures judgment as we give a dollar or two to buy release from the indictment implied in that image.

CARE is well aware of the power of such images and for this reason perpetuates the notion that CARE's primary ambition is feeding starving children rather than administering self-help projects. (CARE does feed children, but that's not where their primary ambitions lie, at least according to the officials I spoke with.) In 1972 I asked Tom Bentley about the ethics of using pictures of starving children to raise funds, when in fact the money is being used for altogether different purposes. "In a television ad," said Bentley, "if you show a guy working with an air compressor, which is what we're doing in Lesotho, let's face it, the average American will not feel a gut response, whereas he will respond to a hungry child—even though the air compressor may be more pertinent to the country's economic development." Frank Goffio amplified on this when I spoke to him that same year. "It's hard to relate to a road or school," he said. "It's easier to think of your money as buying a package. If I show a hungry child and mother, your response is to think that you can feed them. In a thirty-second spot, you have to create a sense of urgency." Goffio admitted that the food-package, starving-kid image was firmly implanted in the donor's mind, but he said that he didn't think the donors would be shocked if he "hit them with the idea that CARE is a development organization." I have noticed that since 1972, CARE ads have been mixing images of hungry children against a background of CARE projects.

CARE's hesitancy to show its real orientation in its ads gives some insight into the nature of the charitable impulse that supports the organization. Clearly, CARE feels that the impulse to give is not an examined impulse, or else CARE would not hesitate to advertise its unfolding involvement in self-help. Rather, CARE is content to be thought of by Americans as an organization that distributes food, because CARE knows that accusing eyes are more effective than appeals to better the lives of others. The consumer society allows the consumer to ignore the plight of others, but leaves the consumer vulnerable to being held a $2 hostage by the eyes of the innocent.

It is when CARE's evolution toward self-help is seen in terms of charity's redemptive functions that the process becomes noteworthy. If at one level charity acts to maintain moral equilibrium in a consumer society by redeeming gross transgressions through token beneficent acts, in actual practice many charities attempt through their programs not just to redeem the sins of capitalism but to vindicate capitalism's very premise. The goal of self-help is basically to improve the climate of investment in the non-Western world to the point where the "villager" can benefit from free enterprise. The argument is: the poor are disadvantaged not because of the system, but because they are not a part of the system. Through self-help the voluntary agencies seem to be arguing against the Communists, who say that free enterprise exploits the poor, by counterarguing that free enterprise will save the poor.

CARE's bureaucratic maturation exemplifies a drift in charity's function (from relief) to the point where a voluntary agency is now promoting free enterprise in the name of charity. But is this surprising? We would expect the fundamental insecurity of the economic missionary to be no less than that of his religious predecessor.

Earlier I suggested various considerations which indicated that CARE's form of charity was tempered by self-interest rather than the pure impulse to improve the lot of the recipient. Now viewed in terms of charity's role in a consumer society, charity seems so divorced from the welfare of the recipient that the question arises whether self-help, impelled and shaped by internal conflicts in the donor society, might actually hurt the people it is supposed to help.

In Lesotho the single most evident dividend of the intense development efforts of the last seven years has been the gradual shift of the Basuto away from communal traditions and toward consumer values. This shift and its manifold ramifications have been invigorated by every development effort regardless of the stated designs of the expatriate framers of those efforts. In fact, there seems to be a singular genius organizing development efforts to accomplish just this stated end, and this genius seems to enlist the guilts and redemptive devices of the donor consumer societies toward accomplishing its transformations in the non-Western world. The fact that the transformations toward consumer values are for the most part unintended as a conscious aim of the expatriate planners, and that the negative cultural repercussions devolving from these transformations are ignored for the most part by expatriate evaluation procedures, leads me to believe that this coherent pattern of effect is authored by a part of the consumer mind of which the consumer is not aware, whether he be donor, planner or administrator of a charitable enterprise.

I suspect that despite the dismay of many expatriates

about their failure to improve the lives of the "natives," expatriate do-gooders achieve precisely what a consumer society demands they achieve: by absorbing guilt money, they help maintain a domestic moral equilibrium in the donor society, and abroad they help create new purchasers to satisfy the consumer society's insatiable demands for growth. There is no more reason for the do-gooder to be aware that this is what he is supposed to accomplish than there is for the Maring tribesman to be aware that the purpose of his gluttonies and wars is to protect his forest. In fact, believing ourselves to be rational and autonomous, we are all the more prone to be deluded and manipulated by the irrational side of our mind.

That charity is fulfilling specific purposes in the donor consumer societies would explain why extraordinary talent in an expatriate or extraordinary care in the design of a project might neither enhance the chances of success of an undertaking nor lessen the chances for producing harmful dislocations. Moreover, the functions of charity in consumer societies make it an irrelevant diversion to look for venality, or blockheadedness as bugs that undermine otherwise noble work. What we have seen in Lesotho is that the most idealistic and efficient organizations have no greater success than their less commendable colleagues. In fact, the more efficient the organization, the more likely it is to effect those changes that are critical to becoming a consumer. Urban migration, the alienation of the young, the abandonment of communal traditions, ribbon development, all dismay the enlightened do-gooder, even though they were authored by the collective consumer mind that orchestrates his actions and prefigures the further advance of the consumer society.

Charitable and aid organizations are if not themselves the root causes of poverty, the cause of the consciousness of poverty. Their projects strip people like the Basuto of the traditional supports which hide their poverty; their projects erode the religious beliefs which offer nonmaterial satisfactions and offer instead the standard of living as an object of worship; and their projects fuel the population explosion and demographic changes that undermine the economic gains that occasionally flow from development. Development smashes the illusions that ennoble the life of the provincial native and confronts him instead with a cold judgment: you may never enjoy the American standard of living in your lifetime, but if you bend to the wheel, you might own a motorcycle.

We often wonder why the Third World hates us, while it seems to embrace Communism. Perhaps it is because the alienated unemployed young come to believe that we have stripped them of their past and dignity and sold them a bill of goods. The Western gestalt forever walls the young from returning to their old way of life—talk of developing within traditional structures is nonsense—but perhaps they feel that they might still recapture part of the past through the Western correlative of the communal past—Marxism. They are in for another disappointment, of course.

As a final irony, we might note that the events which set the stage for the transformation from native into consumer also can lead to the development of a starvation situation requiring emergency relief. For the unemployed trapped in swollen cities with no recourse to the land, any interruption in food supplies might mean starvation. It is possible that organizations whose development projects contribute to urban migration and the development of emergency conditions might also be called upon to provide emergency relief for the situation they helped to create. It's something to think about the next time you reach for your wallet to gain release from the appealing eyes of a starving infant.

Personal Acknowledgments

The researching and writing of this book have indebted me to a great number of people over the past several years. I have benefited from conversations with scores of men and women concerned with different aspects of voluntary-agency work and development, and without exception, the people I have spoken with have been generous with their expertise and helpful in suggesting new paths to pursue. The cooperation and candor I encountered at all points in my research testify to the quality of the people drawn to this type of work. Specifically I must acknowledge the cooperation of CARE, without which this project would have been stymied. From the inception of this project in 1972 throughout my research, CARE made accessible the information and the documents necessary for this investigation to proceed in a thorough manner. The programming department was particularly cooperative in making available documents which articulated the assumptions upon which project decisions were based. The CARE people I encountered were down-to-earth and modest and it was a pleasure to deal with them. As an organization, CARE demonstrated openness that might serve as a model for other voluntary agencies and public agencies alike.

Finally I would like to thank Jim Wilcox for his deft editorial hand.

Index

About the Author

EUGENE LINDEN was born in Plainfield, Vermont, in 1947. He was graduated from Yale in 1969, and has since worked as a free-lance writer, with articles appearing in such publications as the *Saturday Review* and the Los Angeles *Times*. His previous book, *Apes, Men, and Language,* was greeted with nationwide critical acclaim. He and his wife reside in Norfolk, Connecticut.